WHY THIS BOOK HAS BEEN WRITTEN

While considering the idea of this book, I mentioned it to various people to see what their reaction would be. Many had never heard of Katyn at all; of those who had, some appeared to be confused in their own minds as to who was responsible for the crime. Of those others who had a fair idea of who had committed this act, many felt there was little point in resurrecting it thirty years later. I therefore feel it necessary to set down a few of the reasons why this book should be written:

1. To clear once and for all the obscurity which has shrouded for over thirty years the worst crime against prisoners-of-war ever committed, and perhaps the worst single unpunished crime in history.

2. To inspire a sovereign state to seek the setting up of a tribunal for the purpose of re-examining this case at the highest international level.

3. To proclaim the guilt for the act through a clear presentation of all the facts.

4. To remove any doubt as to who is the culprit and thus to forestall the culprit's propaganda which has caused and still causes such doubt and confusion among large numbers of people today.

5. To ensure that the victims are held in honour for posterity.

6. To re-assure the widows and relatives that their murdered men are not being forgotten.

7. To provide, through the sale of this book, some financial relief for such of those widows and relatives as may be in need, and to encourage others to help them.

8. To sound a warning for the future.

Louis FitzGibbon

Louis FitzGibbon

Katyn Massacre

Foreword by the Rt. Hon. The Lord George-Brown, P.C.
Introduction by Constantine FitzGibbon

CORGI BOOKS
A DIVISION OF TRANSWORLD PUBLISHERS LTD

KATYN MASSACRE

A CORGI BOOK 0 552 10455 8

First publication in this form in Great Britain

Katyn Massacre is a compilation, with some additional
material especially written for this edition, of two previous
books by the author – *KATYN – A Crime Without Parallel*,
published by Tom Stacey Ltd., 1971 and *THE KATYN
COVER-UP*, published by Tom Stacey Ltd., 1972

PRINTING HISTORY
Corgi edition published 1977

Corgi Books are published by
Transworld Publishers Ltd.,
Century House, 61–63 Uxbridge Road,
Ealing, London W5 5SA
Made and printed in Great Britain by
Cox & Wyman Ltd., London, Reading and Fakenham

*The author wants to thank his wife, Madeleine, for her
patience and encouragement throughout all the work involved,
especially during those moments when energy and confidence
temporarily deserted him.*

DEDICATION

This book is dedicated to the memory of the 14,500 Polish Officers and leading intellectuals who disappeared from the prisoner of war camps at Kozielsk, Starobielsk, and Ostashkov, U.S.S.R., in the Spring of 1940 of whom the remains of 4,253 were discovered by the German Army in the Forest of KATYN in the Spring of 1943, and to the countless other Poles who vanished in Soviet Russia during and after the war.

R.I.P.

And to their widows and other surviving relatives in many lands.

'No light, but rather darkness visible served only to discover sights of woe'
(Milton: *Paradise Lost, Book 1*)

CONTENTS

FOREWORD

BY LORD GEORGE-BROWN, P.C.
Secretary of State for Foreign Affairs 1966–1968

I am glad to have this opportunity to identify myself with the Katyn case about which I have felt concern for so long. As a member of the Katyn Memorial Fund Committee, I strongly endorse the concept of a monument in remembrance of the massacre victims, but that is not the same as being able to introduce this book and thus add something to the message it contains.

Here is the story of one of the most frightful mass-murders committed in peace-time during recent centuries, and I find it abhorrent that even after thirty-seven years it has never been adjudged.

In a then secret dispatch to the then Foreign Secretary in May 1943, Mr. Owen O'Malley, the British Ambassador to the Polish Government said, *inter alia*: '... We have in fact perforce used the good name of England like the murderers used the little conifers to cover up a massacre ...' Despite a House of Commons motion in April 1971; despite a lengthy debate in the Upper House on June 17th of that year, and notwithstanding over thirty years of pleading by the Poles in exile, this situation remains unchanged.

The lack of a judgment is something which touches the very integrity of this country and, indeed, of the whole free world. That is why the Katyn Memorial is so important, and this is why a fresh edition of Louis FitzGibbon's book is so necessary. Here, again, is the horrid truth, behind which lies the anguish of a nation. It is a story which must be told, and told again if it is to make an impact, and I am therefore pleased to add my name by recommending it to all.

We, and the West generally, have accepted many sacrifices

from the Poles, so that it would be grand indeed if we could take a lead in procuring the international statement about Katyn which is still so lamentably missing. Then, and only then, can we look at our reflection in the mirror of history, confident that eventually we did right.

GEORGE-BROWN

introduction by
Constantine FitzGibbon

INTRODUCTION

WE cannot weigh the dead in some form of moral scales in order to assess the enormity of a crime in our miserable, crime-ridden century and then decide that one crime was 'worse' than another – at least not with crimes on the scale of the one documented in this book. How many people have been murdered by the totalitarian régimes, have been killed in the two world wars and the revolutions that followed them, have been, ghastly euphemism, 'liquidated' so far in this century? One hundred million perhaps? We simply do not know the figures, and if we did we should be none the wiser. Whether the Nazis murdered three or six million Jews does not make that monstrosity half or twice as bad. Whether the Chinese Communists have murdered ten or fifteen million members of the landlord and middle class is irrelevant. Whether five or ten millions died in Stalin's concentration camps has as little moral significance as the light years to Betelgeuse. That more people were killed in the unnecessary air raid on Dresden than died in the probably unnecessary air raid on Hiroshima is no excuse for either atrocity. In our twentieth-century hecatombs 15,000 Polish officers and intellectuals may seem an insignificant figure: more men died in the first hours of the Battle of the Somme. But that is not the point.

When Neville Chamberlain gave Czechoslovakia (which he did not own) to Adolf Hitler in 1938, he apparently believed what Hitler told him, that this was Hitler's last territorial demand. When Stalin signed a treaty of alliance with Hitler a little less than a year later, he apparently believed that Hitler would keep his word, that Poland was to be permanently partitioned between Russia and Germany and hence that, after the conquest of Finland, Russia was to resume its Czarist imperial dimensions. He seems to have continued in this foolish belief until the very moment the Nazis struck at Russia. Meanwhile the Communist apparatus set about, methodically, ingesting the newly acquired territories, the Baltic States and its share of Poland, using the same methods that they had applied, that they continued and continue to apply, to their other conquered territories, the Ukraine, Tartary, the Soviet oriental colonies. Their aim was the destruction of any possible alternative government, their principal method the simple murder of all those who might, in any conceivable circumstances, form the nucleus of a rebellion against Communist tyranny. This meant, in effect, the destruction of more than a 'class' – though such was their explanation – but of anyone who could conceivably act as a leader. Stalin, in the purges, had already decapitated his own army lest that army provide an alternative source of power to that of himself and his apparatus. The man who had killed Tukachevsky and, it is estimated, up to half the Red Army's officer corps including almost all its staff officers, would hardly hesitate to kill the entire Polish élite, in so far as these were within his power. He could rely on Hitler and the Nazis to kill off those who were not. The Polish nation, as a nation, was to be destroyed once and for all and forever by the selective murder of all its potential leaders. The method had worked in the Ukraine, had it not? That, according to the definition given by the United Nations, is genocide. Poland, one of the great historic nation states of Europe, was to be so destroyed that it could never rise again. Those Poles left alive were to be the ignorant slaves of their Russian and German masters.

There are many aspects of this crime that entitles it to be called unparalleled. In a revolutionary situation, whether that of Marat's France or Lenin's Russia, attempts may be made to destroy the old ruling class by expropriation and murder. This is, essentially, a form of civil war and civil wars are notoriously disgusting businesses. The destruction of the Polish officers and intellectuals does not fall into that category. There was no sort of a civil war situation. These men had surrendered to an invader and had every reason to

14

believe that they would be treated as prisoners-of-war, as most of Russia's Polish prisoners were indeed treated. What we call 'Katyn' – but there were other massacres as well – proved yet again that the Soviets are totally uninterested in the accepted conventions, rough though these be, of any morality, personal, political, legal or international.

The massacres by the Nazis were, in theory at least, carried out in the shadow of Hitler's insane racial theories. Here there was a vague precedent in, say, the genocide of the Tasmanians, of the American Indians, of Cromwell's behaviour in Ireland. The submen were relegated to the status of undesirable animals, to be destroyed. The Russians, in Poland, had not even this cruel excuse: they were out to destroy what they regarded as Poland's 'supermen'. Their motive was naked imperialism.

The murdered men were no danger to the Russians: they were all in prison camps. But they just might constitute a threat one day, and they were of course totally defenceless. According to the Marxist 'laws' of historical materialism they must, therefore, disappear as soon as possible. They did.

The methods for killing 15,000 men are complex. Like the Nazi genocide of the Jews such an operation involves men, many men, at all levels, the politicians, the civil service, the army, the railways, the grave diggers, and in this case foresters. Beria's NKVD was primarily responsible, but thousands of others were involved, were accomplices in crime. For criminals, an accomplice chained hand and foot, is, whether he wishes it or not, an ally. The Polish genocide incriminated a great many Russians, thus chaining them more securely to the Communist chariot. The crime thus becomes one not merely against the Polish people but against the Russians too. This method of control was also, of course, practised by the Nazis and is one of the basic techniques of totalitarian misrule, since it is yet another means whereby the rulers can terrorize those over whom they rule.

Finally, there is the question of the big lie. Despite overwhelming evidence from an impartial team of European experts (the Soviets refused to allow the International Committee of the Red Cross to investigate), years later from an

American Congressional Committee of Inquiry, from Poles such as Count Czapski who was one of the tiny handful capriciously spared, the Russians maintained, and still maintain, that it was the Nazis who did it. In this they were given the tacit support, through censorship, of the British and American wartime governments. Fearful lest the Russians sign a separate peace with Hitler, Churchill and Roosevelt – both of whom knew all the facts – were frightened of 'upsetting' Stalin. That sham has lingered on, backed by the whole Communist-dominated apparatus of 'liberal' thought. It is high time that these facts were brought out into the open, and that the next British or American politician who talks smoothly about a 'détente' with the Soviets remembers the sort of men with whom he is dealing. For though Stalin has gone, they have not changed in their immoral tactics. They have proved this again and again, in Hungary, Czechoslovakia, at the time of writing in Egypt and the Middle East. They are trying, not altogether without success, to enlist our support for their future war against China. When will we ever learn that our brutal, lying enemies do not become our friends merely because they happen, for strategic reasons of their own, to be fighting our other enemies? Are 15,000 dead Poles enough? Or do we need ten times or more that number of dead Britons and Americans to open our eyes? Let us hope not.

CHAPTER ONE

THE CRIME

WHAT follows is a dispassionate account of the Katyn Murder, in which the reader is invited to trace the events as they occurred. The author has a duty to place all the evidence before the reader with the utmost clarity. That evidence leaves no scintilla of doubt as to who was murdered, how they were murdered, when the crime was committed and, finally, who are the culprits.

A number of undisputed facts outline the crime.

WHO WAS MURDERED?

Of the figures 4,143 bodies originally exhumed, 2,914 were identified. All the others were identified by rank, by the remains of their uniforms. The bodies included:

Three generals – B. Bohaterewicz, H. Minkiewicz, M. Smorawinski; and one rear admiral – K. Czernicki.

Plus approximately:

    100 colonels and lt.-colonels,
    300 majors,
    1,000 captains,
    2,500 first- and second-lieutenants,
    and more than 500 cadet-officers.

This total included about 200 air force and about 50 naval officers. Officers of the reserve formed about 50 per cent of the group, and amongst them were:

21 University professors and lecturers,

More than 300 surgeons and physicians, military and civilian, some of them outstanding specialists,

More than 200 lawyers, judges, prosecutors, solicitors and court officials,

More than 300 engineers with University degrees,

Several hundred High School and Grammar School teachers, many journalists, writers, industrialists, business men, etc.

A number of officers disabled in the previous war had been deported to the Kozielsk camp, among them two colonels who had lost an arm, Captain Dlugosz of the Sanitary Service who had lost a leg, Captain Horoszkiewicz with one crippled arm.

According to the Testimony of the German authorities, which is confirmed by the Testimony of the non-German journalists and the statement of the members of the Technical Team of the Polish Red Cross – the number of the victims exhumed in the first seven Katyn graves was not less than 4,143. This lowest limit has never been queried by any party.

To the figure of 4,143 bodies exhumed should be added the number of corpses lying in the eighth grave, which was the last to be discovered. This figure amounts to approximately 110 bodies. By adding this figure to the 4,143 total of the other seven graves, we obtain the probable total of the victims buried in the eight Katyn graves – i.e. 4,253.

On the basis of diaries, correspondence and small personal possessions such as wooden cigarette cases and holders with the inscription 'Kozielsk 1940', there is no doubt that the bodies of the men in the Katyn graves are those of officers, prisoners-of-war, who had previously been detained in the camp at Kozielsk, and who were deported thence between April 1st and May 11th, 1940.

Of the 2,914 bodies identified by name, *about* 80 per cent were found in the list of the 'missing' officers, comprising 3,845 names, which was handed by General Sikorski to Stalin on December 3rd, 1941, or in the later additional lists, drawn up by the Headquarters of the Polish Armed Forces in the USSR during 1941 and 1942.

At the beginning of 1940, the inmates of the camp at Kozielsk numbered approximately 4,500 prisoners-of-war. From that total, 245 persons were deported to Pavlishtchev Bor and subsequently to Griazovetz, so that approximately 4,250 were taken by train to Gniezdovo, the nearest railway station to the Katyn Forest. It will be seen that this figure coincides, almost exactly, with the probable total of bodies found in the eight Katyn graves.

Thus, both by comparing the name lists of the bodies identified in Katyn and the total number of bodies of the murdered with the total of the 'missing' inmates of the Kozielsk camp, we arrive at the conclusion that the murdered buried in the Katyn Graves are completely identical with the 'missing' prisoners-of-war from Kozielsk.

HOW WERE THEY MURDERED?

Without exception all the victims whose bodies were found in the Katyn graves were shot in the back of the head. About 5 per cent of the bodies in the Katyn graves had their hands tied behind their backs with a rope. Some had their heads wrapped up in their overcoats and their mouths stuffed with sawdust. These were evidently victims who shouted or resisted at the moment of execution.

The executioners used a strong uncoloured rope for the purpose, which had apparently been prepared beforehand as it was cut in identical lengths. Polish underground authorities of the Armija Krajowa in Poland appropriated several such cords which were secretly taken away from Katyn, together with a few diaries found on the bodies of the victims.

In addition to the pistol shots in the back of the head, which without exception were the cause of death of all the victims, medical examination and dissection showed that a few bodies had jaws smashed by blows or had received bayonet wounds in back and stomach. Presumably these were among those who resisted during or before the execution. A close examination of the flesh wounds showed that they had been inflicted by four-edged bayonets.

WHEN WERE THEY MURDERED?

There are only two possible solutions: in April–May 1940, or in August–September 1941.

Upon the answer as to which of these dates is correct rests the certainty of who was the culprit. Only a close scrutiny of the further detailed facts contained in the chapters which follow will reveal the answer.

WHO WERE THE MURDERERS?

Only the Germans or the Soviet Russians could have committed this crime. Poland lies geographically between those two nations. It must be accepted that a massacre of this scale could only be organized at national level. Only the Third Reich or the USSR were, at any material time, in physical possession of the scene of this act of murder.

CHAPTER TWO

THE INTERNATIONAL SITUATION
1920–1939

In order to grasp the overall historical situation, it is necessary to glance at the various legal instruments which were fashioned between the nations following the Russo-Polish war of 1920. They are as follows:

(1) The Peace Treaty between Poland, Russia and the Ukraine signed in Riga, on March 18th, 1921, by which the Eastern frontiers of Poland were defined. These frontiers were recognized by the Allies at the Conference of Ambassadors on March 15th, 1923, implementing the terms of article 87, para. 3, of the Versailles Treaty. They were recognized by the US Government in April 1923.

(2) The Protocol between Estonia, Latvia, Poland, Rumania and the Union of Soviet Socialist Republics regarding renunciation of war as an instrument of national policy, signed in Moscow, February 9th, 1929.

(3) The Non-Aggression Pact between Poland and the USSR signed in Moscow, July 25th, 1932.

(4) The Protocol signed in Moscow, May 5th, 1934, between Poland and the USSR, extending until December 31st, 1945, the Non-Aggression Pact of July 25th, 1932.

(5) The Convention for the Definition of Aggression signed in London on July 3rd, 1933.

In addition to the above pacts, various pledges of peace resulting from a number of general international agreements and pacts, were in force.

In 1939, the international situation in Europe was extremely tense. Nazi Germany was still smarting from the defeat of 1918 and the humiliation of Versailles. She had prepared herself, only too well, for a further excursion in her search for what she then called *Lebensraum*. In September 1938, the British Prime Minister Mr. Neville Chamberlain, went to talk to Hitler at Munich in an attempt to halt the aggressive plans which – so obviously to others – were about to be put into action. Whatever else we may say about Neville Chamberlain the fact was that he was a kind and sincere man, and one who had in his heart a desire for world peace. But his attempts at Munich failed.

The world knows that this was the moment when the seeds of war were firmly planted in the soil of Europe. It was at this time that Great Britain and France gave a guarantee to Poland. It was announced on March 1st, 1939. In effect, the guarantee meant that England and France would come to the assistance of Poland in the event of German aggression. The idea behind this guarantee was to give Hitler warning that an attack on Poland would lead to a new world war.

Adolf Hitler was not slow to realize that a new problem had been placed before him; but he did not however intend to abandon his plans. He realized however, that he would have to protect himself from Soviet Russia before deciding upon the date of his attack on Poland. The attitude of Soviet Russia and its importance was also understood by the Western powers and in the summer of 1939 a military mission was sent to Moscow. To the apparent astonishment of the Western allies, Stalin preferred to come to an agreement with Hitler, despite the supposed ideological chasm which separated the Soviets from the Germans. It was with Hitler, not with the Western powers, that Stalin signed a pact of non-aggression on August 23rd. One of the most sinister clauses of the Soviet/Nazi Pact was that which anticipated the partition of Poland between the two partners.

Two days later, the British–Polish agreement was signed. Britain was at that time still a world power and Poland was in the process of reconstruction after many years of partition. It therefore anticipated Poland's need of assistance from Britain rather than the reverse. On September 1st, 1939, Germany invaded Poland without a declaration of war. Up to the very last minute Britain and France continued to hope that the Germans would make no such aggressive move. To delay or forestall such an inevitability they had persuaded the Poles not to mobilize in the vain hope that Hitler, without a shred of a protest, would refrain from assault.

Thus when, undeterred, the Wehrmacht, with all its armoured might, descended upon Poland, over ten formations of Polish troops amounting to several hundred thousand men, were being carried in trains to their concentration areas in Poland. Poland therefore was not only hopelessly weaker; she was not ready. The overwhelming technical superiority of the German Army and the German Air Force broke Polish resistance in less than a month. It was hardly surprising. Nevertheless – and these facts are recorded in detail – the Poles fought as gallantly as any army could fight in such circumstances. As many remember today, Polish Lancers on horseback charged the onward rolling might of German tanks.

At the point of time when Polish troops were beginning to withstand the German onslaught, Poland was attacked by Soviet Russia. This treacherous aggression had of course been preceded by the Non-Aggression Pact signed between Hitler's Germany and the USSR – by their two Foreign Ministers, Ribbentrop and Molotov – on August 23rd, 1939, the pact which alone gave Hitler nerve to launch the Second World War.

On September 17th, 1939, Stalin, in defiance of all pledges and agreements with Poland, and without any declaration of war, ordered the Red Army to cross the Polish frontier. At four o'clock in the morning Soviet troops, consisting of several infantry divisions, many armoured brigades and motorized corps with some cavalry formations, invaded Polish territory.

At 3 a.m. the same day the Deputy Soviet Commissar for Foreign Affairs, Potemkin, had summoned the Polish Ambassador in Moscow, Grzybowski, and read out to him a note to the effect that the Soviet Government had ordered their troops to cross the Polish frontier. In view of the reasons given in the note (the annihilation of the Polish State, the non-existence of the Government) misrepresenting the real facts, Ambassador Grzybowski refused to accept the note.

At 8 a.m. the Russian wireless broadcast a statement by Molotov giving a summary of the Note and setting forth the Soviet reasons for the invasion of Poland. Mr. Molotov declared that 'events arising out of the Polish–German war have revealed the internal dissolution and obvious impotence of the Polish State. Polish ruling circles have suffered bankruptcy ... Warsaw as the capital of the Polish State no longer exists. No one knows the whereabouts of the Polish Government ... The Polish State and its Government has virtually ceased to exist ...' In view of this state of affairs, continued Mr. Molotov, the treaties concluded between the Soviet Union and Poland had ceased to operate. A situation had arisen in Poland which called for especial concern on the part of the Soviet Government over the security of its State. Until the last moment the Soviet Government had remained neutral. But in view of the circumstances mentioned, it could no longer maintain a neutral attitude towards the situation that had arisen ... Therefore the Soviet Government had instructed the Red Army to cross the frontier. Molotov concluded with an appeal to the Soviet people to help the Army by their loyalty and devotion.

Among the reasons for Soviet intervention, Molotov mentioned also those which were given to the Polish Ambassador a few hours before, namely – 'to take all measures to extricate the Polish People from the unfortunate war into which they were dragged by their unwise leaders, and to enable them to live a peaceful life.'

Grzybowski sent an immediate protest. The Polish Ambassadors in Paris, Washington and London made their statements on the same day (September 17th). The closing paragraphs of the declaration of the Polish Ambassador in London, Count E. Raczynski, read as follows:

'By the act of direct aggression committed this morning,

the Soviet Government has flagrantly violated the Polish–Russian Pact of Non-Aggression concluded in Moscow on July 25th, 1932, in which both parties mutually undertook to abstain from all aggressive action or from attack on each other. Moreover, on May 5th, 1934, by the Protocol signed in Moscow the above Pact of Non-Aggression was prolonged until December 31st, 1945.

'By the Convention concluded in London on July 3rd, 1933, Soviet Russia and Poland agreed on a definition of aggression, which clearly stamped as an act of aggression any encroachment upon the territory of one contracting party by the armed forces of the other and stated, furthermore, that no consideration of political, military, economic, or any other order could in any circumstances serve as an excuse for committing an act of aggression.

'Therefore, by the act of wanton aggression committed this morning the Soviet Government stands self-condemned as a violator of its international obligations, thus contravening all the moral principles upon which Soviet Russia professed to base her foreign policy since her admittance into the League of Nations.'

On September 17th, at Kossow, a borough in the province of Stanislawow, President Moscicki of Poland issued the following proclamation to the Polish Nation:

'Citizens, at a time when our Army with incomparable courage is struggling, as it has from the first day of war, against the overwhelming power of the enemy, withstanding the onslaught of almost the whole of the armed might of Germany, our eastern neighbour has invaded our land in violation of solemn covenants and the immutable principles of morality.

'Not for the first time in our history we are faced with an invasion overrunning our country both from the West and the East. Poland, allied to France and Great Britain, is battling for the rule of law against lawlessness, for faith and civilization against soulless barbarism, against the reign of evil in the world. From this struggle Poland, through invincible faith, must and shall emerge victorious.

'Citizens, I am sure that throughout the hardest ordeals you will preserve the same strength of spirit, the same dignity and lofty pride, by which you have earned the admiration of the world. On every one of you today rests the duty of guarding the honour of the nation, no matter what may befall you. Almighty Providence will render justice to our cause.'

Great Britain, also, pronounced on the Russian invasion.

The following statement regarding the Soviet action in Poland was issued by the British Ministry of Information on September 18th:

'The British Government have considered the situation created by the attack upon Poland ordered by the Soviet Government. This attack made upon Great Britain's ally at a moment when she is prostrate in the face of overwhelming forces brought against her by Germany cannot, in the view of His Majesty's Government, be justified by the arguments put forward by the Soviet Government. The full implication of these is not yet apparent, but His Majesty's Government take the opportunity of stating that nothing that has occurred can make any difference to the determination of His Majesty's Government, with the full support of the country, to fulfil their obligations to Poland and to prosecute the war with all energy until their objectives have been achieved.'

On September 28th, 1939, the following joint statement was issued by the German and Soviet Governments.

'*Moscow, September 28th, 1939.*

'The Government of the German Reich and the Government of the USSR having, by means of the treaty signed today, definitely settled the problems of the disintegration of the Polish State and having thereby created a firm foundation for a lasting peace in Eastern Europe, they mutually express their conviction that it would serve the true interest of all peoples to put an end to the state of war existing at present between Germany on the one side and England and France on the other. Both Governments will therefore direct their common efforts, jointly with other friendly powers if occasion arises, toward attaining this goal as soon as possible.

'Should, however, the efforts of the two Governments remain fruitless, this would demonstrate the fact that England and France were responsible for the continuation of the war; in which event the Governments of Germany and of the USSR shall engage in mutual consultations with regard to necessary measures.'

Thus, once again in history the mutual crime of Poland's partition bound Germany and Russia together by the bonds of an unholy alliance.

The above-mentioned facts and documents indicate clearly that the Red Army's entry into Poland was not caused by the circumstances which the Soviet Government presented to the world in its official statements. It was an aggression in the full sense of this word, an aggression prepared and worked out carefully before the war broke out, in close partnership with Hitler's Germany.

Soviet troops crossed the Polish border on September 17th, 1939, at a time when the Polish–German campaign was still in full operation and twenty-five Polish divisions were holding their ground. It was the very moment when the impetus of the German advance began to slacken, and the Polish resistance to gain strength, when the very extended communication lines of Hitler's forward troops were overstrained, supplies were running short and operations moving to the Eastern provinces of Poland, where the state of the roads impeded the movements of the mechanized German units.

Moreover the Russian aggression took place on the eve of the day on which, in accordance with the Polish–French military agreement, the French were to launch an offensive in the West against Germany. The timid French held their hand. Consequently the Soviet military intervention had a momentous effect upon the further course of events in the first stage of the war and very considerably curtailed Polish military resistance. The main German strategic aim of 'localizing' operations against Poland and avoiding war on two fronts was thus given effective support by Hitler's Soviet ally.

A few days after this initial USSR assault, the Soviet Army Commander, Timoshenko, issued the following exhortation to Polish soldiers to turn against their officers.

'In the last few days the Polish Army has been finally defeated. The soldiers of the towns of Tarnopol, Halicz, Rowne, Dubno, over 60,000 of them, all voluntarily came over to our side.

'Soldiers, what is left to you? What are you fighting for? Against whom are you fighting? Why do you risk your lives? Your resistance is useless. Your officers are light-heartedly driving you to slaughter. They hate you and your families. They shot your negotiators whom you sent to us with a proposal of surrender.

'Do not trust your officers! Your officers and generals are your enemies. They wish your death. Soldiers, turn on your officers and generals! Do not submit to the orders of your officers. Drive them out from your soil. Come to us boldly, to your brothers, to the Red Army. Here you will be cared for, here you will be respected.

'Remember that only the Red Army will liberate the Polish people from the fatal war and after that you will be able to begin a new life.

'Believe us, the Red Army of the Soviet Union is your only friend.

Commander-in-Chief of the
Ukrainian Front,
S. Timoshenko.'

This invitation made no impression on the Polish soldiers except perhaps to sharpen their anger. Discipline and cohesion between officers and men held firm to the end. The end was only eleven days away.

The nakedness of the USSR's military aggression against Poland was vividly confirmed in excerpts from articles written in the official Soviet press on the occasion of the first anniversary of the attack. They appeared in Krasnaya Zwiezda (17.9.1940, No. 210), organ of the People's Commissariat for the Defence of the Soviet Union.

An editorial entitled *Significant Anniversary* contained the following: '... A year has elapsed since the historic day on which detachments of the Red Army, on orders from the Soviet Government, crossed the frontier. The victories of Grodno and Lwow, the powerful thrust into and smashing of the fortified centre at Sarny and the attacks against the enemy at Baranowicze, Dubno, Tarnopol and many other places, will be recorded for ever in the annals of the Red Army.

'The armoured troops were like an avalanche advancing irresistibly, supported by aircraft, artillery and motorized infantry. Swiftness, an indomitable fighting spirit and lightning action either paralysed or stultified the enemy's resistance. Within twelve or fifteen days the enemy was totally routed and annihilated. At that time one group of the Ukrainian advance forces alone, fighting and outflanking the enemy, captured ten generals, 52 colonels, 72 lieutenant-colonels, 5,131 officers, 4,096 non-commissioned officers, and 181,233 privates of the Polish Army. The swift advance of the Red Army was not facilitated by any lack of enemy resistance. Seven infantry divisions covered the flight of the mean and pitiable government of Poland's landlords to Rumania. In a very short time the main enemy forces were routed by Ukrainian front-line troops under the command of comrade Timoshenko ... At that time we greatly increased the security of our frontiers. All this was achieved by a socialist country at a time when the capitalistic world is going through the turmoil of a second imperialistic war, which the instigators and organizers of this massacre are trying to spread and augment.'

In an article by Corps Commissar S. Kojevnikov, entitled *An historic march*, we read:

'... The leaders of the Polish state together with their

inept generals plunged the country into a war with Germany, but they soon failed ... On September 17th, the Red Army forces, at the decision of the USSR, crossed what was a former Polish frontier ... The attack extended along the entire front-line from the Lithuanian border to the Rumanian frontier. The success of the action was due to a swift advance. The chief task was accomplished by armoured troops supported by aircraft, cavalry and motorized infantry. All resistance, wherever offered, was broken by our troops with energy and determination. Most important parts of the country were occupied and Polish officers and soldiers disarmed and taken prisoner. Our fast advancing army groups were followed by the main body of tanks and cavalry. The attacks were swift as lightning. The armoured troops, advancing under difficult conditions through a trackless country, covered 100–120 km. and the cavalry 80–90 km. a day ...'

The author then indulges in descriptions of the battles and skirmishes fought with the Polish forces. As an example one might select for quotation the capture of Grodno as related by Kojevnikov:

'... In Grodno the Red Army troops met with organized resistance on the part of the enemy. The Niemen bridge had been barricaded and the advancing tanks encounted heavy rifle and machine-gun fire from across the river. The Poles used anti-tank and incendiary shells. In the evening of September 20th, the southern part of the town was captured thanks to a resolute action on the part of our N armoured division. The tanks acted single-handed and routed numerous enemy nests located in buildings and various hiding-places. The enemy tried to encircle our tanks and fired at them from all sides. Some of the tanks broke into the town and fought against overwhelming enemy forces all night through. A part of them was lost. In the morning of September 21st, our artillery on the southern bank of the River Niemen opened fire against the main points of resistance, barracks and trenches. The N rifle regiment, having crossed

the river in boats, built a bridge for the tanks and annihilated a large group of officers in the Poniemun manor. In the
evening the eastern part of the town was captured in fierce
street fighting. Another rifle regiment, following the first,
crossed the Niemen and, assisted by tanks, dispatched a
group of officers (about 250), who were holding the hills east
of Grodno, and took the railway station. On the same day all
resistance on the part of the enemy at Grodno was overcome.
The remnants fled by night towards Sopckinie-Suwalki. In
the Grodno battle 38 senior officers, 28 subalterns and 1,477
other ranks were taken prisoner. At least 350 officers were
killed ... Within a few days 450,000 copies of newspapers
and several thousand copies of different pamphlets were
distributed in the area.'

In the same article the author tells how in the Dubno area
500 officers and 5,500 other ranks were taken prisoner, and in
addition – when General Anders' group was liquidated – two
generals, three colonels, more than 50 lower ranking officers
and 1,000 other ranks. In the Wlodzimierz Wolynski area a
Soviet armoured brigade was said to have taken prisoner
1,500 officers and 12,000 other ranks, and another brigade
commanded by M. Bogomolov about 15,000 prisoners in the
same area and, in the Lublin area, over 3,000 officers and
men.

According to figures quoted by this Soviet newspaper, the
total number of Polish prisoners-of-war taken by the Red
Army in 1939 amounted to 230,000, amongst them twelve
generals and at least 8,000 other officers. This figure is not
complete, as later on, over a certain period, it was increased
by the regular and reserve officers arrested by the Soviet occupation authorities in Poland. To this again must be added
Polish soldiers interned in 1939 in Lithuania and Latvia, who
after the annexation of these countries by the USSR in 1940
found themselves in Soviet hands.

Thus the total number of Polish soldiers taken prisoner by
the Soviets as a result of their operations in 1939 amounted
to some 250,000 men.

The Soviet Command tried to induce Polish units to surrender to the Red Army with a pledge that all officers and other ranks would be released and given the free choice either to return home or to cross the frontier into Rumania or Hungary so that they could enlist in the Polish forces organized there for the purpose of continuing the fight against the Germans. Such proclamations were published in many Polish towns and villages and were signed by the Red Army Commander.

A telling example of how this method worked was the fate of the garrison of Lwow. On September 12th, 1939, German troops approached this town and tried in vain to capture it. An ineffective siege followed and repeated attacks against the town were repulsed. When Soviet troops entered Polish territory and approached Lwow from the other side, they made an agreement with the Germans for joint military action. By September 21st, it was clear that any further resistance was useless. The Russian Command sent representatives to discuss terms. These discussions ended in terms of surrender being offered and accepted. The negotiations were conducted by General W. Langner on behalf of the Poles, and a Soviet General delegated by Timoshenko. General Langner was given a written document setting out the conditions of surrender. These guaranteed, among other privileges, the free passage of officers, soldiers and policemen from Lwow to Rumania through Soviet occupied territory, once arms had been laid down by them at the Polish HQ. Those who preferred to go home instead of crossing the frontier to Rumania were promised food for the journey by the Soviet military authorities.

The surrender terms were signed on September 22nd, 1939, and the Red Army units were to enter the town at 3 p.m. that day. General Langner published a proclamation specifying the time at which the Soviet troops were to enter the town. He justified the surrender of the town by the necessity of preserving it from complete and useless destruction. He further ordered the Polish officers to foregather in front of the building that served as the Corps HQ. After laying down arms they were to march out from the city in military order along Lyczakowska Street towards the village of Winniki.

But the Soviet Army broke its pledge and entered the town before the time agreed, disarming all the Polish units it encountered on its way. The officers who had laid down their arms with a view to being sent to Rumania were directed on foot through Winniki towards Tarnopol. Thence were transported by rail not to Rumania, but to Russia.

A Polish officer, Jozef Czapski, who was also an eminent painter and writer, was there in person, one of the very few survivors of what was to follow. He has described these events in his book *Memoirs of Starobielsk*:

'The negotiations between the Deputy of the Commander-in-Chief, Timoshenko, and General Langner's Staff concerning the fate of several thousands of Polish officers who took part in the defence of Lwow were the most typical example of the methods employed by the Red Army on Polish territory. As a result of these negotiations the garrison of Lwow received a guarantee that after the capitulation of the town the soldiers and officers would not only retain complete freedom of movement but would be allowed to go to Rumania or Hungary and from there to France in order to continue fighting. This agreement was a deliberate deceit on the part of Soviet Army Headquarters. The majority of the Polish officers were deported to special camps in Russia.

'After the surrender the Soviet authorities ordered a supplementary registration of all Polish officers who remained in the town, regardless of whether or not they were called up during mobilization in September 1939. The officers who reported for registration were told that they would receive the same treatment as Red Army officers. In spite of this, on December 9th and 10th, 1939, about 2,000 Polish officers both on the active list and the reserve, were arrested on the strength of the registration records, put into Brigidki prison and then deported.'

Even within the minds of the Russians, there existed a duality of basic conceptions. Some of them clung with the greatest obstinacy to the 'basic theory' of the non-existence of the Polish State and all the logical consequences of this theory. Others had a more realistic approach – an actual military operation against the organized armed forces of the Polish State.

Polish soldiers taken prisoner by the Soviets had absolutely no knowledge of these ideologies. As prisoners-of-war they assumed they would be accorded the well-known (to them) international rights and privileges laid down by the Geneva and Hague Conventions. At that time it did not occur to them that these would be withheld or violated. In fact the USSR had never signed the Geneva conventions regarding the treatment of prisoners-of-war.

The Soviet administrative machinery, unprepared for so large a number of prisoners, had considerable difficulty in making up its mind as how to treat the prisoners they had captured. According to the official communiqués of the General Staff of the Red Army, they were 'normal' prisoners of war and as such entitled to be treated in accordance with the rules of international law. According to the proclamation of the commander of the Ukrainian front, General Timoshenko, they were Soviet sympathizers who had voluntarily come over to the side of the Red Army, and should therefore be treated as friends.

But, according to the 'Theoretical conception' of the 'non-existence' of the Polish State, held by the People's Commissariat for Foreign Affairs (official note of 17.9.39) and the declared opinion of the Soviet press, (undoubtedly shared by the NKVD, i.e. Russian Secret Police) these prisoners were 'members of armed bands' resisting the armies of the legal Soviet authorities, thereby causing the great sufferings to the local population. Their treatment from the point of the Soviet law should therefore be that for ordinary 'criminals', and 'malefactors'.

It was this third view that prevailed. Between it and Polish thinking a great gulf yawned. It was to lead directly to the events of Katyn.

CHAPTER THREE

THE THREE SPECIAL CAMPS 1939-1940

It was between the three special camps at Kozielsk, Star-obielsk and Ostashkov that some 15,000 Polish Army Officers, Frontier Guard Officers, Military Police Officers and various leading intellectuals were detained. Examination of the evidence demonstrates a singular similarity in the setting up, organization and clearing of these camps.

The privates, NCOs and officers in Soviet captivity were kept in about a hundred prison camps, some of which were situated on Polish territory (almost exclusively for privates), others in the interior of Russia (all containing officers, most NCOs and some privates). A number of these camps were only rallying points and were soon liquidated; others existed until the outbreak of the German-Soviet war. After May 1940 many of the camps inhabited by Polish NCOs and privates were transferred to the far North, to the Koma Republic and the Kola peninsula, between the White Sea and the Arctic Ocean (region of the Ponoi river). This was the foundation of the widely circulated rumour that Polish officers were sent to the distant northern territories of Russia.

During the first few weeks after September 1939 many thousands of people were herded into these prison camps, in terribly overcrowded and insanitary conditions, either in half-ruined barracks or in monasteries destroyed by the Revolution. They usually slept on the ground without mattresses or blankets. Once every twenty-four hours, at varying times, food was brought to them, usually consisting of thin lentil soup and a piece of bread.

From the first the treatment of officers (and sometimes

NCOs too) went against all internationally accepted convention. They were not separated from the ranks. In camps in the interior of Russia they were obliged to perform particularly heavy and unpleasant tasks (carrying water, peeling potatoes, cleaning latrines etc.). This was done with the

object of humiliation and as a method of 'propaganda' and 'agitation' aimed at subverting the respect and loyalty of the men.

Here follow descriptions of the three camps containing officers.

The Kozielsk camp was situated in the grounds of a former Orthodox monastery, five miles from the Kozielsk railway station on the Smolensk–Briansk line in the USSR.

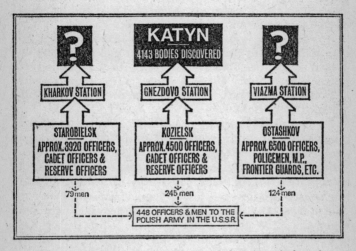

Of 14,920 Polish prisoners-of-war, the great majority of them officers, captured by the Russians after their invasion of Poland in September 1939, and held in the three camps of Starobielsk, Kozielsk and Ostashkov, only 448 were ever seen alive again. The bodies of 4,143 (a total which later rose to 4,253) were found buried at Katyn, USSR – all of these victims having been former inmates of Kozielsk camp.

N.B. The spelling of various place-names in the USSR varies in transliteration from the Russian – e.g. Gnezdovo/Gniezdovo.

About 600 yards from the Monastery and separated from it by woods was the 'Skit' namely a complex of huts comprising the hermitage, outside the monastery wall where the Eremite monks formerly lived. After the extinction of monasteries in the post-revolutionary period, the main monastery building was converted into 'The Gorki Rest Centre for Workers' and the Skit into a 'House for Mothers and Children'. The monastery farm became a 'sovkhoz' (collective farm).

The whole monastery camp was derelict and gloomy. To judge from the graffiti on parapets, windows and walls, Soviet workers frequently expressed their desire to return home from their 'rest' spent in darkness, dirt and boredom. A common pastime was hunting bed-bugs.

In September 1939 both rest houses were earmarked for Polish prisoner-of-war camps. Machine-gun-nests were installed on the four towers and between the towers stood elevated sentry boxes for the guards. The grounds were surrounded by barbed wire entanglements, carefully guarded by special armed guards of the NKVD.

At the end of November 1939 Kozielsk became an officers' camp accommodating about 5,000. Until the beginning of April 1940 only small groups or particular individuals were sent away from Kozielsk and from Starobielsk; most of them disappeared without trace. Just before Christmas, 1939, all the priests with the exception of Father Ziolkowski were removed from the Kozielsk camp, among them the Right Reverend Col. C. Wojtyniak, deputy to the Polish Bishop, and the Reverend Col. Nowak. The only one of them to survive was the Reverend K. Kantak, a professor of the Seminary in Pinsk.

The recollections of survivors are of value here. Professor S. Swianiewicz, one of the survivors of the Kozielsk camp, has written:

'In spite of the magnitude of the Polish disaster, the general mood of the prisoners tended to be optimistic. The Kozielsk prisoners believed in the might of the Allied forces. They hated Germany and never imagined that she could win the war. These strong Western sympathies of the prisoners greatly irritated the Soviet officers who guarded them.

'The Polish prisoners naïvely thought that by stubbornly demanding to be handed over to England and France they

38

could realize their dream of joining the Allied forces. But even those who were aware of the Soviet distrust of the West felt obliged to proclaim and stress that they were officers of an army allied with the Western powers. When the rumour spread that the officers who before the war had lived in Central and Western Poland would be sent home (i.e. – to the territories occupied by the Germans), General Minkiewicz, the highest-ranking officer in the camp, issued an order that all the prisoners in question should refuse any offer to be sent to German-occupied Poland. Under the Polish Military Code, it was the duty of every serviceman in enemy hands to do everything possible to escape and join the fighting forces of his country. At that time the fighting forces of Poland were mostly in France and partly in Syria with General Weygand's Army, and all the thoughts of Polish prisoners in POW camps in Russia were naturally centred on the chance of joining one of these forces.

'Soviet political theory recognizes two methods only of dealing with a defeated enemy: he must either be forced to work for the good of the Soviet Union (and if so, he can and ought to be "re-educated") or else be annihilated. The Soviet authorities had to decide which of these two methods should be applied to the Polish officers in their hands. It was the task of Kombrig Zarubin and his NKVD team to examine the problem with a view to enabling their superiors to reach a suitable decision.

'When they embarked upon their task the NKVD team first tried to create tolerable material conditions in the camp as far as this was possible. There was an improvement in the food and, though still scanty, it was sufficient to keep the prisoners in fairly good physical shape. Accommodation was still cramped: there was not enough room to sleep and a great shortage of laundry facilities. Lice, that plague of Russian life, continued to torment the prisoners.

'Interrogation of the prisoners-of-war now began. Poland was regarded as a tool of Anglo-French capitalism, and though at this stage it was being used against the Germans, it might in altered circumstances be turned against the Soviet Union. The Soviet authorities therefore attached great importance to a thorough examination of the Polish officers.

'The interrogation was no easy task. Every one of those foreigners had to be sized up, and his opinion and value to Soviet Russia assessed. Every prisoner was interrogated separately. Occasionally the interrogation lasted several hours; some prisoners were interviewed four or five times or even more, very often in the middle of the night. Every Polish officer had to give an account of his life, to express his views on various philosophical, political and social subjects, to disclose his social origins, his way of life in Poland, to give details about his family, his friends, etc. At the same time, the officers of the NKVD collected data about every prisoner from various other sources. A prisoner undergoing interrogation would sometimes be astonished to learn how many details of his past life were already known to the officers of the NKVD. To spring a surprise was a favourite trick of the NKVD. One prisoner, who before the war lived in the Polesie area, was struck dumb when the examining officer described in detail even the furniture in this man's house in Poland. In addition, each prisoner was photographed from every angle. The photographs were included in his personal dossier in the camp office and sent to Moscow.

'Some of the prisoners had the privilege of a special interview with Kombrig Zarubin himself. Mostly he invited senior officers, but sometimes selected juniors, especially those who had held some more or less important position in civilian life before the war. An invitation to call on the Kombrig was always an indication of special interest on the part of the Soviet authorities.

'The authorities also tried out re-education. The camp was plastered with propaganda posters; big boards with the complete text of the USSR constitution printed in capital letters were put up and agitators were constantly moving between barracks, expatiating upon the superiority of the new order which the USSR had introduced. Hundreds of propaganda pamphlets were sent to the camp and sold at ridiculously low prices; the camp was also supplied with Moscow newspapers. Loud-speakers transmitting broadcasts from Moscow were installed in the courtyard.

'These efforts at re-education met with no response. The Polish officers were quite willing to read the newspapers and listen to the wireless, because they hoped to learn how the war was going. Propaganda pamphlets were also bought because they were cheap and paper for everyday needs was short. But they told the NKVD officers frankly that they did not believe in the superiority of the Soviet way of life. They said, almost to a man, that they would heartily welcome Russia as an ally against Germany, but did not want Poland to become part of the USSR. They revered the memory of Marshal Pilsudski, whom the Russians regarded as their arch-enemy. In 1940 the name-day of Marshal Pilsudski (March 19th) was celebrated in the camp in spite of all the precautions which the Soviet authorities had taken.'

Of religious life at Kozielsk, another survivor (who remains anonymous because of relatives surviving in Communist Poland) writes about a certain Captain Bychowiec:

'I saw Captain Bychowiec relatively seldom while at Kozielsk. We had our quarters in different buildings; moreover, our intellectual interests were dissimilar and it was clear that our views on many matters did not coincide. But we shared the comradeship established during the days when we fought against the German invaders. I am sure we both felt the specific tie between companions at arms which tells them that they can rely upon each other. Today, recalling the day when Captain Bychowiec left Kozielsk Camp for Katyn, I should like to salute the passing of a comrade with whom I served during the dramatic days of September 1939.

'The task of the re-educating authorities was further complicated by the strong religious beliefs of the prisoners. The uprooting of "religious prejudices" formed a part of the programme of re-education. But in this respect the prisoners were recalcitrant and openly showed their contempt for the propagators of "godlessness".

'Communal evening prayers are an old tradition in the Polish Army, and the prisoners attempted to keep up this practice, which was, however, strictly forbidden by the camp authorities. These orders were ignored and the prayers went

41

on, but after some of us had been punished for taking part in them, we substituted a few minutes' silence for reciting the prayers aloud. Imagine the interior of the former Orthodox church, in which six hundred prisoners were accommodated. Bunks in five tiers covered every inch of the floorspace. The church building was in semi-darkness, which a few electric-bulbs could not dispel; here and there private candles or small kerosene lamps added a flicker of light. Every night, about nine o'clock, the hum of voices and the din of comings and goings which filled the place was silenced abruptly by a cry from the pitch dark choir, 'Silence, please!' At once every movement in this human beehive stopped and everyone stood still. A silence fell as at the Consecration of the Host during Mass. The remote sounds from the outside barely penetrated the walls of the church. People of various faiths – Roman Catholics, Protestants, members of the Orthodox Church, Jews, Free-thinkers – they all observed these few minutes of spiritual life.

'I remember one occasion when an NKVD captain entered our church building during the minutes of silence. He was taken aback, and asked one of the prisoners for an explanation, and the echoes of his voice (he got no reply) seemed to fill every corner of the building, still further increasing the weird effect. Then, after five minutes, suddenly the human beehive returned to normal life, everyone moving and shouting again. The NKVD captain left the church, and there is no doubt that he was convinced that he had witnessed a new manifestation of hostility towards the USSR.

'In November and December 1939, Divine Services were organized in the camp at night time. Army chaplains said Mass and administered Holy Communion with the aid of ordinary ration bread. The night, the darkness, the Ortho-dox atmosphere – all added a queer and impressive touch to the age-old Latin service. Very soon the camp authorities got wind of these services and some of the priests were punished by solitary confinement in the so-called "Carcer". But it was of no avail, and real religious feelings grew notwithstanding all the efforts of the re-educators.

'Special measures were taken by the authorities on Christmas Eve, 1939, when nearly all our chaplains were arrested and sent to unknown destinations during the night. Only one of them was ever heard of again, Father Kantak, who is now in the Middle East. He owed his survival to the fact that he was a Danzig citizen. The others disappeared without a trace.

'There was another exception: Father Ziolkowski. In December 1939 he was put in the camp jail because the authorities found out that he was taking part in religious services. Apparently he was overlooked when the other priests were removed. It is also possible that at that time the authorities were not aware that he was a priest. In his major's uniform he could be easily mistaken for a regular officer. After several weeks he was released and lodged in a separate building, where majors were accommodated – and he carried on with great devotion as secret chaplain of the camp until it was wound up in April 1940. His copy of the *Imitation*, by Thomas à Kempis, and a few prayer books which he possessed were constantly in circulation and a source of moral strength to many prisoners.

'Father Ziolkowski was particularly busy in March 1940, the period of Easter duty for Catholics, when he had to hear the confessions of hundreds of prisoners. He was then often seen walking with an officer, and every time a different one. We knew that these friendly talks should not be disturbed. Indeed, this was a very unusual form of confession under the watchful eyes of Soviet re-educators. Father Ziolkowski said Mass in great secrecy in remote corners of various camp buildings and afterwards administered Holy Communion; the whole service had to be performed very quickly so that the authorities would not realize what was going on. For the overwhelming majority of prisoners it was their last Holy Communion.

'Father Ziolkowski was not an intellectual. Of peasant origin, he was rather rough in manner and down to earth, but his inner force was strong and his faith unshakeable, and he knew the secret of making other men share the strength of his spirit. In appearance he looked more like a soldier than a clergyman, and actually he was a soldier of

43

the Church. Other officers were deeply aware of their inactivity at a time when the very existence of their country was at stake. But this was not the case with Major Ziolkowski; he was still on active service, he fought on to save souls – and he was on duty to the very end. Having known him personally, I am certain that even at the time of his execution he succeeded in giving absolution to those who were going to their death with him.'

Lieutenant 'K', another of the few survivors, whose full name is withheld for reasons of danger to family members in Communist Poland, has described the Soviet authorities at Koziesk, and especially the members of the notorious NKVD.

'Little is known about two high-ranking officers of the NKVD who played a specific role in the annals of Kozielsk Camp. One of them was Kombrig Zarubin, who directed the NKVD team which investigated and recorded the history and background of prisoners and – in all probability – drew up recommendations upon which the ultimate fate of the Polish officers depended. The other man was an NKVD colonel who turned up in the Kozielsk camp before it began to be wound up. The groups of prisoners sent off in the direction of Smolensk came under his control the moment they entered Kozielsk, and another source reports that he was seen at Gniezdovo railway station in April 1940 supervising the transport of the groups that were leaving the trains for Katyn Forest.

'Kombrig Zarubin was the highest Soviet authority with whom the Polish officers who were detained in Soviet POW camps could enter into direct contact, and the picture of that suave, educated and well-mannered general is still vivid among the few survivors from those camps. There is a mystery about Kombrig Zarubin, and it is hard to tell whether he should be regarded by Poles as an enemy or as a friend.

'The Kombrig had overriding authority over his team of NKVD men. It was difficult to define his position precisely, without being familiar with the secret hierarchy of the NKVD; but it was obvious that he ranked very high. He was not the commandant of the camp; actually the major in charge of it was subordinate to him. He was usually referred to as "The Kombrig", and everyone in the camp – the gaolers as well as the prisoners – knew that he was the highest authority on the spot.

'The behaviour of the Soviet officers in Kozielsk towards the prisoners was more or less correct, but the correctness of the Kombrig had even a touch of the distinction of a cultured man. As a rule the prisoners did not salute Soviet officers. But General Minkiewicz, the senior Polish prisoner in camp, issued an order that they were to salute the Kombrig. The Kombrig always returned the salute politely and often his face brightened with a friendly smile on these occasions.

'The Kombrig did not take part in the usual interrogations of prisoners, but from time to time a prisoner was asked to call on him for a talk. Sometimes these talks took place without anyone else being present, sometimes in the presence of other Soviet officers, mostly the chief of the so-called third (Intelligence) department in the camp office. The Kombrig was a very agreeable man to talk to. He was an educated man, he knew not only Russia, but the West as well. He spoke fluent French and German and had also some knowledge of English. Usually he asked prisoners their opinion on various social, political and philosophical problems. He would say, "We belong to two different worlds, but I like to discuss our differences with an educated man from the opposite world." And usually he would offer his victim cigarettes of good quality. Sometimes also tea, cakes and even oranges were served.

'The Kombrig had a small but select library with Russian, French, English and German books, some 500 volumes in all. He was kind enough to allow the prisoners to use these books. Thus *The World Crisis*, by Winston Churchill, became the most popular book in the Kozielsk camp.

'The Kombrig did not take any direct part in the re-education campaign in the camp. He seemed to stand above the daily nonsense of Communist propaganda. Yet he was clearly the man who was required to form an opinion about the problem of the Polish prisoners and to report to the highest authorities in Moscow. What was his real opinion?

45

Nobody outside the NKVD knew it. Neither did anyone know whether he made any suggestions as to what should happen to the prisoners. Nevertheless, when later on it was rumoured that a major decision had been taken, the Kombrig suddenly left the camp. His departure made no impression at the time, since he often went to Moscow for a few days. But this time he left for good.

'The prisoners were extremely curious about "Brigadier-Commander" Zarubin. We did not know whether this was his real name or an assumed one, though various unconfirmed rumours concerning his past were rife. According to one of these, he was supposed to have been a Soviet ambassador accredited to some Western country after having been attached to the Soviet Embassy in Warsaw for a long time. It is, howeyer, not possible to say how much truth there was in all this. But it seems certain, that he had some connection with the Soviet diplomatic corps, as witness his knowledge of other languages and the special interest he showed in relations within the Polish Ministry of Foreign Affairs – as I noticed when talking with him.

'It may well be asked: Was his friendly and courteous approach the cunning trick of a professional, or was it sincere? No clear-cut answer can be given. Quite possibly, both attitudes were simultaneously present and interwoven.' Although this book is concerned with the Katyn massacre, and therefore with the camp at Kozielsk, from which the Katyn victims were exclusively drawn, it is proper that mention be made of the other camps – Starobielsk and Ostashkov.

STAROBIELSK

Starobielsk is a small township in the eastern part of the Soviet Ukraine (Voroshilovgrad province) situated to the south-east of Kharkow. The Polish camp was located in the precincts of a former monastery, and comprised some 15 acres surrounded by a wall with, in the centre, a large Orthodox church facing the gate. On the left side stood another smaller church, and more than ten miscellaneous brick and wooden buildings. During the first years after the outbreak of the Revolution, this monastery was used as a transit concentration camp for prisoners being deported further east. In a remote part of the camp a large number of bullet marks could still be seen in the wall, recalling that period. The Polish prisoners had the feeling that this had been a place of executions. Afterwards, until the arrival of the Polish prisoners in 1939, the buildings of the former monastery were used as granaries.

From the end of November until the first days of April, i.e. until the time when the final winding-up began, the camp was occupied almost exclusively by Polish officers, both regular and reserve, totalling some 4,000. About half this number were officers taken prisoner after the surrender of Lwow and deported eastwards, contrary to the surrender conditions. Others were seized by the Soviets as prisoners-of-war or arrested in various parts of Eastern Poland, partly as a result of the registration order issued for occupied territories.

This number, as well as the general character of those detained at Starobielsk, remained unchanged until the beginning of April 1940. Small groups or single individuals only were taken away (these included a priest, moved, as were those from Kozielsk, on Christmas Eve, 1939) and most of them disappeared without trace. At the time when the winding-up of the camp started there were in captivity there, eight generals – L. Billiwicz, S. Haller, A. Kowalewski. K. Lukowski, K. Plisowski, F. Sikorski, L. Skierski, P. Skuratowicz, according to information in the possession of the Polish authorities.

The number of officers of lesser rank were approximately as follows:

150 colonels and lieutenant-colonels,
230 majors,
1,000 captains,
2,450 first- and second-lieutenants,
30 cadet-officers, as well as
52 Polish civilians.

The total of prisoners was 3,910.

From the service branches there were several hundred Air Force officers, the entire personnel of the Military Anti-Gas Institute, surgeons, chaplains of all denominations – i.e. Catholic priests, Protestant ministers and Rabbis.

The reserve officers held at Starobielsk were:

Several hundred University professors and lecturers. About 400 surgeons and physicians, both civilian and military.

Several hundred engineers with University degrees.

Several hundred lawyers – judges, public prosecutors, solicitors and civil servants.

A great number of High School and Grammar School teachers. Many poets, writers, journalists.

A great number of social welfare workers and politicians, among them A. Eiger, Vice-President of the Anti-Hitlerite League in Poland.

As in other camps, there were amongst the inmates of Starobielsk also men disabled in previous wars who had been arrested as serving officers by the Soviet authorities.

OSTASHKOV

Ostashkov is a provincial town situated north-west of Kalinin (Tver) on the Seliguer Lake and served by the railway line that runs between Wielkie Luki and Bologoye. The camp was some 15 kilometres from the town on an island on Lake Seliguer, and like the other two camps occupied the precincts of an old monastery.

From November 1939 until the beginning of April 1940, i.e. until the date when the winding-up of the camp began, it held about 6,500 prisoners. Unlike the two camps already mentioned, this was not an officers' camp; there were only about 400 officers, of whom 300 belonged to the Polish Police militarized after the beginning of the war in September 1939. In addition there were officers, non-commissioned officers and privates of the Intelligence service, Military Police, Frontier Guards, State Police and Prison Warder Corps, several scores of priests, ex-servicemen settlers (mostly from the north-eastern regions), landowners and court magistrates. The latter prisoners, coming under the heading 'bourgeois', were, like the officers, considered by the Soviets to be potentially particularly dangerous.

The number of Polish prisoners-of-war held in the three above mentioned camps in the early spring of 1940 therefore totalled nearly 15,000, mostly officers. In mid 1941, i.e. after the beginning of the German–Soviet war and the resumption of Polish–Soviet relations, only about 400 of them could be traced. These were mostly officers who had been taken from the camps before mid-March 1940, passed through the Pavlishchev-Bor Camp, and were then transferred to the Griazovietz Camp. Of the many generals detained in these camps in the spring of 1940, only one escaped, General Wolkowicki. In all, some 14,500 Polish prisoners-of-war, of whom over 8,000 were officers, vanished without trace: that is, about 97 per cent.

The following is an account of one of the survivors of the camp at Ostashkov, senior-sergeant Jozef Rychalski:

'The detachments of the Frontier Guard (in which body I served) operated in the region of Rawa Ruska and Zolkiew and were incorporated in various formations organized on an emergency basis as they fought skirmishes with the forward detachments of the Wehrmacht in the "no-man's-land" between the invading German Army and the Soviet armies. It was not until September 26th, 1939, that I finally parted with my uniform, a thing beyond price, for I had spent most of my life in uniform. Having divested ourselves of our arms, we carefully packed rifles, pistols and ammunition and buried them near a forester's lodge when almost in sight of a detachment of the "victorious" Red Army. To this very day I cannot recall that moment – one of the most melancholy in my life – without a sigh. Looking each other straight in the eye, we parted with this silent farewell – pals who had spent so many years together on the borders of our native land. We all set off in different directions.

'After several days of wandering on foot and by bicycle I reached Bolechow, where I expected to find my family temporarily installed. I had been stopped and detained by the Bolsheviks at various places en route, but each time I had managed to get away. At Bolechow I began to look for work, any kind of work that would enable me to buy some bread for my wife and three little children. The Bolsheviks paid little heed to the empty stomachs of the "liberated" population of that part of Poland which they had seized. They attached far more importance to what they called "victory-work", whereby the Polish element which might influence the masses in any way was deported deep into Russia. Then came an order that all newcomers to Bolechow must register on October 25th, 1939. I went to register my family and myself. Yes, I went, but never returned. They arrested me, took me to the prison in Dolina the same day, and thence on November 2nd, transferred me to the prison in Stanislawow. During the night of November 10th, all the prisoners there were loaded into wagons adapted for this purpose and transported via Tarnopol, Podwoloczyska, Ploskirov, Shepetovka, Kiev, Konotop and Briansk to Babinino, our destination, where we arrived on November 25th. Thence, many miles on foot to Pavlishchev-Bor camp. Fifteen days of nightmare journey.

'Here, members of the police force were separated from the others and transferred somewhere else on December 21st, leaving members of the Frontier Guard and of the Borderland Defence Corps. Formed into a separate group, we left Pavlishchev-Bor on January 30th, 1940, struggling through waist-deep snow to Babinino railway station. Here we were loaded into authentic Soviet prison-wagons, painted green – symbol of hope – or a quick death. Like animals in barred cages, we were trundled on and on for thirteen days, with frequent stops at various places as the war with Finland had disrupted traffic on this railway line.

'We reached our destination, Ostashkov railway station,

on the morning of February 11th, 1940. We were so stiff, having been confined for such a long time in the cages without room to move, that it was difficult to get us out on to the snow-covered ground; the glaring light blinded us, thus adding to our misery. We were lined up in a column (of living corpses) and, guarded by an ample escort, set off through one of the absolutely deserted streets of the town.

'Passing through the town, I noticed only one striking feature: the ruins of what had once been an impressive church. It now bore a large signboard which announced that some club or other was housed there. The street ran to the shore of an ice-bound lake studded with numerous distant islands, between which tracks had been dug in the snow to facilitate motor traffic. We were marched down one of these tracks and it was evening before we reached an island. Long before we "landed" on it, the cupolas of an imposing church came into sight and then a number of single storey buildings around it: we assumed it must once have been a monastery. When we got nearer the fencing of the little island, we noticed lines of people standing on the embankment and then saw that most of them wore the navy blue uniform of the Polish police. We soon realized what use was being made of the buildings on the island. It was still a "monastery", only now it had been made into a temporary abode of suffering for the Polish victims of Soviet subjection and brutality. We were led on to the camp parade ground. We recognized people whom we had met at Pavlishchev-Bor. I was allocated to the 4th Corps, housed in a long, low brick building at the lower end of the island which must once have contained the workshops used by the monks. In the long room we entered new bunks had been installed in tiers, looking as if they had never been used before. We took up our positions in these together with our beggarly belongings.

'Quarantine lasted nearly to the end of February 1940. This time was occupied with de-lousing, having baths, the clipping-off of our beards, etc., and we received prophylactic injections. In addition, we were submitted to endless investigations and registrations, besides being photographed with our registration numbers on our chests and having prints made of all the fingers on each hand. At the end of this period we began to make contact with inmates who had come before us. As far as I could see, the camp had none of the organization to which Poles were accustomed in such a situation. This was due to the fact that the camp had only recently been set up, and to the rumours that we would not be staying there long.

'I learnt from chums who had arrived in the camp before me that we were on one of the many islands of Lake Seliguer, about 35 square miles in area and believed to be one of the sources of the River Volga. Our particular little island had two names: Ilovaya and Stolobnoye. The western part of the island is higher than the eastern part and it was there that the buildings had been erected. These were surrounded by a high wooden fence, while the island as a whole was encircled by barbed-wire fencing. The ruins of what had once been a church still stood on the highest point of the islet; around them were two-storey buildings which used to serve as living quarters for the monastery personnel and give shelter to pilgrims. Here too, were the kitchens. The buildings around the church ran in a continuous ring broken only by two gateways, one that led from the interior of the island and the other from the landing stage, formerly used by small ships which provided communication between the various small islands during the summer. Outside this ring of buildings round the church, there were other ones: stables of one or two storeys, workshops and other administrative quarters. Some had been destroyed by Bolshevik shellfire during the years when the island was being besieged: it appears that anti-Communist White Russian forces had put up a stubborn defence there before disaster finally overtook them. Rumour had it that the defenders were massacred by the victors or drowned in the lake and in the well of the miracle-working spring; the well-head was then destroyed so that no trace remained by the time we came there; but the site was pointed out to us.

'Though of the original inhabitants of the island few can have been spared, one of the survivors, a monk (he may not have been the only one) lived and worked there during our stay; his job was to cart out the excrement from the latrines every day with a single horse lugging his "tanker" along. This monk was a tall man, with expressionless face and deep-sunken eyes. He looked like a walking corpse and never said a single word, even when somebody spoke to him – a living automaton. It was said that in Tsarist times, the islet was famous because members of the royal family celebrated their weddings there. As far as we were concerned, the place was a monument to the unending martyrdom of the Polish nation: when we found the inscription "Kowalski 1863" carved on one of the stones in the foundations of the landing-stage gateway, we realized that Poles taken prisoner during the insurrection in 1863 had laid the foundations under the monastery which now served as a staging post on our way to destruction.

'Buildings not used by the NKVD, the camp guard and the camp administration, were crammed full of Polish prisoners-of-war. There were about 7,000 of us. Those quartered in the church building were the worst off. The dark, gloomy, fusty naves and aisles of the enormous church building were filled with three-tier bunks to reach which phantom-like men had to clamber painfully up – like monkeys climbing the posts of dovecotes. The place was indescribably overcrowded; the stench was overpowering.

'Most of the prisoners-of-war had belonged to the police, but other classes and professions were well represented. Policemen from Silesia (Slask) were very numerous indeed, and they occupied the middle block of buildings surrounding the church; it was called the Silesian block for that reason, though not all the Silesians were quartered there. Officers of the police and the Frontier Guard regardless of rank inhabited a separate building outside the church precincts and their housing conditions were more bearable.

'Beyond the camp fence stood a building that had been set aside for the most part for officers whose cases, from the Bolshevik viewpoint, required special investigation. It was reported that Beria himself came there from time to time.

'The only woman prisoner-of-war in the camp for a time

was a Pole with the rank of second-lieutenant of the air force.

'From time to time I would drop into the "officers" building, since I knew many of the occupants from pre-war times; I cannot, however, remember their names now. The officers helped us by sharing their bread ration with us and by organizing collections of money in aid of the sick other ranks most in need. I made contact with Lt. Jozef Downar, whom I had known personally as an instructor in the Frontier Guard Central School in Rawa Ruska; he later served as an officer in the headquarters of the Frontier Guard for the Silesian Region of Katowice – the region in which I was stationed up to the last.

'Amongst the other ranks, I had closest relations with platoon-leader Josef Sieradzki of the Frontier Guard: we had served together for many years in the same commissariat, the one in Nowa-Wies. In Ostashkov, amongst my pre-war acquaintances in the police force of the district where I served, were: Senior Sergeant Emil Walder, constable Jan Kryska, Senior Sergeant Jan Wojcik and his deputy, as well as commandants and constables of some other police-posts. But I no longer remember their names. Nothing more was heard about all these people after they were taken away from Ostashkov.

'The prisoners-of-war were put to work in the following manner. The Bolsheviks decided to join our islands with the mainland by means of high embankments with a wooden bridge in the middle to allow for the passage of ships and boats. The earth for the embankments was taken from the island and the shores of the peninsula, and work was begun at both ends simultaneously. As the embankments became longer, the earth was transported on what might be described as shallow sleighs pulled by humans and horses. One day, two officers engaged on transporting earth (by means of two horses harnessed to a sleigh) at the mainland end got on to their sleigh when the guards were not looking and tried to escape; they drove their horses for as long as possible and then abandoned them, after which they continued their flight on foot. But they were caught the same day: it was quite easy to track them on the snow. They were cast into the camp prison where they were kept under terrible conditions before being transported elsewhere.

'Everybody was anxious to participate in this work for two reasons: it was a welcome interruption in the monotony of camp life and, most important, those who worked received supplementary food rations. As I did not work, all I received was a small piece of darkbrown bread (it looked like peat), three half-litre helpings of fish soup made of pilchards and stinking to high heaven, and two tablespoonfuls [sic] of barley groats. Those who worked, however, could eat their fill of bread and groats. Our basic food ration just sufficed to keep body and soul together, but we suffered constant pangs of hunger. Incidentally, these supplementary rations for the workers were at the cost of the non-workers: there was a notice in the kitchen which stated the daily ration per prisoner, but no information was given regarding the ration for those doing heavy manual work.

'Another group of workers granted the same food privileges as the embankment labourers were those engaged in cutting and transporting ice. Lake-ice a metre thick was sawn into blocks. These were loaded on to long sleighs, pulled by humans, to be taken to an enormous cellar under one of the camp buildings for storing. My friend Sieradzki (mentioned above) and constable Regowski had been given this work. Both of them, but particularly the former, contributed substantially to my nourishment by supplying me with bread and groats from their supplementary rations. Several score men were engaged on this work. Apart from those employed on the above two jobs, several hundred were detailed off to work on tidying-up the camp and in the storehouses, and digging roadways through the snow on the icebound lake; others did odd jobs on other islets utilized by the NKVD for purposes known only to that organization. These workers, however, received no supplementary rations, although they were given some cold helpings of food when work outside the camp lasted longer than usual. Once, I even received a small piece of sausage.

'Towards the end of March, when the sun began to warm the southern walls of the camp buildings, men like phantoms with sunken cheeks, pale faces and expressionless eyes could be seen plastered against these walls like so many flies. The vitality and enterprise which marks Poles even in the most difficult of situations, now began to make themselves felt, both in a positive and a negative manner. A music group was formed: with violins made of plywood, concerts were held at which folk melodies dear to the Polish heart brought many a tear to the eyes. Others fashioned what were often small masterpieces in the shape of rings, religious ex-votos and carvings from bone and in fact from every available material under the most primitive conditions. Some ruthless types, of low moral fibre, gave expression to their enterprise by under-cover trading: acting as intermediaries between the camp staff and the prisoners, they secured food-stuffs and tobacco, and then mercilessly stripped their comrades in misfortune by bartering these products for everything of any value at all, managing to retain these in spite of countless searches of their belongings by the Bolsheviks.'

CHAPTER FOUR

THE WINDING-UP OF THE CAMPS

In the first days of April 1940 the general winding-up of the three camps, where the majority of Polish officers and special categories of prisoners in Soviet hands were concentrated, was started simultaneously, and was carried out systematically.

Although the camps were situated in widely separated administrative districts, the closing-down procedure was evidently based on a single plan. This suggests that the entire operation had been prepared beforehand and decided by the Soviet authorities at the highest level. The fate of these Polish prisoners-of-war was sealed in the beginning of 1940, by a decision taken with cold-blooded calculation at a time when the USSR was at peace, and collaborating smoothly with Hitler's Germany.

The clearing of the camps at Kozielsk, Starobielsk and Ostashkov took from five to six weeks. By about mid-May they had ceased to exist. A new camp at Pavlishchev-Bor was set up, to which some 400 of the 15,000 inmates of the three camps were transferred. It was from those who survived among these remaining prisoners-of-war, who were later transferred to Griazovietz and liberated in 1941, that the Polish military authorities obtained reports and information concerning the winding-up of the three camps. It enables us to reconstruct a picture of the method by which this operation was conducted and the mood and hopes of the prisoners. Professor S. Swianiewicz [some of whose accounts have already been quoted] describes the last days before the winding-up of the Kozielsk camp:

'March 1940 was a joyful month in the Kozielsk camp. From the surrounding fields and forests came the breath of spring. Deep snow still covered the ground but spring was in the air. The nights were still very cold but the pure, frosty air acted like a tonic whilst the aromas of awakening nature caressed the senses. The snow dazzled with its whiteness and reflected the stars at night. We prisoners assembled during the day where the church walls sheltered us from the wind, unbuttoned our greatcoats, took off our caps and exposed ourselves to the gentle rays of the sun; some of us acquired nearly as deep a tan as after skiing excursions before the war.

'There were several reasons for the sense of joyful antici-pation pervading the camp. First of all, everyone believed the spring would bring the longed-for Anglo-French offensive that was expected to destroy Hitler's power and humble his freshly recruited ally, the Soviet Union. Sec-ondly, it became known that the Soviet authorities had come to some decision regarding the closing-down of Kozielsk camp. Here nobody knew the plan, but everybody expected a change for the better. It was believed that we would all soon be free. True, there were two schools of thought as to how this would come to pass, represented by the optimists and the pessimists respectively. The optimists reckoned we would shortly be handed over to the Allies. Some even expected that the Russians would move us southwards in order to hand us over to the Western powers, said to be assembling a large army in the Near East under the command of General Weygand.

' "Gentlemen," such an optimist assured us in the low, earnest tones which implied access to a special source of in-formation which he could not disclose, "there can be no doubt that the Soviet authorities are very embarrassed by the whole affair. They were incautious enough, in the autumn of last year, to take an enormous number of Polish officers into captivity, and now they don't know how to extri-cate themselves from the situation. We are, after all, officers of the Allied forces. Because of us, the Soviets risk a conflict with the powerful Anglo-French alliance. The French will start an offensive on the western front any day now. The Soviets cannot run the risk of a further worsening of relations: after all, Weygand's air force can in case of need bomb Baku within a few hours and knock out the chief sources of Russia's oil supplies. Not so long ago, a political commissar visiting our block blurted out that we can't begin to imagine how great is the outcry in the world on our account!"

'And all the time the sun poured down the brilliance of its rays to gild the weather-beaten walls of Kozielsk monastery; the snow sparkled in its whiteness and gradually contracted as the thaw set in. The world was so beautiful and everything around pulsed with such promise of reborn, pulsing life, that even the most hardened sceptics tried to accept this optimistic reasoning.

'Even the pessimists supposed that our captivity in Russian hands was nearing its end. They did not believe, however, that we would be handed over to the Western Allies, but that we would be simply sent back to our homes: to central Poland, western Poland under German occupation or to the Wilno district under Lithuanian administration – depending on the place of domicile given in our records. Opinions were divided as to the fate of those whose homes were in Polish territories under Soviet occupation. Some thought they would be sent home; others doubted whether the Russians would agree to leave so many educated, army-trained people on the western borders of their strategic area. It was supposed therefore that the Russians would be more likely to keep many of them in camps or settle them elsewhere in Russia, even directing officers of the reserve to work in their civilian professions. The more pessimistic ones thought that all of us would be handed over to the Germans, who would, of course, intern us with their other prisoners-of-war; but even this held the promise of our being allowed to see our families while on the way to the German prisoner-of-war camps.

'The most pessimistic theories, then, had their hopeful side. True, they precluded all hope of further participation in the war against Germany. Everybody wanted to take part in the war, just as all of us believed in ultimate victory; it was therefore irksome to remain inactive while our luckier colleagues were reorganizing themselves in France, with thousands of volunteers slipping out of Hungary, Rumania and Poland to join them, and while the forces of the Polish Home Army were growing apace. All the same, there was one consoling thought. It was rarely mentioned, but practically all of us cherished it: the hope that we would soon see our loved ones. To see one's wife once again, to hug the children, to spend even a few days in the family circle – and then, come what may. This modest private hope brought some consolation to nearly every heart.

'An NKVD private strode from the sunlit assembly ground into the murky interior of the church which housed some 600 prisoners: a runner from the camp administration came to say one of us was to report to the camp command. Nothing unusual; somebody or other was always being summoned because the authorities constantly had something that needed supplementing in the records of the prisoners kept by the NKVD personnel in a most scrupulous fashion. The officer thus summoned had probably been dozing in his bunk; he began to get down slowly and unwillingly, the NKVD rifleman urged him to hurry: "Get a move on, Mister. Get up quick: you'll soon be going back to your lady." And the broad, good-natured face of the NKVD private would be wreathed in smiles. The officer in question would smile palely, and his fellow-prisoners would also smile. For, in the rough wit of the messenger there was a glimmer of a mirage – a mirage which never leaves a prisoner, even one condemned to a life sentence: the mirage of freedom.

'I was strolling along the camp assembly ground at the close of one of these sunny and joyful days. A tall, burly NKVD man was striding some twenty steps or so in front of me. His greatcoat, boots and cap told me that he was an officer. I did not recognize his figure and gait as belonging to any high-ranking member of the camp administration. So I increased my pace a little and glanced at him as I passed. The lapels of his greatcoat bore the insignia of an NKVD colonel, an important officer considering that ranks in the security police service have higher hierarchical significance than in the Red Army. (Thus, a sergeant of the NKVD, i.e. a sergeant in the State Security Service, receives the rank of lieutenant when detailed off to the Army, whilst the rank of major in that service is equivalent to that of colonel in the Army.) But what struck me most was his face: it was the ruddy-purplish face one associates with a butcher. It made such a powerful impression upon me that I was scarcely aware of anything else about him. "Surely," the thought came to my mind without any logical reason, "the arrival of this butcher must be connected with the liquidation of the camp." The feeling would not leave me that I had brushed against the secret of the fate prepared for us; but the nature of the secret could not be read from his face. I turned and looked at the NKVD colonel again but our eyes did not meet: his glance slid indifferently from one inanimate object to another, but he showed no interest in the prisoners who wandered all around him.

'And yet his face reminded me of something and, on my way back to my quarters, I tried to identify it. Suddenly, from amidst the multitude of images buried deep in my memory, a scene slowly began to take shape, a scene which I had subconsciously associated with that face: a nursery, the fair unruly hair of little children and, scattered on the floor, illustrated story-books. In one of them was the picture of a giant intent on preparing a roast from little children. In the colouring and expression of the NKVD colonel's face there was something that closely resembled those of the creature shown in the story-book.

'Having established the association, my thoughts wandered farther away from the butcher's face of the NKVD official and from any attempt to explain the reason for his arrival in Kozielsk. My thoughts passed to matters nearest my heart. I strolled along, breathing in the pure frosty air laden with the smells of approaching spring, whilst memories of the past gradually asserted themselves. I could almost feel the physical presence of my dearest ones. The beloved world I had left at home seemed to be the only real and actual one, whilst all that now surrounded me – the

NKVD, the camp, and all that Nazi-Soviet world – seemed as unreal as the story-book giant. I reached my quarters, clambered up the tier of bunks to my place and the rhythm of the reality I had conjured up lulled me to sleep.

'The first group bound for Katyn left a few days later.' Professor S. Swianiewicz goes on to describe the first transport.

'It was on April 3rd, 1940, an hour before dinner. We were all in our living quarters, a small room in the building opposite the bath house and crammed with two-storey bunks to accommodate about forty officers. These comprised mainly cavalrymen, most of whom had tried to break through to Hungary during the last week in September 1939, under the command of General Anders. An NKVD rifleman came in briskly and called for Lieutenant K. Such a summons was in itself nothing unusual, as somebody or other was always being called to the camp office to provide supplementary data for the card-index. But in this case, the rifleman added, "Sabierai sia s vieshchami" – "Take your things with you". These routine words, familiar in all the camps and prisons throughout the Soviet Union, meant that Lieutenant K. was to be separated from us and sent to some unknown destination. We were surprised, as there seemed to be no reason why the Soviet authorities should show any special interest in the person of Lieutenant K. He was an officer in the regular army (combat force) who certainly had nothing to do with Military Intelligence and had never even served in the Frontier Defence Corps. We were just trying to guess why he had been singled out when another officer hurried into our quarters and told us that Captain Bychowiec had been summoned in just the same way. Immediately afterwards, in swift succession, came news that a number of other officers had been taken from the other buildings for transfer elsewhere. All had been summoned individually, by name, told to take their belongings and report for departure. Obviously, the long-awaited liquidation of the Kozielsk camp had begun.

'Soon afterwards, a fresh piece of sensational news swept through the camp like wildfire, namely that groups of fifteen

or so officers apiece were beginning to arrive from the "Skit".
This was a complex of hermits' huts outside the monastery
walls where were quartered Polish officers who had homes
situated on Polish territory incorporated with the Soviet
Union by decree of the Supreme Soviet. Officers domiciled in
territories under German occupation or in that part of the
Wilno region which had been handed over to Lithuania by
the Soviets were housed within the monastery walls. Now, it
must be remembered that shortly after our arrival in
Kozielsk, the place of birth and home address of each prisoner were scrupulously noted down by the camp administration.

'In all, about 4,000 officers and 100 civilians were interned
at Kozielsk and about 1,200 of these – as far as I remember –
were transferred to the "Skit". The camp administration
made every effort to isolate the two groups as completely as
possible. There was, however, no bath-house in the "Skit"
and the officers there were allowed to use the one within the
monastery walls; groups of these officers were usually escorted by political commissars and NKVD riflemen whose
task it was to prevent any communication between the
"hermits" and the monastery dwellers. None the less, whenever a "hermit" group passed across the monastery courtyard, they always shouted out some news – our only source
of information regarding life in their part of the camp.

'This segregation of prisoners according to an artificial
and imposed new State allegiance caused us great distress: it
was eloquent proof that the Soviet Government meant all its
declarations about the elimination of Poland's statehood to
be taken quite seriously and ruled out any possibility of its
ever being restored. The fact that the groups leaving the
camp comprised officers from the Polish eastern provinces
and prisoners whose homes were in central and western
Poland before the war suggested that the attitude of the
Soviet Government had changed. It was also significant that
the "Skit" prisoners who passed with their belongings
through the monastery courtyard were now no longer forbidden to stop and chat with friends from whom they had
been separated for so long. The curtain of isolation which

had separated us was raised; as was to be expected, this change was the subject of very optimistic and hopeful comments.

'The officers who were due to be sent away were conducted to the "club-house", which had a large hall where propaganda films were sometimes shown. The entrance was guarded by NKVD riflemen who admitted only those on the list. The remaining prisoners crowded in front of the building, leaving a passage free for those entering it. Some of those about to leave the camp had no belongings apart from a greatcoat or a rug; they were mostly combat officers who had fought to the bitter end and then, manoeuvring between German and Soviet detachments, had tried to break their way through to Hungary. Others, however, carried suitcases – sometimes more than one; most of these officers had been serving in hospitals, auxiliary services and institutions evacuated to eastern Poland where Soviet troops subsequently rounded them up. The departing officers were greeted with cries of "God-speed", interlarded with optimistic assurances for the future and expressions of hope that they would see further war service. The "hermits" were greeted and seen off with special enthusiasm. It was as if, though in captivity, we were celebrating the unification of the Polish Army: there was not the slightest suspicion that this unification was taking place in the shadow of Lady Death – who unites and levels all, who weaves her sombre background to the colourful highlights of life and has a special affection for soldiers in time of war.

'A dinner, much better and much more abundant than the normal one, was brought to the officers in the "club-house". Both those about to leave the camp and the other prisoners interpreted this as a Soviet attempt to produce a favourable last impression on the former – an attitude which implied the unspoken surmise that we were being handed over to some non-Soviet authorities. The corollary was: Into whose hands? To Poland's allies or to the Germans?

'In addition, every officer leaving the camp received the following rations for the journey: 800 grams of bread, some sugar and three herrings. The manner in which the herrings were handed out caused an even greater sensation than the re-uniting of the "hermits" with the monastery dwellers. Every ration of herrings was wrapped up in brand-new, unused grey paper! Only those acquainted with life in Soviet camps can truly appreciate how great was the impression this made; it was always quite a problem to secure a piece of paper – to write a letter, to roll a cigarette, or simply for use in the latrines. Cigarettes were rolled for the most part in strips torn from newspaper or from the propaganda pamphlets that were handed out to us and which found a ready market as a source of paper. And yet, suddenly, absolutely new, unused paper was now being used to wrap up herrings, without it would seem, any attempt at economy. "They probably want to produce the impression that there is culture in the Soviet Union," the prisoners remarked, using the terminology to which the political commissars so often had recourse when explaining the beneficial aspects of Soviet life. But even the suggestion that the Soviet authorities wanted to produce a favourable impression on someone outside the USSR carried pleasant and hopeful implications.

'This first transport of prisoners who left Kozielsk on April 3rd, 1940, consisted of about 300 officers and inaugurated the winding-up of the camp. Thereafter groups left more or less regularly – sometimes on successive days, sometimes at intervals of several days – and the average number of men in each transport was kept at this figure. We also managed to find out, from Russian civilian workers engaged on jobs inside the camp, that the transports proceeded in a westerly direction. This seemed to clash with the optimists' opinion that we were to be handed over to our British and French allies and supported the view of the pessimists that the Germans were to take us over. On the other hand, the possibility that we should be transferred to some other camp in Russia now seemed less likely – since in that event the transports would not be going westwards.

'Whenever a transport was about to leave, the same procedure was adopted. Until noon, nobody as a rule knew whether a group of prisoners would be going that day or not;

the prisoners certainly did not know and I am convinced that the great majority of the NKVD men were equally in the dark. Most probably, there was not a single person who knew this with certainty. True, the Russian workmen told us fairly regularly that on the railway siding just outside the township of Kozielsk wagons were being prepared for a transport; but the mere fact that wagons were being marshalled did not necessarily mean a transport would leave that day.

'Usually, at about 10 a.m., Moscow would telephone the camp commandant ordering the transport for that day and giving the names of the officers who were to go. It was always a very long telephone call because about 300 names had to be dictated and many of these must have sounded very foreign to Russian ears and had to be spelt out. As a rule the news that such a telephone call was in progress spread very quickly through the camp. In fact, when the ventilation panes of the office windows were open, anyone standing outside could plainly hear the names being repeated or spelt out by the official who was receiving the telephone call. As soon as the first page of names was ready, NKVD riflemen hurried off to summon the officers listed. These gathered up their belongings and, as a matter of routine, proceeded to the "club-house" where they had their dinner and received the regulation rations for the coming journey – including the herrings wrapped in nice, clean paper.

'The fact that all the officers who were to leave were selected individually by Moscow impressed the prisoners. This seemed to support the view that the Soviet central authorities were seriously concerned over the fate of the Polish officers. Some of us hazarded the guess that a Franco-British-Soviet mixed commission (or perhaps a Russo-German one) was deciding which Polish officers were to be sent abroad and that the telephone messsages from Moscow to Kozielsk meant that such decisions were being put into effect. Once the probability had been accepted that we were being evacuated from the Soviet Union, this was a perfectly logical assumption, the more so since the remarks made by some of the political commissars lent it further credence. They would say, for instance, "You'll go abroad, but not all of you." Commissar Alexandrovich, of the camp administration, who attended to the prisoners' personal matters and was very courteous in his attitude towards us, accepted a colonel's camera, sealed it and promised the apparatus would be handed back to the owner on arrival at his destination. Everybody interpreted the words "on arrival at destination" to mean "after crossing the Soviet frontier".

'I, personally, did not believe we were to be handed over to any foreign power. I assessed the military and political position of Britain and France much less optimistically than most of the other prisoners-of-war in the Kozielsk camp; to me it seemed most improbable that Poland's allies – as matters stood in 1940 – could force Russia to hand over to them her Polish prisoners-of-war. If the Germans were involved on the other hand, I failed to see how it could be in their interest to get the Polish officers transferred from Russian to German captivity. But, though I discounted both hypotheses I was unable to substitute one of my own to explain why Moscow should telephone the names of the officers to be sent away from Kozielsk on each given day.

'I was standing in the monastery courtyard one day. A group of officers from the hermitage area were marching across the sunlit square on their way to the bath-house. Lieutenant Krahelski, who owned a country estate in Slonim County, detached himself from the group and stepped up to me – this was at a time when the "hermits" were no longer forbidden to speak to us. The lieutenant, a most likeable young man, was full of enthusiasm. "What do you say now?" he said to me; "I always said things would turn out well! And you see, they [the Russians] have naturally been forced to get off their high horse!" I looked at him and thought, "My dear young friend, your rejoicing is naïve nevertheless". Though, I must admit that I was in a state of pleasant anticipation myself.

'Lt.-Colonel Nowosielski, my commanding officer and closest companion during the last ten days of fighting in September 1939 came up to me immediately after and asked in a joking way, "Well, Lieutenant, what have you to say about all this? You're one of the pessimists after all." I answered: "I don't know, Sir, how to explain all this, but one thing seems clear: there is no longer a Kozielsk monastery and a Kozielsk hermitage camp. We are once more, in Soviet eyes, prisoners-of-war from a single homogeneous Polish Army. Obviously, something must have happened to make the Soviet authorities adopt such an attitude."

'The colonel abandoned his jocular tone as he regarded me closely. "So, that's what you think, is it? Perhaps you're right. Maybe—" Somehow, his cryptic smile, charming as it was, expressed scepticism. But, for an instant, his face reflected some nagging thought left unexpressed. Today, when I recall this conversation, I often wonder whether this really excellent officer and commander, who boosted the morale of others and strove to keep alive their faith in ultimate victory, was the only one amongst us who succeeded in guessing the mystery of those telephone messages from Moscow.

'On April 21st, 1943, Lieutenant W. J. Furtek, a Polish officer, ex-prisoner-of-war from Kozielsk camp, who had been a cadet officer while there, wrote in the *Polish Daily* in London:

'... About 3,500 officers had already left the camp when I myself was sent away.

'Everybody very naturally tried to guess what the future held in store for those who had to leave.

'In spite of the atmosphere of mistrust the majority opinion was that they were going home. Our talks with "poli-trouks" and lower camp officials lent added credence to this view. They openly declared that people taken from the camp would be handed over to the Germans, and Brest-Litovsk was even mentioned as the place where the handing-over would take place. This seemed to us the most likely interpretation, since the majority of those leaving the camp came from central and western Polish provinces.

'I remember that the first officer from our row of barracks to have his name read from the list was Captain Bychowiec, a young artillery officer, the commandant of that building. The men that were to leave were at first anxious, but soon grew cheerful. When the group headed by generals Minkiewicz, Smorawinski and Bohaterewicz was leaving, the Soviet authorities gave them a farewell dinner at the local "Club" and then the whole camp turned out to see them off.

'I, myself, left the camp on April 26th, 1940. Everybody making up the party was carefully searched before departure. The Camp Commissar, Dimidovich, approached our group as we were queueing before being searched and said: "Nu, tak vy kharasho popali." We could not make out whether he was being ironical or meant what he said. Now I see that those words which could be translated as: "Well, yours was a lucky draw," really signified good news, for, as it later transpired, we were one of the only two groups to escape the Katyn slaughter.

'We were put into large lorries outside the camp gates and were driven to the railway station of Kozielsk after making a big detour through the woods to avoid the village. There we were locked into special railway carriages. The train consisted of six coaches and we occupied two of them. We waited on a siding for two hours and during that time another group from the Kozielsk camp was loaded into the other coaches.

'We left Kozielsk and, judging from the position of the sun, we seemed to be going south-west. After several hours we reached a junction, probably Sukhiennitse. After a short stop, we set off in a north-easterly direction. Lying on the top berth of the compartment during the journey, I noticed some words written on the wall with a pencil or a burnt match. They read: "Two stations beyond Smolensk. We get out. We are loaded." The writing was partly defaced and the date could have been April 12th or 17th. It aroused great interest in the compartment, and there was much conjecture as to what it might mean. Lt.-Colonel Prokop, who was with us, thought that it was probably written by Lt.-Colonel Kutyba, as they had promised each other to leave some message behind.'

Another account of the winding-up of the camp at Kozielsk comes from Wladyslaw Cichy, who also was a cadet-officer at the time of his imprisonment there.

'At the beginning of 1940,' he writes, 'rumours started spreading that the camp was to be closed down. Added strength was given to these rumours by the fact that owing to the camp being so overcrowded the chances were that by the time spring arrived we were likely to be decimated by epidemics. From time to time members of the Camp Head-quarters staff would hint that we were soon to leave Kozielsk. But if so, where to? In the absence of any precise information, speculation was rife. The optimists were convinced that we would be handed over to our Western Allies ... or be allowed to return home. The realists resigned themselves to the idea that our camp would be broken up into smaller camps ...

'Finally, on April 3rd, 1940, the camp was all agog. Our Bolshevik guards visited a number of blocks and read out the names of certain prisoners, ordering them to assemble in the Club. The selected men, amounting to some 300 all told, were given a special meal and handed some food for the journey and marched through the gate. The following day the same procedure was repeated, and from then on nearly every day a batch of prisoners left the camp ... What was their destination? ...

'On April 26th, my name was called out. At last the mystery was to be solved! I collected my few earthly possessions and embraced my friends: Au revoir! The highest-ranking officers in our group of 107 men were General J. Wolkowicki and Colonel M. Boleslawicz. In the guardroom, outside the wall, the Bolsheviks made a thorough search of everyone. They were after sharp objects and took away from me a broken mirror. After that we were loaded on the lorries and soon were approaching, not the railway station, but a deserted railway siding. I could see prison wagons. Until then we had always enjoyed the luxury of travelling in cattle trucks. This time we were degraded to the level of common criminals. The guards crammed us into the coaches – 16 prisoners to each compartment meant to seat eight – and locked the doors with chains.

'The train is on the move,' continues Cichy, 'but where to? We examine our surroundings. On the wall of the compartment are some notes scribbled in Polish. On the ceiling we can read the words: "Detraining at Gniezdovo station". The name is unfamiliar. Two days later the train stops at a station – Babynino. From a neighbouring compartment comes a message from Lt.-Colonel Mara-Meyer: "There is a camp near-by, called Pavlishchev-Bor." And indeed, after several hours waiting we are ordered off the train and soon find ourselves in a neat-looking camp, beautifully situated among pine trees. The camp is empty. Plenty of room and much better conditions. The following day we noticed a commotion at the gate: Polish uniforms! It was a group of 63 prisoners from Starobielsk, among them I have noticed Lt.-Colonel Berling. During the following week we were joined by further groups of prisoners from Ostashkov, Kozielsk and Starobielsk. Our number increased to nearly 400.

'From our colleagues from Starobielsk and Ostashkov we learned that their camps and their living conditions had been similar to ours and that the breaking-up of their camps had followed the same pattern as in Kozielsk. There were nearly 4,000 officers and cadet-officers in Starobielsk and approximately 6,500 men, mainly police officers and Frontier Guards (KOP) in Ostashkov. By now we were firmly convinced that other convoys had been directed to similar small camps and we were grateful to the Bolsheviks for improving our miserable conditions.

'Towards the end of May Commissar Alexandrovich, who had been on the staff of the Kozielsk Camp Administration, mentioned to a friend of mine that we were soon to be transferred to another camp. This is the only instance I can remember when advance information given by the Bolsheviks proved correct. And indeed, at the time when in the West the Germans were imposing surrender terms on France, our small group of 390 POWs was in transit by rail to Griazovietz

71

camp situated some 300 miles due north of Moscow in the direction of Archangel.

'In August 1940 some four months after we had left I received a letter from my sister from German-occupied Poland. Among other things, my sister wrote: "There was with you in Kozielsk a Lieutenant X. [The actual name is suppressed for obvious reasons.] Please ask him to write to his fiancée who is very worried at the lack of any news from him. I assume that Lt. X is together with you ..." I answered my sister in good faith: "Lt. X is not with me. No doubt he is in another camp and I am sure that his fiancée will soon be hearing from him."

'Similar letters inquiring after fellow prisoners from previous camps were received by my colleagues. At that time these inquiries did not arouse any suspicion in our minds. Somehow we felt that the Bolsheviks had adopted a more lenient attitude towards us; nor was it unusual for our correspondence to be interrupted for periods of up to several months at a time. But inquiries kept coming in, became more insistent and involved always more names. I remember the discussions we had on the subject. What made us ponder was the fact that all the news from other prisons had stopped since Kozielsk, Starobielsk and Ostashkov days, and that we had heard no mention of any new camps but our own. This weighed upon our minds and filled us with foreboding. Months passed, Russia was overrun, and ultimately the hour for our release, and yet for a period of 14 months there had been not a single sign of life from our comrades.

'Our worst fears were confirmed two years later, when on April 13th, 1943, the German radio gave the news of the discovery of the Katyn graves.'

In June 1942, Professor Stanislaw Swianiewicz recounted what he had seen at a small railway station near Smolensk to General Wolikowski, Chief of the Polish Military Mission in the Soviet Union. On April 30th, 1960, he gave his first public account of it.

'As luck would have it, I am the only surviving Polish officer who travelled with a group of fellow prisoners-of-war from Kozielsk to a railway station in the vicinity of Katyn. It is exactly twenty years ago to the day, namely, on April 30th, 1940, that I was near that place of execution, though I did not know at the time what was happening there...

'I was summoned on April 24th. Amongst those who were sent away with me I recall the names of 2nd Lt. Leonard Korowajczyk, 2nd Lt. Tadeusz Tucholski (an assistant professor in Warsaw Polytechnic), and Professor Marceli Zoltowski.

'Isolated in a separate building, we were given a little bread and some herring for our journey, after which we were handed over to a fresh escort team who very thoroughly searched all our effects and confiscated every sharp object amongst them. We were then taken by motor lorry to the marshalling yard near the railway station where six Stolypin-type prison wagons were ready for us in a siding. Fourteen men were packed into every compartment-cell.

'We travelled all night with hardly a stop on the way. It was on the morning of April 30th that we caught sight of the church towers of Smolensk lit by the first rays of the rising sun. The train was held up for ten minutes outside the station and then went on. We tried to establish in what direction we were travelling by observing the shadows outside and came to the conclusion that it was northwest. This greatly encouraged us. Were we really being repatriated to Poland?

'But the train stopped after covering about ten miles or so. The outer wall of our compartment had no windows, but we could hear the throbbing of a powerful internal combustion engine and the sound of many people tramping about. Somebody in the next compartment shouted that our group was already beginning to leave the train.

'Some time later, a colonel of the NKVD entered our wagon and ordered me to get my belongings together and follow him. The whisper went from compartment to compartment: "Lithuania has probably claimed him." I got out of the wagon. It was a fine, sunny day; the scents of spring came from the fields and, here and there, small patches of snow lay on the ground. There was a small railway station some two hundred yards away, but not a soul was to be seen on the platform. The colonel led me to another wagon, an empty one, and had me locked up in one of the compartment-cells. A guard was stationed at the grille which served as the door of the cell.

'Again, I heard the throbbing of an internal combustion engine and some commotion behind the blind wall of my compartment. At that moment, I noticed a small hole in the wall just under the roof; so I climbed up on to the upper shelf, normally used for bundles of belongings, in the hope that I would be able to look through the opening. To my surprise, the guard did not order me down, so I lay down on the shelf and pretended to fall asleep. I glanced at the guard after a time and, finding him gazing through the corridor window with his back to me, I looked through the hole.

'I saw a fairly large open area, with patches of grass. It was bounded on the left by a road running parallel to the railway track. A low, slatted fence ran beside the road, and seemed to border the garden of one of the little station buildings, but I could not see any inhabitants. The horizon was screened by trees and bushes. Numbers of NKVD guards with fixed bayonets occupied the area in front of me and an ordinary passenger bus stood there; it was of medium size and had whitewashed windows. The bus had a rear entrance, so that when it was backed up to the railway wagons, the prisoners could step straight into it. NKVD soldiers stood on both sides of the bus with bayonets fixed. When about thirty prisoners had boarded the bus, it drove off and disappeared behind the trees. The vehicle returned after about half or three-quarters of an hour to take off the next batch.

'A black prison-van without any side windows stood a little to one side; an NKVD captain, aged about 50 and with grizzled fair hair, stood beside it. The NKVD colonel who had picked me out from my group stood, with hands in the pockets of his greatcoat, in the middle of the area: he was a tall, stout, middle-aged man, with dark hair and a ruddy face. He was obviously directing the whole operation. I wondered what kind of operation it was. Clearly, my companions were being taken to a place in the vicinity, probably only a

74

few miles away. It was a fine spring day and I wondered why they were not told to march there, as had been the usual procedure on arrival at camps. The presence of a high-ranking NKVD officer at what was apparently the simple operation of transferring several hundred prisoners from one camp to another could be explained if we were actually going to be handed over to the Germans. But, in such a case, why these extraordinary precautions? Why the fixed bayonets of the escort? I could think of no reasonable explanation. But then, on that brilliant spring day, it never even occurred to me that the operation might entail the execution of my companions.

'The grille which served as the door of my cell was opened some time later and I was told to get out. The grizzled NKVD captain transferred me to the prison van and transported me to the so-called internal NKVD prison in Smolensk where I was kept for six days. I was then sent, escorted by four special guards, to the Lubianka prison in Moscow, where I was handed a document charging me with espionage and signed by the Prosecutor-General of the Soviet Union.

'A new chapter in my life as a prisoner now began. I was sentenced, in 1941, to a term of eight years hard labour in a penal labour camp. It was not until the spring of 1942 that I was released after numerous representations had been made by Ambassador Kot and after the Polish Foreign Ministry had handed a special Note to the Soviet Ambassador accredited to the Polish Government in London. When I came to the Polish Embassy in Kuibyshev in June that year, I was bombarded with questions about the fate of the officers in Kozielsk.

'It was then that I filed an official report in writing with General Wolikowski, Chief of the Polish Military Mission, giving the facts which I have just narrated. The report astounded all those interested in the matter; for, despite the constant, insistent inquiries made by General Sikorski, General Anders and Ambassador Kot, the Soviet authorities had never even mentioned that the Kozielsk officers had been transported to the Smolensk district. It was only when news was received of the discovery of the Katyn mass-graves in

1943 that the various unco-ordinated elements of the mystery which puzzled so many of us began to fall into place and produce a coherent whole.'

By collecting all the available information it is possible to ascertain details of the convoys which left the camp at Kozielsk in April and May 1940, and these are set out in chronological order below.

April	3	62	men including among others:	J. Niemczyński, Wojciechowski.
,,	4	302		
,,	5	280	ditto	Fryga, Burdziński, Westerowski, Wolyszyn.
,,	7	92	ditto	Gen. Minkiewicz, Gen. Smorawinski, Gen. Bohaterewicz, Col. Stefanowski, Lt.-Col. J. Kutyba, Mjr. Solski, Capt. Szyfter.
,,	8	277	ditto	Kruk, Zalasik.
,,	9	270		
,,	11	290	ditto	Wajda, Wajs, Bogusławski, Przygodziński, Iwanuszko, Prof. Pieńkowski, Ulrich, Skupien.
,,	12	204	ditto	Kotecki, Ochocki.
,,	15	150	ditto	Col. Pawlikowski, Bilewski.
,,	16	420	ditto	Lt.-Col. dr. Moszczeński, Capt. Trojanowski, Znajdowski, Sołtan.
,,	17	294	ditto	Roguszczak, Liliental, Majewski.
,,	19	304	ditto	Jóźwiak, Handy, Leitgeber, Rumianka, Domania, Rzążewski.
,,	20	344	ditto	Kowalewicz, Prausa, Jabłoński, Prof. Morawski, Paciorkowski.
,,	21	240	ditto	Dr. Jakubowicz, Capt. Trepiak.
,,	22	120	ditto	J. Zięcina.
,,	26	100	ditto	(All survivors sent to Pavlishchev-Bor and Griazovietz.)
,,	27	200		
,,	29	300	ditto	Prof. Świaniewicz, Dr. Tucholski, Lt. Zóltowski, Zóltowski, Lt. Korowajczyk.
Total		4,249		

In May 1940 the last three convoys left Kozielsk.

May	10	50 men	
„	11	50 men	
„	12	90 men	(All survivors sent to Pavlishchev-Bor and Griazovietz.)
Total		190 men	

Of these 190 men, the last convoy of 90, and the one which left Kozielsk on April 26th, arrived at the camp of Pavlishchev-Bor.

The evidence suggests, then, that out of a total number of 4,440 deported men only two convoys of about 200 men in all and a few individuals detached from various convoys *en route*, have been traced.

As already mentioned, some prisoners were taken away from Kozielsk, either singly or in small groups, before the camp started to be wound up at the beginning of April 1940. Stanislaw Lubodziecki, then colonel and a public prosecutor of the Supreme Court, after joining the HQ of the Polish Army in June 1942, made the following statement:

'I was removed from Kozielsk on March 8th, 1940. In the evening of that day soldiers of the camp guard began to collect officers from the various huts. Their names were typed on a short list.

'After these persons had been identified by the seniors, the NKVD soldiers ordered them to collect their possessions immediately, whereupon they were driven brutally to the camp administration building. Here the prisoners were rather superficially searched and all state property was taken away from them. They were conducted in groups of two or three to the railway station about eight miles away. Each group was escorted by two NKVD men armed with revolvers.

'It was difficult to march in a temperature of minus 20 degrees C., heavily laden, along dark, rough paths covered with frozen and slippery snow; particularly as the guards were constantly prodding the prisoners on. When an old retired colonel was clearly beginning to tire the guards shoved him on brutally, abusing this "officer of the White Guard", who "now cannot walk, though last year he was able to march with the troops against the Red Army", and tauntingly urged the "old warrior" to get back on his feet and hurry to his "little wife", whom we would see tomorrow.

'After travelling for three days, during which time the train was more often standing at stations than moving, the prisoners, having travelled only about 130 miles, arrived at Smolensk. Here at some distance from the station they were unloaded from the truck and formed into ranks. One of the guards ordered them to march in formation, without speaking to each other or to any passer-by, to look straight ahead and not to break ranks; he warned them that if anyone took even half a step sideways this would be regarded as an attempt to escape and the guards would open fire immediately. After crossing the railway yards, the prisoners were halted in front of a closed gate, leading on to a road, and were ordered to kneel down in the deep, dirty snow. After a few minutes a black, closed bus arrived and the prisoners were ordered to stand up in turn and get into the bus.

'The bus was specially designed for transporting prisoners. A narrow corridor ran up the centre, on both sides of which were many low and narrow doors. When a prisoner stepped into the corridor, he was ordered by an NKVD standing there, to enter backwards into one of the cabins. These compartments were unlit and so small that the prisoners were forced to adopt a crouching position. This was the prisoners' first experience of the "tshorni voron" (black raven) well known to Soviet citizens. Some of the prisoners were already extremely anxious because of having apparently been especially picked out from about the 5,000 other POWs. They were also bewildered by the journey of several days in what to them had hitherto been inconceivable conditions and by the constant abuse hurled at them by the guards. They were therefore reluctant to enter the dark, narrow holes, assuming that this was some unknown method of torture or even execution. The guard, however, pushed each one in and, after shutting the door, called out for the next prisoner.

'As the prisoners had been taken singly from their huts at Kozielsk, conducted to the station and loaded into the train in twos or threes, they had no idea who the rest of their fellow-travellers were. They did not see them until their arrival at the station in Smolensk. Just as during the journey every prisoner had tried in vain to puzzle out the reason for his removal from Kozielsk by going over his past life and particularly the period of imprisonment, so now in the bus each one tried to guess what the future held in store for him by analysing the composition of the group, in which everyone had one or two acquaintances. But they could think of nothing all these men had in common.

'There were altogether 14 officers in the group, including Colonel A. Starzenski, a cavalry officer and formerly Polish Military Attaché in Belgium; Captain J. Radziszewski, an officer formerly attached to the military Replacement Office, and Lieutenant Graniczny, a naval officer who had played an important part in the Polish rising against the Germans in Silesia in 1921.

'After travelling for less than twenty minutes, we were offloaded in a small yard, surrounded by buildings with barred windows. Five prisoners were separated from the group and conducted to one of the buildings; the rest were ordered to re-enter the "tshorni voron". After a few minutes they were ordered out again and four more were put into the prison building. Then the bus drove off with the remaining five.'

Thus in the yard of the Smolensk prison on the afternoon of March 13th, 1940, this group of prisoners from Kozielsk was broken up. Except for Colonel S. Lubodziecki, the author of the report, who was sent from the Smolensk prison to prisons in Kiev and afterwards to the Forced Labour Camp, nothing more was heard of any of the other officers of the above-mentioned group.

The prisoners' families, who had remained at home in Poland or were deported to the Soviet Union, received letters from the three camps more or less regularly, until the spring of 1940. But after the disbandment of Kozielsk, Starobielsk and Ostashkov, this correspondence ceased except in the case of the four hundred transferred to Pavlishchev-Bor and afterwards to Griazovietz.

Some of the members of the families that had been deported to Soviet Russia, in an attempt to find out the whereabouts of the missing prisoners, made inquiries at the Soviet authorities. The answers, where received, were all the same – to the effect that the camps had been disbanded and the prisoners in question transferred to an unknown destination. We record two typical cases:

One of the Polish soldiers who arrived in Great Britain from Russia in 1942 reporting to the Polish authorities, stated that his father, a policeman in Zdolbunow (Poland), had been arrested there by the Soviet authorities and was subsequently sent to the camp for Polish prisoners-of-war at Ostashkov, from where he communicated by letter with his family in Poland.

On April 13th, 1940, his family (wife, son and daughter) were deported by the Soviet authorities from Zdolbunow to southern Kazakhstan, from where they still tried to correspond with the father. Not receiving any reply from him, the deported family approached various local and central Soviet authorities – the NKVD, public prosecutors, etc., even Stalin himself – with a request for information as to what had happened to this prisoner. After a long delay, in the spring of 1941, they received the following answer, signed by the public prosecutor of the Ostashkov district:

'The camp in which your father was living was disbanded in the spring of 1940. The present whereabouts of your father are unknown.'

The following interesting document was found in the record of the Smolensk branch of the NKVD and published:

A Polish citizen, Alexandra Urbanska, was deported with her family from Poland to Rodnikovka, province of Aktyubinsk, Kazakhstan. When she requested the NKVD to inform her of the whereabouts of her husband, Lieutenant Richard Urbanski, who had been at Kozielsk but from whom she had received no news since March 1940, an official of the Smolensk NKVD, Filipovitch, was alleged to have made the following comment:

'Inform her that he was transferred to an unknown camp. 6.5.40.'

The body of Richard Urbanski was found in one of the Katyn graves.

SUMMARY OF FACTS

1. In the first days of April 1940 the simultaneous disbandment of the camps at Kozielsk, Starobielsk and Ostashkov was started.

2. As similar evidence from survivors (e.g. Joseph Czapski, Lt. Ilynarski, J. Rijchalski) the winding-up was everywhere carried out in an almost identical manner. The prisoners were given the same reasons for being moved, the transports were formed at the same time of the day and followed the same procedure. The numbers were more or less the same everywhere, and the selection was made according to some unintelligible scheme which the prisoners failed to decipher.

3. The winding-up of the camps, carried out in accordance with an overall plan, was directed from Moscow, where all decisions concerning the selection of personnel for the transports were taken and the lists were dictated by phone to the camp commandants at the last minute.

4. Transports from Kozielsk which could not afterwards be traced were directed to a station some 10 to 15 kilometres west of Smolensk, and unloaded there.

5. At the camp of Pavlishchev-Bor about 400 prisoners-of-war arrived, officers, and cadet-officers transported from Kozielsk, Starobielsk and Ostashkov, who, for a variety of obscure reasons which are still a mystery to most of the men themselves – were the sole survivors of about 15,000 prisoners-of-war, amongst them about 9,000 officers. Soon, these 400 were to be transported to the camp of Griazovietz, from which in 1941 they were released after the outbreak of the war between the USSR and Germany.

6. The surviving prisoners-of-war soon began to receive from Poland inquiries about those who had been with them in the three camps, and it could be seen from these inquiring letters that all correspondence from these men had ceased after the liquidation of the camps in question. Nor did the families of these missing prisoners deported to Russia receive any letters from them.

CHAPTER FIVE

THE SEARCH AND THE GERMAN ATTACK ON RUSSIA 1940-1943

FROM mid-April 1940 nothing whatever has been heard from the 14,500 Polish prisoners-of-war from Kozielsk, Starobielsk and Ostashkov. No letter, no postcard, no message of any kind was ever again received by the relatives of those who were missing. All they got were their postal packets officially stamped 'return to sender'.

In view of the state of war, with all the confusion and disruption it entailed, and taking into consideration the vast size of the territories over which that war was raging, the relatives at first sought justification for the 'delay' in hearing from their captured menfolk. Time moved on, and still they heard nothing. Apprehension grew – an apprehension not diminished by what those relatives saw their new oppressors doing around them. During the whole year, summer 1940 to summer 1941, wives, mothers, sons and daughters wrote again and again, still in hope – but no answer came. On June 22nd, 1941, Germany attacked the USSR. In the first months of the war the Russians suffered heavy defeats. The German armies advanced swiftly, penetrating deep inside Russian territory. The number of prisoners taken by the Germans rose steeply and reached very high figures.

Under the stress of a highly critical political as well as military situation, the attitude of the Soviet Government began to shift not only towards the Western Allies, but also towards Poland. The Russians were obliged to ask the Allies for assistance: they were threatened with complete destruction.

Though Poland was at war against Hitler – while at the

same time being stabbed in the back by the Soviet Union – she made no special reservations nor asked for any compensation from the Soviet Union save only for a return to the *status quo* that had preceded the Soviet aggression. Such a request was of course an essential condition for any agreement with Soviet Russia. Poland also requested the immediate release of all Polish prisoners held on Russian territory. This attitude was made clear in the Note delivered to Anthony Eden, the British Foreign Secretary, by the Polish Foreign Office on July 8th, 1941, and in the draft of the Polish–Soviet agreement of July 12th, 1941.

Eventually the Polish–Soviet agreement was signed on July 30th, 1942. Its additional protocol read as follows:

'The Soviet Government grants an amnesty to all Polish citizens now detained on Soviet territory either as prisoners-of-war or on other adequate grounds as from the resumption of diplomatic relations.'

The agreement and the protocol were to come into force immediately upon their signature and without ratification.

On August 14th, 1941, the Polish–Soviet military agreement was signed. From this moment the Polish prisoners-of-war and civil internees deported from Poland by the Soviet authorities during the invasion of Poland, released from camps and prisons, began to join the Polish units organized on Soviet territory.

Very soon, however, the members of the Polish Headquarters in the USSR realized that many officers who were personally known to them and who according to their own most reliable information had been taken prisoner by the Soviets in September 1939 were still missing. Among the missing were also nearly all the officers of General Anders' group from 1939, including Major Soltan, Chief of Staff, Major Furman, for many years General Sikorski's aide-de-camp, and many senior officers.

During the very first weeks after the signing of the agreement the attention of the Soviet liaison officers was drawn to the fact that many officers were unaccounted for. The Russian liaison officers stated that they were unable to give any definite information as to the fate of the officers in question, and continued to come out with an old, semi-official story to the effect that a great number of Polish officers had been released in 1940 and sent back to Poland.

The Polish authorities at once regarded this explanation with suspicion, since letters received from Poland by prisoners who had been in Griazovietz camp made it clear that the missing officers had not returned home. In view of this the Polish authorities ordered the Underground Army in Poland to investigate whether these missing persons were detained in German prisoner-of-war camps after their alleged delivery into German hands by the Soviets.

At the same time a special department was instituted at the Polish Headquarters in the USSR for the purpose of drawing up a list of the missing officers. As early as September 1941 both the Polish Government in London and the Polish Military Authorities in the USSR made strong representations demanding the whereabouts of the missing prisoners.

The Polish Government in exile, in London, still refused to question the loyalty of the central Soviet authorities and clung to the explanation of why so many Polish citizens had not been released that either the authorities of local camps and prisons were unreliable or the fact that transporting them from faraway in the north or east was a difficult and cumbersome process.

Even before the Polish action took the form of methodical and repeated request, General Anders had taken up the matter in August 1941. On August 4th, the General was released from Lubianka prison in Moscow. That same night Lt.-Colonel Berling and Lt.-Colonel Dudziński called on him. They were his sole visitors for the next few days. It was not until August 8th, that General Anders met General Szysko-Bohusz, sent to Moscow from London as Chief of the Polish Military Mission.

From Lt.-Colonel Berling and Lt.-Colonel Dudziński General Anders received positive information that there were three big prisoner-of-war camps, mainly for officers but also for non-commissioned officers of the military police, the police and constabulary of frontier guards, at Kozielsk, Starobielsk and Ostashkov. They reckoned that the number of inmates of these camps was about 15,000, a figure that later proved to be accurate.

The same two officers also informed General Anders that in the spring of 1940 about 400 officers from these camps were removed to the camp at Pavlishchev-Bor and subsequently transported to Griazovietz, where they were joined by the so-called 'Lithuanian Group', that is to say, Polish officers previously detained by the Lithuanians who had a quarrel with Poland over Wilno. All this information was later confirmed in conversation with other officers.

On August 16th the first official meeting between General Anders and representatives of the Soviet military authorities took place with General Panfilov presiding. General Zhukov of the NKVD also attended. Already at this first conference General Anders asked the Soviet delegation how many soldiers were still detained as prisoners-of-war, and who would be available for the Polish Army being formed in the USSR. He was told that 1,000 officers and 20,000 ORs might be considered as being available. This answer made a deep impression on General Anders and he immediately asked about the camps at Kozielsk, Starobielsk and Ostashkov. The Soviet representatives replied that they were unable to answer this question, but that they would try to obtain exact information. General Anders kept on putting this question at each of five consecutive conferences, but without obtaining any satisfaction. It was significant that no mention of this was ever made by the Russians in the minutes of the meetings.

Eventually General Anders received from the officers at Griazovietz all the details of the winding up of the three large POW camps in the spring of 1940.

On September 20th, 1941, the Polish Ambassador, Professor Stanislaw Kot, had his first conversation with the Deputy Commissar for Foreign Affairs, Andrei Vyshinsky.

On September 27th Kot handed to the Soviet Government a note which pointed out that:

(a) many Polish citizens were still being held, individually and in groups, in forced labour camps and prisons,

(b) they were prevented from establishing contact with the Polish Embassy,

(c) many other Polish citizens were denied the right to choose or change their place of residence,

(d) they were compelled to work as prisoners,

(e) they were refused certificates of amnesty.

The next Kot–Vyshinsky conversation took place on October 7th, 1942. At the end of it the Polish Ambassador returned to the problem of the missing Polish prisoners-of-war, mostly officers.

Kot said: 'I now wish to quote some figures. Altogether 9,500 officers were taken prisoner in Poland and deported inside the USSR, while there are only 2,000 in our army. What happened to the remaining 7,500 officers?'

Vyshinsky tried to convince Kot that these figures could not be right but was unable to find valid arguments.

Kot replied: 'We have tried everywhere to find them. Thinking that they might have been handed over to the Germans, we have made inquiries in German prisoner-of-war camps, in occupied Poland, everywhere they might be. I could have understood it if a few dozen individuals were missing, or let us say, several hundred, but not several thousand.'

Vyshinsky, evidently embarrassed, gave no clear answer.

On October 13th, the Polish Embassy again presented a note stating that the Soviet Government was not abiding by its pledges in the matter of the release of Polish citizens.

On October 14th, a further conversation took place between Kot and Vyshinsky. In the course of it the Polish Ambassador, referring to the proposed visit of General Sikorski to Moscow, said: 'I venture to hope that General Sikorski will find all his officers when he arrives.'

'We will deliver to you all the persons we have,' Vyshinsky replied, 'but we cannot hand over those who are not with us. The English, for instance, have given us the names of their nationals who are supposed to be in the USSR, but who have actually never been here.'

The Polish authorities in London eventually checked up in Poland the initial information given by the Soviet liaison officers, according to which the prisoners-of-war from Kozielsk, Starobielsk and Ostashkov had been released and sent home in 1940. The Polish Underground Organization reported that the officers in Soviet hands had not returned home during the German occupation nor were they being held in German prisoner-of-war camps; moreover all correspondence with their families had stopped since April–May 1940.

The most disturbing reports were at that time coming from the USSR; these stated that a considerable number of Polish citizens were still awaiting release. For this reason, before his intended visit to the USSR, General Sikorski sent a personal note to Mr. Bogomolov, the Soviet Ambassador to the Polish Government, on October 15th, 1941. There was no reply to this note.

Ambassador Kot referred to his previous conversations with Vyshinsky. 'I specified to Mr. Vyshinsky several parts of Soviet territory where the amnesty has not been observed and pointed out the categories of our citizens, such as officers, judges, public prosecutors and members of the police forces who had not been released.'

Mr. Molotov replied that, in principle, all Polish citizens had been set free on the strength of the amnesty; but he admitted that 'owing to a great shortage of transport and administrative difficulties in several districts they undoubtedly still remain in places where they have been living up to the present.'

These vague and non-committal remarks of Mr. Molotov's were interpreted by the Poles as a kind of official confirmation by a member of the Soviet Government of the Polish supposition, that the missing officers were far away in the north or east and could, for purely technical reasons, not be sent back at the time.

On November 1st, 1941, the Polish Ambassador handed over to Commissar Molotov a confidential note in which he again tried to persuade the Soviet Government to release all prisoners-of-war before the arrival of General Sikorski in Moscow. The Fourth Kot–Vyshinsky talk took place on November 1st, 1941.

The Polish Ambassador asked Vyshinsky to supply him with information about the whereabouts of these men and to grant him an opportunity of getting in touch with them, at least by telegram.

The Deputy Soviet Commissar for Foreign Affairs shrugged his shoulders when the names of camps where Polish citizens might still be detained were mentioned; he answered that all prisoners had been released.

Kot: 'It is so long since the agreement was signed and so many of our men have still not been set free in spite of their right to liberty under the agreement. We have not even received letters and telegrams from them. We do not have their addresses, in spite of the promise made during our conversation on the 14th of October to supply me with the list I asked for by the following day.'

Vyshinsky: 'I did say so, but on the 15th we left Moscow and it became difficult to maintain contact between the different administrative branches. This accounted for the delay in supplying you with the data...'

Kot: 'The NKVD or Gulag Headquarters* have all the necessary information. Will you please let me send delegates who, accompanied by NKVD officials, could visit the camps where these men are detained, in order to render them some assistance and raise their spirits, which would enable them to get through the winter.'

Vyshinsky: 'Mr. Ambassador puts the question as if we wished to conceal some Polish citizens. Where could they be hidden!'

Kot: 'The information I possess has been collected from the reports and accounts of eye-witnesses. They have observed at one time or another many of our officers being

* Gulag – Glavnoie Upravlenie Laguerey – Headquarters of the Forced Labour Camps.

deported to an unknown destination. If you had given me precise information it would have been useful to me. People are not like steam, they cannot evaporate . . .'

Vyshinsky: 'Some people on the lists given by Mr. Ambassador have now been found. We are looking for the others. When I have exact details regarding these I shall be able to contact the responsible authorities and even punish where necessary. But you are making a mistake, Mr. Ambassador, in thinking that these things do not concern me. In the Commissariat of Foreign Affairs Polish questions are within my province.'

The Polish authorities, having despite all their representations and continuous efforts failed to get the Soviet authorities to honour the July Agreement and release all Polish citizens, approached the British authorities with a request to mediate.

It is possible that the Polish note of November 1st, as well as the steps taken by Great Britain on November 3rd precipitated the issue by the Soviet Government of the statement 'on the full implementation of the Decree on Amnesty towards the Poles'.

On November 8th, 1941, Molotov sent a note in which he declared:

'In accordance with the decree of the Presidium of the Supreme Council of the USSR of the 13th of August, 1941, on the amnesty, all Polish citizens who were detained as prisoners-of-war or for any other adequate reasons, have been released. To the said categories of released persons and prisoners-of-war the Soviet authorities gave all necessary assistance.'

From the wording of this note it was reasonable to conclude that all Polish citizens entitled to be released had already been set free. But where were those thousands of missing Polish prisoners-of-war? Where were the generals and senior officers so badly needed for the new Polish Army? Where were several thousand junior officers?

On November 14th, 1941, Mr. Bogomolov, the Soviet Ambassador to the Polish Government in London, handed to Count Raczynski a note which reiterated the main statement of Commissar Molotov's note of November 8th. It contained the following passage:

'Also released were all Polish officers detained on the territory of the USSR. The assumptions made by the Polish Prime Minister that numerous Polish officers were dispersed in the northern areas of the USSR appear to be based on inaccurate information.'

Two days before, on November 12th, 1941, Ambassador Kot had had his fifth talk with Mr. Vyshinsky who maintained:

'In my opinion all officers have already been released. It is now only a matter of stating their whereabouts. Should anyone of them not yet have been set free, he certainly will be released. As far as I am concerned, this problem no longer exists.'

Eventually, after three and a half months of vain attempts to find the missing men, during which not one Soviet office was able to give a satisfactory answer to the question as to what could have happened to all those thousands of Polish prisoners-of-war, mostly officers, the Polish Ambassador was able, on November 14th, 1941, to obtain an audience with Stalin. The interview took place in the presence of Molotov.

The following minutes of the conversation were made immediately after the meeting:

Kot: 'I have already taken up a great deal of your time, Mr. President, when you have such important business to attend to. But there is still one more important question; may I raise it?'

Stalin (*politely*): 'Certainly, Mr. Ambassador.'

Kot: 'You are the author of the amnesty for Polish citizens in the USSR. Would you care to use your influence to have this initiative fully implemented?'

Stalin: 'Are there still any Poles who are not released?'

Kot: 'Not one officer has yet reached us from the camp at Starobielsk, which was closed down in the spring of 1940 . . .'

Stalin (*interrupting*): 'I will look into the matter. But after release many things may happen. What was the name of the commander at the defence of Lwów? Langner, if I am not mistaken?'

Kot: 'General Langner, Mr. President.'

Stalin: 'Exactly, General Langner. We released him last year. We had him brought to Moscow and talked with him. Then he escaped abroad, probably to Rumania.'

Molotov nodded.

Stalin: 'There are no exceptions to our amnesty, but the same thing may have happened with other officers as with General Langner.'

Kot: 'We have the names and lists. For example, General Stanislaw Haller has still not been found: officers from Starobielsk, Kozielsk and Ostashkov, who were removed from those camps in April and May 1940, are missing.'

Stalin: 'We have released everyone, even people who were sent to us by General Sikorski to blow up bridges and kill Soviet people; we have set free even those people. Actually it was not General Sikorski who sent them, but his Chief of Staff, Sosnkowski.*'

Kot: 'My request to you, Mr. President, is that you will give instructions for the officers, whom we need for the organization of the army, to be released. We possess records with the dates when they were removed from the camps.'

Stalin: 'Are there any accurate lists?'

Kot: 'Each name is recorded by the Russian camp commanders who held a roll-call of all prisoners every day. In addition the NKVD carried out an investigation of every individual. Not one officer of the Staff of General Anders' Army, which he commanded in Poland, has been handed over.'

Stalin, who had stood up a few minutes before and begun to pace slowly round the table, smoking a cigarette, but listening carefully and answering questions, walked quickly to the telephone on Molotov's desk to get himself put through to the NKVD.

Molotov (*also getting up and going to the telephone*): 'It

---

* General Sosnkowski was a Minister in General Sikorski's Government from 1939 to 1941, not Chief of Staff.

does not connect like that.' He turned the switch and sat down again at the conference table.

Stalin (*into the receiver*): 'Stalin here. Have all Poles been released from prison? (Silence for a moment while he listens to the reply.) I have with me here the Polish Ambassador, who tells me that not all have been.' (He again listens to the reply, then puts down the receiver and returns to the conference table.)

After a few minutes' discussion on another subject the telephone rang. Stalin left the conference table and listened for a while, presumably to the answer to the question previously asked concerning the release of Poles. After replacing the receiver he returned to the table without saying a word.

This scene might have produced the impression on the Polish side that Stalin himself had not been informed of the fate of the missing Polish officers and had to make inquiries from subordinate officials. On the other hand, in view of the great centralization of the Soviet administration, it is difficult to believe that such an important decision, concerning the fate of some 15,000 prisoners of war, mostly officers, could have been taken by anyone without the personal approval of the Soviet leader. It was therefore probably a piece of play acting purposely staged in order to give the impression that Stalin had not been personally involved in the fate of the Polish prisoners-of-war.

Simultaneously with discussions on the diplomatic level, the inquiries and researches instituted by General Anders in August 1941 and conducted by him personally, were continued by Polish Army Headquarters in the USSR. The Embassy, as a diplomatic mission, could only approach the Commissariat for Foreign Affairs. General Anders on the other hand was not handicapped by diplomatic protocol and was able to make a direct approach to the NKVD, which had all Polish prisoners and prisoners-of-war under its control and was responsible for their fate.

In a letter to the NKVD dated November 4th, 1941, General Anders assessed the number of missing officers at 8,722, adding that this list was not complete. The Polish military authorities received no reply to this letter.

Apart from this move, a special branch of the Headquarters of the Polish Army in the USSR was, as mentioned previously, set up in order to go into the problem of the missing officers. When sending the Polish Embassy copies of some reports, General Anders commented:

'The Soviet authorities have several times declared that a considerable number of the officers listed above were released and sent home in the autumn of 1940. This information cannot be true, as

(1) there is not one family of the above-mentioned prisoners who have had any news of their relatives;

(2) inquiries carried out in German prisoner-of-war camps for officers have yielded negative results;

(3) our own Intelligence Service in Poland has stated that those officers were not on Polish territory.

Polish military and civilian authorities were agreed as to what was the probable fate of the missing prisoners-of-war. They did not believe the statements that the prisoners had been released in 1940; they supposed that they had been sentenced to live under great hardship and very far away, but they did not suspect that of the whole body of prisoners-of-war not one remained alive.

The difficulties met with by Polish diplomatic representatives in the USSR and by the Polish military authorities in their dealings with the Soviet authorities made General Sikorski attempt a definite solution of this problem by personal intervention on the highest Soviet level.

For General Sikorski's use in his conversation with Stalin the Embassy prepared a 'Note on the question of captive soldiers of the Polish Army from the camps at Starobielsk, Kozielsk and Ostashkov, deported to forced labour camps in the Far North and not released by 1.12.41,' dated December 1st, 1941. In its introduction the 'Note' referred to the 'irrefutable fact' that 'over 95 per cent of all servicemen from the aforementioned three camps had been removed and all trace of them lost'.

The meeting between General Sikorski and Stalin, with

General Anders and Molotov present, took place at the Kremlin on December 3rd, 1941. The parts of the protocol relating to it run as follows:

Sikorski: 'I wish to state in your presence, Mr. President, that your declaration concerning the amnesty is not being implemented. Many of our most valuable people are still in labour camps and prisons.'

Stalin (taking notes): 'That is impossible because the amnesty applied to all, and all Poles have been released.' The last words were directed towards Molotov, who nodded.

Anders (after giving details regarding General Sikorski's request): 'This does not conform to the real state of affairs.'

Sikorski: 'It is not within our province to provide the Soviet Government with the detailed lists of our people; these are in possession of the camp commandants. I have with me a name-roll of about 4,000 officers, who were forcibly deported and who are still in the prisons and labour camps, and this list is not even complete as it contains only those names which could be listed from memory. I took steps to verify whether they were at home, as we are in close touch with Poland. It has been ascertained that not one of them is there, nor in prisoner-of-war camps in Germany. These people are here. Not one has returned.'

Stalin: 'This is impossible. They have escaped.'

Anders: 'Where could they escape to?'

Stalin: 'Well, to Manchuria.'

Anders: 'All of them could not possibly have escaped ... The majority of the officers mentioned in this roll are personally known to me. My staff officers are there, and commanders who served under me ...'

Stalin: 'They have certainly been released, but have not yet arrived.'

Sikorski: 'Russia is vast and the difficulties are great. Perhaps some local authorities have not obeyed instructions ... Should anybody have escaped beyond Russia's boundaries, he would have reported to me.'

Stalin: 'Please realize that the Soviet Government has no reason for detaining even one Pole.'

Molotov: 'It seems quite impossible that your people could still be in camps.'

Anders: 'But I can positively state that they are ...'

Stalin: 'This will be settled. Special instructions will be issued to the executive authorities. You must take into consideration, however, that we are engaged in a war.'

General Sikorski's conversation with Stalin gave support to the belief of the Poles that the missing officers were alive and were detained in labour camps in the Far North or East. This belief was strengthened especially by Stalin's assurance that the missing officers 'have certainly been released, but have not yet arrived', and by his promise that 'special instructions will be issued to the executive authorities.'

Captain Czapski had been a prisoner at Starobielsk. For some reason still unrevealed – possibly because he was already an established writer, and the Russians (entirely mistakenly) felt his talents could be twisted to their purposes – he had been spared the liquidation. It is Czapski who has since given the most vivid description of this period of doubt and growing suspicion concerning the fate of his comrades at Starobielsk, Ostashkov and Kozielsk.

The formation of the Polish Army in the USSR began in September 1941, in Tatishchev, near Saratov, and in Totskoie, on the railway-line from Kuibishev to Tchkalov. Each day hundreds flowed into the summer camp at Totskoie. A sort of information office was created. It was his duty to interrogate all those who arrived. Every one in turn, those from Vorkuta and Magadan, Kamtchatka and Karaganda, was concerned above all with two matters: trying to trace their deported families and giving long lists of their fellow prisoners not as yet released. From the beginning, he began by asking every Pole who arrived whether he had news of any of their comrades from Starobielsk, Kozielsk and Ostashkov. He still believed that they would arrive at any moment ... But none of them did arrive; moreover, there was no news as to their fate, apart from a few secondhand and contradictory reports ...

'Day after day we waited for our comrades, drawing up new lists and supplementing earlier ones. A month had passed but none of the one-time prisoners from Starobielsk, Kozielsk and Ostashkov appeared. On the arrival in Moscow of General Sikorski, Commander in Chief of the Polish Armed Forces, in early December 1941, our list contained more than 4,500 names: it was taken to Moscow by General Anders...

'In early January 1942 I was sent by General Anders to Tchkalov as officer in charge of the mission concerned with missing prisoners-of-war, with the object of clarifying the situation with General Nasyedkin, Head of the Directorate of Labour Camps ("GULAG"). He told me that in the spring of 1940, when the POW camps in question had been disbanded, he was not the head of "GULAG" and that he did not deal with prisoners-of-war, but with those detained in labour camps; namely, political and criminal prisoners. It was possible that some Polish soldiers were amongst them, but he knew nothing definite about it. He would look into the matter and would give me an answer the next day. In my presence he gave an order by telephone that the situation in all three camps was to be investigated. When giving this order he repeated the words of General Anders' letter: "po prikazanyu towarishcha Stalina" – "on the instructions of Comrade Stalin". So my first conversation with the General ended.

'At about 11 p.m. on the same day I was received by the head of the NKVD of Tchkalov "Oblast" (District) Bzyrov ... He received me with affability and appeared willing to help. At first he told me that I would not learn anything except from the central and highest authorities (there were two NKVD officials present at the conversation). He gave me to understand that Merkulov or Fiedotov would be able to help me. (The head of the NKVD of the USSR was at that time Beria; Merkulov was his deputy and, in the following order, Kruglov, Fiedotov and Rajchman were assistants.) When I started to speak of Novaya Zemlya and Franz Joseph Land, he did not show surprise; on the contrary he pointed out to me the port of Dudinka on the River Yenisei, whence the largest transport of workers were sent to these islands. He told me that there were no unreleased Poles in his "Oblast".

'Next day, I was received once more by General Nasyedkin. He told me that he had nothing to report, that only the central authorities would be able to give me information. I again mentioned Novaya Zemlya, saying that we had some information about Polish prisoners-of-war there. That very day I had received some news supporting this. Nasyedkin reacted differently from the day before. "It is not impossible," he said, "that some of my subordinate labour units in the north sent some small groups there but there could be no question of the many thousands of which you speak."

'In the middle of January I was sent by General Anders to Kuibishev and Moscow on the same errand, with letters of introduction to General Zhukov. General Anders wrote explaining to what extent the problem of the missing officers was hampering the organization of the Army, emphasizing the distress it was causing him and his colleagues; and added that, being unable to deal with the matter himself, he was sending me to Moscow and requesting they render me the same assistance that would have been accorded him. I knew that these Soviet generals whom I was to see, held very high positions in the NKVD; that they were instructed to assist in the organization of the Polish Army, that General Rajchman himself had interrogated many of our colleagues during the last two years. I thought that these generals, knowing all about the matter, would be able and willing to help me and that they would arrange my visit to the all-powerful Beria or Merkulov. From Kuibishev I was sent to Moscow but it was not until February 3rd, 1942, that after many difficulties and even being briefly placed under arrest – allegedly due to a mistake – I reached the Lubianka prison and saw General Rajchman ...

'I asked him to help me to obtain an interview with Beria or Merkulov, and received a polite refusal. I then submitted my memorandum to him, and, following every line with his pencil, he read it in my presence. The history of the three camps was given up to the time of their final disbandment,

i.e. May 1940. After having dealt with the historical part, I
had written:

' "Since the publication of the amnesty for all Polish prisoners on August 12th, 1941, groups of officers and men as
well as individuals who have been set free from camps and
prisons are flowing into the Polish Army now in process of
being formed ... In spite of the amnesty, in spite of the
solemn promise given to our Ambassador Kot by Stalin himself in October 1941, and in spite of the decisive order given
by Stalin on December 3rd, 1941, in the presence of General
Sikorski and General Anders (whereby our prisoners were to
be located and freed), not a single prisoner-of-war has come
from the camps at Starobielsk, Kozielsk and Ostashkov.
Moreover, no request for help or assistance had reached us
from any of the prisoners from these camps. We have interrogated thousands of people released from labour camps
and prisons but we have not gleaned any information as to
where they might be; excepting indirect rumours concerning the transportation of from six to twelve thousand
officers and NCOs to Kolyma through Buchta Nachodka in
1940, the concentration of more than 5,000 officers in some
mines in Franz Joseph Land, the sending of prisoners to
Novaya Zemlya and Kamtchatka, the deportation of Polish
officers to the Northern Islands and their being shipped on
huge barges carrying 1,700 to 2,000 each, which eventually
were sunk, *etc.*

' "Knowing with what accuracy every prisoner was regis-
tered and how his dossier, containing the results of his interrogation, photographs and various verified documents,
was carefully kept in special files, none of us ex-prisoners-of-
war was prepared to admit even for a moment that the lo-
cation and fate of such a large group of prisoners-of-war
could be unknown to high NKVD authorities. The personal
promise of Stalin himself and his order that the fate of
Polish prisoners-of-war be investigated, lead us to hope that
we may at least know where our comrades in arms are and, if
they perished, when and how it happened."

'Then followed the numbers ascertained with the greatest
possible accuracy ... The General's face did not move a

muscle. He read the memorandum with complete indifference, then answered that he did not know anything of the fate of these people and that it was not his responsibility, but that to please General Anders he would try to solve the problem and to send me the answer. He asked me to wait in Moscow for his telephone call.

'The parting was icy. I waited ten days and then received a night telephone call: General Rajchman himself informed me in a very affable manner; that unfortunately he was leaving the next day, that he was sorry he would not be able to see me, that his advice to me was to return to Kuibishev as all material concerning the affair had been handed over to the Deputy Commissar for Foreign Affairs, Comrade Vyshinsky. I plucked up courage to tell General Rajchman that I knew very well that Vyshinsky would not give me an answer, for prior to my visit, Ambassador Kot had seen Mr. Vyshinsky eight times without any result. This was the end of my Moscow visit.

'We were left with a glimmer of hope, skilfully fed by the NKVD officers attached to our Army. We hoped that our colleagues deported to some remote islands would appear in July or August, that is to say in the only period when the navigation of those northern seas is possible. Many a time we were told in great secrecy: "Be calm, be patient, your comrades will come back in July or August." July and August passed and nobody had returned.'*

In Moscow, on February 2nd, 1942, on orders of General Anders, Captain Czapski handed the above-mentioned memorandum to General Rajchman, one of the closest assistants of the NKVD chief, Beria. It ended with the following general remarks, stressing the true significance of the problem for the common Allied war effort against the German invader:

'Though unable to give exact figures of all missing prisoners, we can assess with great accuracy the number of prisoners-of-war detained at Kozielsk, Starobielsk and Ostashkov at about 15,000, mostly officers (about 8,700).

* Memoirs of Starobielsk, Józef Czapski, pp. 48–60.

'In our efforts to build up the strength of our army, which is being formed in the south of the USSR in accordance with the agreement between Stalin and Sikorski, we greatly miss these men, as we have lost our best military experts and most distinguished commanding officers.

'It would be superfluous to discuss how much the disappearance of thousands of our fellow officers hampers the creation in our army of the atmosphere of confidence and goodwill towards the USSR so indispensable for the development of normal relations between two armies allied in the struggle against the common foe.'

After General Sikorski's visit to Moscow there was an interruption in the diplomatic representations of the Polish Ambassador in the matter of the missing prisoners. Czapski, returning via Kuibishev, informed the Ambassador of the failure of his mission.

Since Soviet diplomats, in the course of the talks, categorically denied that they were detained with the knowledge and approval of the central authorities, renewed requests for information were pointless. In these circumstances it was decided that no alternative remained but to wait patiently for the summer, when transport conditions would improve, and meanwhile to carry on the search throughout the USSR.

In the meantime the Polish Government in London again made an official move in the matter by delivering Note No. 49, dated January 28th, 1942. This note too had no effect.

On March 18th, 1942, General Anders, accompanied by his Chief of Staff, Colonel L. Okulicki* had an audience with

---

* Colonel L. Okulicki, subsequently promoted to the rank of General, was on May 18, 1944, parachuted on to Polish territory, occupied by the Germans, and assumed one of the highest commands in the Polish Underground Army. When the Commander-in-Chief of the Home Army was taken prisoner, Okulicki succeeded him. In this capacity he took part in the 'negotiations' initiated by the Soviet Government; as one of the 16 leaders of the Polish Underground Movement, which under German occupation directed the struggle against the Germans. This delegation, instead of being seated round a conference table, was thrown into a Moscow prison and then placed

Stalin and again took up the matter of the missing Polish prisoners-of-war. Here is an extract from the record of the talk:

Anders: 'Apart from that, many of our people are still in prisons and labour camps. So far not one officer removed from Kozielsk, Starobielsk or Ostashkov has reappeared. Therefore you certainly must have them. [Here he handed over two lists of names, which are taken by Molotov.] Where can they be? We have traces of their whereabouts on the Kolyma river.'

Stalin: 'I have already given orders that they are to be freed. They say they are even in Franz Joseph Land, but there is no one there. I do not know where they are. Why should we keep them? It may be that they were in camps in territories which have been taken by the Germans and came to be dispersed.'

Okulicki: 'Impossible – we should have known of it.'

Stalin: 'We have detained only those Poles who were spying for the Germans.' [Then he changed the subject.]

In the words which Stalin let fall 'en passant' during this conversation, was first put forward what, later on, after the Germans had discovered the Katyn graves, became the official Soviet version of the fate of the missing Polish prisoners-of-war.

On May 12th, 1942, the Polish Embassy delivered to the People's Commissariat for Foreign Affairs (NKVD) a memorandum on the subject of the fulfilment of the Additional Protocol to the Polish–Soviet Agreement of July 30th, 1941. It ran:

'Although the Soviet authorities are in possession of complete lists of their former prisoners-of-war who, for reasons unknown to the Poles, have to date been unable to return to

---

in the dock and tried in the spring of 1945. The case of these 16 men was for some time the focus of international attention but soon sank back into oblivion. General Okulicki was sentenced to ten years' imprisonment in Moscow. After some years Moscow official sources reported him as dead.

active service, comprehensive lists of the missing Polish officers were drawn up by the Polish Prime Minister and Commander-in-Chief, General Sikorski, on 3.12.41, and by the Commander of the Polish Forces in the USSR, General Anders, on 18.3.42, at the request of the Soviet authorities and in order to help them in their inquiries.

'The above lists were reconstituted with great difficulty from memory by a few former prisoners from Kozielsk, Starobielsk and Ostashkov, who had escaped the fate of the officers departed in groups from those camps by the Soviet authorities in May and June 1940 ... None of the missing men has so far returned to active service, nor are there any signs of them being alive.'

On June 13th, 1942, following new information received from the Far North by the Polish Embassy, the Embassy once again took up the question of the missing prisoners in a note to the Soviet Government:

'In many talks with the highest-ranking officers of the USSR the question has been raised of setting free the members of the Polish Army, mostly officers, who were in the prisoner-of-war camps at Kozielsk, Starobielsk and Ostashkov. Those camps were disbanded in 1940, and the prisoners were dispatched in groups in April and May of the same year in a direction unknown to the Embassy. Since then all trace of them has been lost. Hitherto the NKVD has given the Embassy no explanation of this matter ... The Polish Embassy would be very grateful for the earliest possible reply regarding the former prisoners-of-war from the camps of Starobielsk, Kozielsk and Ostashkov, the more so as ten months have already elapsed since the conclusion of the Agreement of 30.7.41.'

It must be added that as much as eleven months had passed since the capture of Smolensk by the Germans ...

This note from the Embassy remained unanswered.

A Soviet aide-memoire was received on July 10th, 1942. It constituted a reply to the Polish memorandum of May 19th, 1942. In it the NKID (Soviet Foreign Office) stated:

'It is known that many Polish citizens who were released

before the issue of the Amnesty Decree left the USSR for their own country. It should also be pointed out, that many of the Polish citizens who were released in accordance with the terms of the amnesty decree escaped abroad, some of them to Germany ... Finally, as a result of spontaneous migrations from the northern to the southern provinces of the USSR in the winter of 1941, undertaken in spite of reiterated warnings issued by the People's Commissariat, a number of Polish citizens fell ill on the way and were left behind at various railway stations. Some of them died during the journey. All these circumstances may well account for the fact that a certain number of Polish citizens have given no sign of life.'

The case of the 'missing' prisoners was discussed for the last time on July 8th, 1942, when Ambassador Kot, accompanied by the Polish Charge d'Affaires – Henryk Sokolnicki, paid a farewell visit to Vyshinsky. It was the latter who brought up the subject:

Vyshinsky: 'As to the detention of Poles in prisons or camps and forced labour camps, I must assure you, Mr. Ambassador, that we have looked into the matter and have ascertained that they really are not there. There are no officers in the Far North nor in the Far East, nor anywhere else. Perhaps they are outside the USSR, perhaps some of them have died. All have been freed. Some were released before our war with Germany, some afterwards.'

Kot: '... as for the officers, I must tell you that it is precisely from Poland that I receive the largest number of inquiries from their families, who are extremely worried about their fate and their continued absence. Not one of them is there.'

Sokolnicki: 'If our prisoners have been freed, then please let me have a list of them and the date and place of their release. The Soviet authorities made several lists of prisoners in the camps and to produce these lists cannot present any difficulties.'

Vyshinsky: 'Unfortunately we have no such lists.'

The question of the prisoners was raised for the last time

in diplomatic correspondence – before the Katyn revelations – in a note of the Polish Ministry of Foreign Affairs in London, dated August 27th, 1942, dealing with the refusal of the Soviet authorities to allow further recruiting for the Polish Forces on the territory of the USSR.

'The negative attitude of the Soviet Government towards the further augmentation of the Polish Army is also confirmed by the fact, that over 8,000 Polish officers, who in the Spring of 1940 were in the prisoner-of-war camps at Ostashkov, Starobielsk and Kozielsk, have still not been found, despite repeated interventions by the Polish Government and in spite of the fact that incomplete lists of those officers were handed to the President of the Council of People's Commissars by General Sikorski in December 1941 and by General Anders in March 1942.'

Among the Polish citizens who had been deported to the USSR were a large number of relations, friends and acquaintances of the 'missing' officers. Those friends and relations, on being released from their prisons, labour camps and places of deportation, began to search for the missing men. In consequence of the ever-increasing anxiety in Polish circles concerning them, the question of publishing an official communiqué in *Polska*, the Embassy official journal appearing in Kuibishev, was raised.

This communiqué couched in exceptionally circumspect terms, recalled the promises given by representatives of the Soviet authorities on many occasions in answer to Polish requests and, on the strength of these promises, appealed to people to wait patiently for the probable return of the prisoners in the summer. This communiqué was approved by the Ambassador on March 8th, 1942, but never appeared in *Polska*, having failed to pass the Soviet censorship. Soon afterwards the censorship prohibited the families of the missing persons in all the territories of the USSR from publishing their names in *Polska*.

Apart from official negotiations and diplomatic contacts concerning the missing Polish prisoners-of-war, mostly officers, the Polish Headquarters in Soviet Russia obtained some confidential information on the subject.

This was provided by a group of officers on the Polish General Staff who had been transferred by the Soviet authorities in the autumn of 1940 from Griazovietz camp to Moscow. Among them were Col. E. Gorczyński, Lt.-Col. Z. Berling, Lt.-Col. L. Bukojemski and Lt.-Col. L. Tyszyński. This group, being regarded as pro-Soviet sympathizers, were separated from all the other prisoners; they were brought to Butyrki and Lubianka prisons and later confined in a dacha near Moscow. Beria and Merkulov, then respectively head and deputy head of the NKVD, summoned them to discuss the Soviet plan for organizing a nucleus of Polish Red Army units. During these conversations the problem of the missing officers from Kozielsk, Starobielsk and Ostashkov was raised.

Joseph Czapski, in his *Memoirs from Starobielsk*, writes:

'In October 1940 – eight months before the outbreak of the Soviet-German war – the Bolsheviks brought to a special camp near Moscow and then to Moscow proper several of our staff officers, among them Col. Berling, and suggested they should organize a Polish Army to fight the Germans. Berling was in favour of it, but made one definite stipulation, namely that all officers and other ranks should be permitted to join this Army regardless of their political affiliations. Beria and Merkulov participated in this conference.

' "But of course," they said, "Poles of all political opinions will have the right to join this army."

' "Very well, then," replied Berling, "There are excellent cadres for this army in the camps at Starobielsk and Kozielsk."

'Then Merkulov blurted out:

' "No, not those. We made a great mistake with them." Unfortunately Merkulov was not at that time asked to explain his remark.'

From what has been recorded in this chapter the following conclusions can be drawn:

1. None of those Poles who passed through forced

labour camps spread all over the territory of the USSR ever met any of the prisoners-of-war from the camps in Kozielsk, Ostashkov and Starobielsk (apart from those who were brought to the Griazovietz camp).

2. In all their talks with the Polish representatives, at which the problem of the missing men was discussed, and all the diplomatic notes which were exchanged concerning this matter, the Soviet authorities, including Stalin himself, firmly asserted that all prisoners-of-war, particularly the officers, had been freed and the fate of the missing ones was not known to them.

3. When provided with proof of various kinds that those prisoners had neither joined the Polish Army nor given any sign of being alive and when their nominal lists had been presented, the Soviet representatives put forward vague and contradictory hypotheses, in order to divest themselves of responsibility regarding the fate of the lost men and to avoid any further inquiries. Stalin's suggestion, made in the conversation with Generals Sikorski and Anders, that the missing officers escaped to Manchuria, and hints to the effect that they were taken over by the Germans, fell into this category.

What happened to the men? What was the meaning of Merkulov's outburst, 'No, not those, we made a great mistake with them'?

Contrary to Polish hopes the year 1942 brought no clarification of the question of the missing Polish prisoners-of-war. They did not return after the resumption of communications with the Polar Regions and no news of them had been received. Nevertheless, Polish circles still hoped that they were still in the Far North and that if a conciliatory attitude was taken towards the Soviet Government they would be released. The Polish Government, therefore, tried to prevent this question gaining too much publicity, although Polish public opinion was actively concerned about it.

During the autumn and winter of 1942, as a result of the evacuation of the Polish Forces from the USSR to the

Middle East, rumours that Polish prisoners-of-war were in the northern regions of the Soviet Union rapidly increased in number, taking at the same time a far more detailed form. On October 19th, 1942, the Polish Minister of National Defence in London, General Kukiel, in a conversation with the Soviet Ambassador, Bogomolov, raised the question of the missing prisoners. Having these rumours in mind, he announced that before long the Polish Government would perhaps be in a position to supply the Soviet authorities with certain facts which would facilitate further search. Bogomolov, who had so far given evasive and rather negative replies, merely stating that the Polish officers were not on Soviet territory, suddenly broke off the conversation, 'disturbingly helpless'. This behaviour on the part of the Soviet Ambassador alarmed the Polish Minister of Defence, who wrote in his notes directly after the conversation: 'It seems to me, unfortunately, that the question of the 8,000 officers must be considered hopeless and that Bogomolov knows they have perished.'

Besides these rumours, others began to reach London, namely of Merkulov's remark about the 'great mistake' made to Berling and his friends in Lubianka. This information, and the eighteen months of waiting for the return of the missing prisoners, caused growing pessimism in Polish circles which was reflected in the Polish press.

In the weekly *Polska Walczaca – Zolnierz Polski na Obozyznie* ('Fighting Poland – The Polish Soldier Abroad') of January 30th, 1943, an article by 'S.W.' entitled 'Visit to the Soviet Union', appeared. In this article the Polish war correspondent sharing his impressions of his visit to the USSR with his readers, clearly implied that the Soviet authorities had made a 'great mistake' with regard to the missing Polish prisoners, as a result of which 'those people are lost for ever'. The following is an extract from the article: '... Our elementary demands for the rescue of our people are: protection for a large number of Poles still remaining alive. The whereabouts of the 15,000 – not yet recovered – prisoners-of-war should be disclosed to us. If we receive the reply that those people are lost for ever, then we shall demand that for that price the remaining Poles shall be properly cared for and that we shall be given every possibility of helping them. We have still hundreds of thousands of human lives to save. Rescue must be rapid – very rapid. From the mouths of several high Soviet officials has not the timid confession been uttered that a "bolshaya oshibka" ("great mistke") was made about our prisoners. A great mistake, bloody perhaps as well as great? Now we wish that this mistake will not be repeated, that the Soviet State will make amends for it as far as may be possible – by saving the rest from extermination.'

Polish minds were beginning to realize that what once seemed a remote and unthinkable possibility was now a distinct and ghastly probability.

CHAPTER SIX

KATYN

At 2.15 p.m. London time on April 13th, 1943, the following news was broadcast by Radio Berlin:

'A report has reached us from Smolensk to the effect that the local inhabitants have mentioned to the German authorities the existence of a place where mass executions had been carried out by the Bolsheviks and where 10,000 Polish officers had been murdered by the GPU.* The German authorities accordingly went to a place called Kozy Gory [i.e. "Goats' Hill" – a small forested hill inside Katyn] a Soviet health resort situated twelve kilometres west of Smolensk, where a terrible discovery was made. A ditch was found, 28 metres long and 16 metres wide, in which the bodies of 3,000 Polish officers were piled up in twelve layers. They were fully dressed in military uniforms, some were bound, and all had pistol shot wounds in the back of their heads. There will be no difficulty in identifying the bodies as, owing to the nature of the ground, they are in a state of mummification and the Russians had left on the bodies their personal documents. It has been stated today, that General Smorawiński from Lublin has been found amongst other murdered officers. Previously these officers were in a camp at Kozielsk near Orel and in February and March 1940 were brought in "cattle" freight-cars to Smolensk. Thence they were taken in lorries (trucks) to Kosogory and were murdered there by the Bolsheviks. The search for further pits is in progress. New layers may be found under those already discovered. It is estimated that the total number of officers killed amounts to

* These initials stand for the previous name of the Soviet secret state police, at the time already the NKVD.

10,000, which would correspond to the entire cadre of Polish officers taken prisoner by the Russians. The correspondents of Norwegian newspapers, who were on the spot and were thus able to obtain direct evidence of the crime, immediately sent their dispatches to their papers in Oslo.'

In its further transmissions Radio Berlin announced that medical commissions from neutral countries had arrived on the spot to investigate the crime and were proceeding with the exhumation of the bodies. New mass-graves continued to be discovered up till April 16th, bringing to light an additional 1,500 bodies.

In London the news given by Radio Berlin was received with diffidence. Moscow however reacted swiftly. At 7.15 a.m. on April 15th, 1943, Radio Moscow broadcast the following:

'In the past two or three days Goebbels' slanderers have been spreading vile fabrications alleging that the Soviet authorities carried out a mass shooting of Polish officers in the spring of 1940, in the Smolensk area. In launching this monstrous invention the German-Fascist scoundrels did not hesitate to spread the most unscrupulous and base lies, in their attempts to cover up crimes which, as has now become evident, were perpetrated by themselves.

'The German-Fascist report on this subject leaves no doubt as to the tragic fate of the former Polish prisoners-of-war who in 1941 were engaged in construction work in areas west of the Smolensk region and who fell into the hands of German-Fascist hangmen in the summer of 1941, after the withdrawal of the Soviet troops from the Smolensk area.

'Beyond doubt Goebbels' slanderers are now trying with lies and calumnies to cover up the bloody crimes of the Hitlerite gangsters. In their clumsily concocted fabrication about the numerous graves which the Germans allegedly discovered near Smolensk, the Hitlerite liars mention the village of Gniezdovo. But, like the swindlers they are, they remain silent about the fact that it was near the village of Gniezdovo that the archaeological excavations of the historic "Gniezdovo burial place" were made.'

The Poles reacted also. That same day, April 15th, two

days after the Katyn revelations, General Anders sent from his HQ in the Middle East the following telegram to the Polish Minister of Defence in London:

'From the moment of my release from prison I tried to find our soldiers from Starobielsk, Kozielsk and Ostashkov. I always received evasive replies from the Soviet authorities. The Commander-in-Chief of the Polish Army, General W. Sikorski, when in Moscow made a personal appeal to Stalin and received the answer that they had probably escaped. During the whole time I was in the USSR, I for my part, made prodigious efforts to discover something about their fate from the Soviet authorities and from Stalin himself.

'I sent people in all directions to search for them ... In private conversations some of the high Soviet officials declared that a "rokovoya oshibka" [fatal mistake] had been made over this. News reached us that some of our officers had been deliberately drowned in the Arctic Ocean. But it is quite possible that those moved from Kozielsk were murdered near Smolensk. A number of the names given by the German radio are in our card index. It is a fact that not one of the 8,300 officers from the camps at Kozielsk and Starobielsk, nor any of the 4,000 NCOs of the military and civil police from the Ostashkov camp, have joined the army. In spite of tremendous efforts on our part, we have received absolutely no news of any of them. It has long been our conviction that none of them are alive, but that they were deliberately murdered. Nevertheless, the announcement of the German discoveries made a tremendous impression and caused deep dismay. I consider it necessary for the Government to intervene in this affair with the object of obtaining official explanations from the Soviets, especially as our soldiers are convinced that the rest of our people in the USSR will also be exterminated.'

At the same time the German Press started a violent propaganda offensive, exploring the tragedy of the thousands of murdered Polish officers to further their own political aims. The following details were given in countless communiqués, reports and articles:

In the summer of 1942, several Poles from Labour units attached to the German Army as well as some civilians who had escaped from Soviet captivity, learned from the local population that Poles had been shot by the Russians in the region of Smolensk. From the disclosures of local peasants and workmen they gradually learned that the murdered Poles were probably buried in Katyn Forest to the right of the narrow, unsurfaced road joining the Smolensk–Katyn highway to the NKVD resthouse in the woods. Transports of Polish officer prisoners-of-war arived at regular intervals at Gniezdovo railway station and these officers were removed in lorries to the neighbouring Katyn Forest.

Poles from the Labour units – so the German reports ran, anxious to learn something more about the fate of their countrymen, started to excavate a mound which obviously did not harmonize with the surrounding country and had an artificial appearance. They soon came upon the body of a Polish officer in uniform. At first they did not realize that they had found a mass-grave. As the German unit to which these workers were attached had to go elsewhere, the search was discontinued.

The local inhabitants, terrorized by the Soviet régime, were not willing to recount their experience of 1940. It was not until the spring of 1943 that the news about the trenches containing bodies of murdered prisoners reached the German authorities. They then initiated systematic investigations on a large scale, which brought to light details of all the events that preceded this monstrous crime. Little by little the appalling scope of this mass-murder was revealed. The sworn evidence of numerous witnesses gave a clear picture of the situation, which was consistent with the facts disclosed by the excavations. These statements proved that the Katyn Forest had been used by the GPU (NKVD) for many years as a place of execution and that recently nearly the entire cadre of Polish officers, after falling into the hands of the Red Army, had become victims of a colossal mass-murder.

On April 17th, 1943, four days after the Berlin com-

muniqué, the following statement was published in London
by the Polish Government:

'London, April 17th, 1943,
'On Saturday a cabinet meeting of the Polish Government
was held in London at which all information concerning the
discovery of the mass-graves near Smolensk and the news
received from Poland in connection with this discovery, was
examined; after which the following communiqué was
issued:
' "No Pole can help being deeply shocked by the news to
which the Germans are now giving the widest publicity, that
is to say the discovery of the bodies in a common grave near
Smolensk of the Polish officers missing in the USSR, and
of the mass execution which was their lot.
' "German propaganda is trying to give the greatest possible publicity to this news. The Polish Government have
instructed their representative in Switzerland to request the
International Red Cross in Geneva to send a delegation to
investigate the true state of affairs on the spot. It is desirable
that the results of the investigations of this protective institution, which is entrusted with the task of clarifying the
matter and establishing the responsibility, should be made
public without delay." '
Simultaneously with the statement of the Polish Government, General Kukiel, Polish Minister of National Defence,
issued a communiqué which, after presenting the whole
case, concluded with the following sentences:
'We have been accustomed to the lies of German propaganda and we understand the purpose behind its latest revelations. In view, however, of abundant and detailed German
information concerning the discovery of the bodies of many
thousands of Polish officers near Smolensk and the cat-
egorical statement that they were murdered by the Soviet
authorities in the spring of 1940, it has become necessary to
have the mass-graves investigated, and the alleged facts
verified by a competent international body, such as the
International Red Cross. The Polish Government has therefore approached this Institution with a view to their sending

a delegation to the place where the massacre of the Polish prisoners-of-war is said to have taken place.'

At the same cabinet meeting on April 17th, 1943, the Polish Government decided to make one more attempt to obtain direct from the Soviet Government an explanation of the fate of the lost prisoners-of-war.

This approach was made in a note addressed to the Soviet Ambassador on April 20th, 1943.

After recalling the fact that the question of the missing prisoners-of-war had been raised many times in conversations and correspondence with the Soviet authorities in 1941 and 1942, the Polish Foreign Minister expressed his regret 'at having to call your attention, Mr. Ambassador, to the fact that the Polish Government, in spite of reiterated requests, have never received either a list of prisoners, or definite information as to the whereabouts of the missing officers and of other prisoners, deported from the three camps mentioned above. If, however, as shown by the communiqué of the Soviet Information Bureau of 15.4.43 [i.e. the Russian reaction to the German revelations, quoted above] the Government of the USSR should be in possession of fuller information on this matter than was communicated to the representatives of the Polish Government some time ago, I beg you once more, Mr. Ambassador, to communicate to the Polish Government detailed and precise information as to the fate of the prisoners-of-war and civilians previously detained in the camps at Kozielsk, Starobielsk and Ostashkov.

'Public opinion in Poland and throughout the world has quite rightly been so deeply shocked, that only irrefutable facts can outweigh the numerous and detailed German statements concerning the discovery of the bodies of many thousands of Polish officers murdered near Smolensk in the spring of 1940.'

No reply to this note was received from the Soviets.

On April 16th, the German Red Cross sent the following message to the International Red Cross in Geneva:

'Reference the news published on the discovery of thousands of bodies of Polish officers in Katyn Forest near Smolensk. In view of international importance of the affair we regard the participation of the International Committee as very desirable, particularly in view of many cases of disappearance of persons in the USSR reported by the German Red Cross, the Polish Red Cross and other bodies. According to information obtained by the German Red Cross all facilities will be given to the representatives of the Committee to enable them to proceed forthwith to the place to take part in the investigations. (Signed) Grawitz.'

A similar message was later sent to Geneva by Prince von Koburg, the President of the German Red Cross.

At 4.30 p.m. the next day, in accordance with the instructions of the Polish Government in London, the deputy of the Polish Red Cross delegate in Switzerland, Prince S. Radziwill, handed a note from the Polish Government to Mr. Rueger, a representative of the International Red Cross, requesting this organization to have the massacre of Polish prisoners-of-war at Katyn investigated by a delegation of neutral representatives.

In view of the fact that similar proposals had been put forward by two parties between whom a state of war existed, the International Red Cross representative – in accordance with the rules laid down by the International Red Cross at the beginning of the Second World War with regard to the participation in international investigations – told Prince Radziwill that the proposals would most probably be considered by the Executive Council, and announced that a meeting of a special commission of the International Red Cross would be held on April 20th, 1943, to appoint a neutral delegation.

This meeeting, however, did not take place, the attitude of the International Red Cross having changed as a result of Russian opposition. Instead, the Executive Council replied with a short Memorandum, the third point of which reads as follows:

'(3) the context of the memorandum of September 12th, 1939, does not permit us to consider sending experts to take part in the technical procedure of identification except with the agreement of all interested parties.'

According to private information supplied to Prince Radziwill, the International Red Cross intended to send an investigatory commission to Katyn composed of Swedish, Portuguese and Swiss experts, under the leadership of a Swiss. But, as was clear from the foregoing letter, everything depended on Russia's agreeing to this. The International Red Cross therefore suggested that the Polish Government should approach the USSR either directly or through the medium of the Anglo-Saxon Allies.

A similar letter was sent by the International Red Cross to the German authorities, suggesting that they endeavour to obtain the consent of the Soviet Government to an investigatory commission through the medium of the 'puissance protectrice'.

In view of the wide interest aroused by the Katyn affair, the International Red Cross in Switzerland published the following communiqué on April 23rd, 1943:

'The German Red Cross and the Polish Government in London have approached the International Red Cross with a request for its participation in the identification of bodies which, according to German reports, have been discovered near Smolensk.

'In both instances the International Red Cross replied that in principle it is prepared to afford assistance by selecting experts, on condition that similar appeals are received from all other parties interested in this question. This is in accordance with the memorandum sent by the International Red Cross, on September 12th, 1939, to all belligerent nations, defining the principles on the basis of which the International Red Cross may participate in this kind of investigation.'

The International Red Cross in Switzerland agreed in principle to undertake the investigation at Katyn. In its opinion, however, participation was subject to the concurrence of all parties concerned. In this case, there were three parties concerned: the Polish Government, the German Government and the Soviet Government.

The messages and declarations cited above prove that both the Polish and the German Governments agreed that the whole matter should be entrusted to the International

Committee of the Red Cross. But the Soviet Government did not reply. It might have been expected that they would be only too glad to place the whole affair into the hands of a neutral body such as the International Red Cross, which enjoys the respect and confidence of all nations of the world. This solution would have offered the Soviet Government a chance to clear itself of all accusations, and of proving incontestably that this terrible crime had been committed by the Germans, as was stated by the Soviet Government in its first wireless communiqué. But they did not reply.

Instead, the Russians attacked the Polish Government for drawing attention to the massacre. Already on April 21st in referring to an article in *Pravda* entitled 'Polish Collaboration of Hitler' Radio Moscow launched a bitter accusation against the Polish Government in London under General Sikorski, for 'collaborating' with the Nazis. The Soviet newsagency Tass declared that the Polish Government's appeal to the International Red Cross in Geneva 'showed what an enormous influence this pro-Hitlerite element had in Polish Government circles.'

Then, on the night of April 25th (Easter Sunday), 1943, at 12.15 a.m., the Polish Ambassador in the USSR was summoned to the Commissariat for Foreign Affairs (NKID), where Molotov attempted to hand him a note, which he had previously read aloud.

The note read as follows:

'Moscow, April 26th, 1943.

'Mr. Ambassador,
'On behalf of the Government of the Union of Soviet Socialist Republics, I have the honour to notify the Polish Government of the following:
'The Soviet Government consider the recent behaviour of the Polish Government with regard to the USSR as entirely abnormal, and violating all regulations and standards of conduct between two allied States. The slanderous campaign against the Soviet Union launched

by the German Fascists in connection with the murder of the Polish officers, which they themselves committed in the Smolensk area on territory occupied by German troops, was at once taken up by the Polish Government and is being fanned in every way by the Polish official Press.

'Far from offering a rebuff to the vile Fascist slander of the USSR, the Polish Government did not even find it necessary to address to the Soviet Government any inquiry or request for an explanation on this subject.

'Having committed a monstrous crime against the Polish officers, the Hitlerite authorities are now staging a farcical investigation, and for this they have made use of certain Polish pro-Fascist elements which they themselves selected in occupied Poland where everything is under Hitler's heel, and where no honest Pole can openly have his say.

'For the "investigation", both the Polish Government and the Hitlerite Government invited the International Red Cross, which is compelled, in the face of a terroristic régime with its gallows and mass extermination of the peaceful population, to take part in this investigation farce staged by Hitler. Clearly such an "investigation", conducted behind the back of the Soviet Government, cannot evoke the confidence of people possessing any degree of honesty.

'The fact that the hostile campaign against the Soviet Union commenced simultaneously in the German and Polish Press, and was conducted along the same lines, leaves no doubt as to the existence of contact and accord in carrying out this hostile campaign between the enemy of the Allies – Hitler – and the Polish Government.

'While the peoples of the Soviet Union, bleeding profusely in a hard struggle against Hitlerite Germany, are straining every nerve for the defeat of the common enemy of the Russian and Polish people, and of all freedom-loving democratic countries, the Polish Government, in support of Hitler's tyranny, have dealt a treacherous blow to the Soviet Union.

'The Soviet Government are aware that this hostile campaign against the Soviet Union is being undertaken by the Polish Government in order to exert pressure upon the Soviet Government by making use of the slanderous Hitlerite fake for the purpose of wresting from it territorial concessions at the expense of the interests of the Soviet Ukraine, Soviet Byelorussia and Soviet Lithuania.

'All these circumstances compel the Soviet Government to recognize that the present Government of Poland, having embarked on the path of accord with Hitler's Government, have in effect discontinued friendly relations with the USSR, and has adopted a hostile attitude towards the Soviet Union.

'On the strength of the above, the Soviet Government have decided to sever relations with the Polish Government.

Molotov'

So, at the height of the common struggle against Hitler the Russians had refused to have any more to do with the Polish Government. At the same time they at once set about forming a 'Polish Committee' in Moscow formed entirely of Polish communists.

On April 28th, 1943, the Polish Government in London issued the following statement:

'The Polish Government have emphatically declared that their policy, aiming at a mutual friendly understanding between Poland and Soviet Russia on the basis of the integrity and full sovereignty of the Republic of Poland, was and continues to be fully supported by the Polish nation.

'Conscious of their responsibility towards their own nation and towards the Allies, whose unity and solidarity the Polish Government consider to be the cornerstone of future victory, they were the first to approach the Soviet Government with a proposal for an understanding in spite of the many tragic events that had taken place from the moment the Soviet Armies set foot on the territory of the Polish Republic, that is from the day of September 17th, 1939.

'Having established their relations with Soviet Russia by

the Agreement of July 30th, 1941, and by the Declaration of December 4th, 1941, the Polish Government have strictly discharged their obligations.

'Acting in close union with its Government, the Polish nation, making unheard-of sacrifices, fight unswervingly in Poland and abroad against the German invader. It produced no traitor Quisling and countenanced no collaboration with Germany. In the light of facts known throughout the world, the Polish nation and the Polish Government have no need to defend themselves from any charge of contact or under-standing with Hitler.

'In a public statement of April 17th, 1943, the Polish Government categorically denied to Germany the right to abuse the tragedy of the Polish officers in order to further her own perfidious aims. They unhesitatingly denounced the efforts of Nazi propaganda to create mistrust between the Allies. About the same time a note was sent to the Soviet Ambassador accredited to the Polish Government asking once again for information which would help to elucidate the fate of the missing officers.

'The Polish nation and the Polish Government look to the future. They appeal, in the name of the unity of the Allies and of elementary human principles, for the release from the USSR of the thousands of families of soldiers of the Polish Armed Forces engaged in the fight or preparing in Great Britain and the Middle-East to take their part in the fight, tens of thousands of Polish orphans and children for whose education they would take full responsibility and who now, in view of the German mass slaughter, are particularly precious to the Polish people. The Polish Army, in waging the war against Germany, needs as reinforcements all able-bodied Polish men who now find themselves on Soviet soil. The Polish Government appeal for their release. They reserve their right to plead the cause of all these persons before the world. Finally, the Polish Government appeal for the con-tinuation of relief for the large number of Polish citizens who remain in Russia.

'Whilst defending the integrity of the Republic of Poland, which accepted the challenge of war with the Third Reich, the Polish Government never claimed and do not claim, in accordance with their statement of February 25th, 1943, any Soviet territories.

'It is, and will be, the duty of every Polish Government to defend the rights of Poland and of Polish citizens. The principles for which the United Nations fight and the strengthening by all means of their solidarity in this struggle against the common enemy, remain the unchanging basis of the policy of the Polish Government.'

The severing of diplomatic relations with Poland by the USSR surprised public opinion in the West, where the possibility of such drastic action had not been envisaged. It shifted the Katyn affair from a moral to a political plane: fears that the USSR might make a separate peace with Germany were again revived. Fears which had never quite abated.

The British Government, immediately attempted to appease both parties.

On May 4th, 1943, the British Foreign Secretary, Anthony Eden (the late Lord Avon), said in the House of Commons:

'The House will no doubt wish me to make a brief statement about the unfortunate difficulties between the Soviet and Polish Governments which have arisen since the House rose. There is no need for me to enter into the immediate origins of the dispute. I would only draw attention, as indeed the Soviet and Polish Governments have already done in their published statements, to the cynicism which permits the Nazi murderers of hundreds of thousands of innocent Poles and Russians to make use of a story of mass murder in an attempt to disturb the unity of the Allies.

'From the outset His Majesty's Government have used their best efforts to persuade both the Poles and the Russians not to allow these German manoeuvres to have even the semblance of success. It was, therefore, with regret that they learned that, following an appeal by the Polish Government to the International Red Cross to investigate the German story, the Soviet Government felt compelled to interrupt relations with the Polish Government. His Majesty's Government have no wish to attribute blame for these events to anyone except the common enemy. Their sole desire is that these differences between two of the United Nations shall be repaired as swiftly as possible and that relations between the Soviet Union and Poland shall be restored on the basis of collaboration established, in spite of all the difficulties, between Marshal Stalin and General Sikorski, which has proved of such benefit to the cause of United Nations and is of far-reaching importance for the future well-being of Europe.

'In pursuing this policy, His Majesty's Government are, of course, working in the closest consultation and collaboration with the Government of the United States. They trust that the statesmanship which led to the conclusion of the Soviet–Polish Agreement of July 30th, 1941, will succeed again where it succeeded before. One thing at least is certain: the Germans need indulge no hope that their manoeuvres will weaken the combined offensive of the Allies or the growing resistance of the enslaved populations of Europe.'

The official attitude of the Soviet Government however remained unchanged to the end. They continued to refuse to allow the International Red Cross in Geneva, to take part in the inquiries made into the affair of the Katyn mass-murder.

One must here, however, call attention to an important point. If Radio Moscow on April 15th, 1943, that is to say, two days after the discovery of the Katyn crime, could declare without hesitation that the bodies found were those of 'the former Polish prisoners-of-war who, in 1941, were engaged in construction work in the areas west of Smolensk, and who fell into the hands of the German-Fascist hangmen in the Summer of 1941, after the withdrawal of the Soviet troops from the Smolensk area,' why is it that the Soviet authorities did not give the same information to the Polish representatives during the ten long months of negotiation during 1941–42, the object of which was to trace these same Polish prisoners-of-war?

Why did the answer come only after the Germans had discovered that these prisoners-of-war were lying in the Katyn graves?

'This question could perhaps be answered in the same way as this second question: Why did the Soviet Government not agree to an investigation by the International Red Cross?

CHAPTER SEVEN

OFFICIAL GERMAN DOCUMENTARY EVIDENCE

IN 1943 the German authorities published a special report under the title 'The Official Statement Concerning the Mass Murder at Katyn. Collected, prepared and edited by the German Information Bureau on the basis of documentary evidence by order of the German Foreign Office'.

This volume of 330 pages begins with a short introductory section entitled 'General Outline', followed by the 'Documentary Evidence', divided in five chapters.

The 'General Outline', six pages long, gives a résumé of the whole case. The first few sentences present the Katyn crime in broad outline. There follows the account of events in chronological order, beginning with the discovery of the graves and the exhumation of 4,143 bodies. The total number of Polish victims buried in Katyn Forest is estimated to be 10,000–12,000. The gist of the official Soviet Statement, issued in reply to the German revelations, is then given, and the final conclusion is that the crime had been committed by the Russians. The third paragraph shows the development of Polish–Soviet relations and finally presents the attitude of Great Britain and the United States towards the Polish–Soviet conflict.

The evidence concerning the discovery of the mass-graves of Polish officers was given by Ludwig Voss, Secretary of the Secret Field Police, in the presence of the Judge, Doctor Iuris Conrad, and an Official of the legal office of Bornemann's Army.

This witness gave the details of the case and his personal data; he then explained that his duties consisted in supervising the exhumation work at Katyn and the police investigations.

His evidence was given on April 26th, 1943, and the gist of it is as follows:

The first news of the mass-graves of Katyn was received at the beginning of February 1943. Mounds with young pine-trees planted on them were found in the Katyn forest; on closer inspection it was discovered that they were caused by human agency. Preliminary excavations, carried out during the February frost, proved the existence of mass-graves. In view of the prevailing cold, work on a large scale could not be undertaken.

People living in the neighbourhood were called as witnesses in order to ascertain the facts. Then follows a list of the witnesses.

By special order of the German High Command (OKW), the excavation of the first grave was commenced on March 29th, 1943. So far 600 bodies had been identified. There were about 3,000 bodies in the first grave. It was estimated that in the nearby graves a further 5,000 to 6,000 bodies would be found.

The identification so far carried out showed beyond all doubt that they were, almost without exception, the bodies of officers of the Polish Army.

All entries in the diaries and notebooks found on the bodies ceased on dates between April 6th and April 20th, 1940.

In this part of the German report, the exact wording of the statements given by the witnesses during their interrogation is recorded. Three local inhabitants were interrogated on the subject of the Kosogory Hill, near Katyn: Kusma Godonov, Ivan Krivozertsev, Michal Shigulov.

They all certified that since 1918 the hill had been generally known as a place of execution. It was used for executions in the time of the Cheka, which later was replaced by the 'GPU', and then by the NKVD (today the KGB).

In 1931 the area in question was surrounded by an enclosure, and special signs were erected warning the inhabitants not to enter. From 1940 on, Kosogory was also guarded by sentries and police-dogs.

· The report of the German Field Police, dated April 10th, 1943, states that the graves Nos. 8–11 (a sketch was attached) contained the bodies of numerous civilians killed by means of pistol shots in the back of the head. The state of decay of those bodies indicated that the executions were carried out at various times prior to September 1939, when the war began.

Five local men were interrogated on the subject of the transporting and killing of the prisoners-of-war in 1940.

Ivan Krivozertsev saw trains arriving every day at Gniezdovo railway station during March and April; they were composed of three to four carriages with gratings over the windows.

Matthiew Zakharov, who was working at the railway station at Smolensk, also stated that train-loads of prisoners-of-war were arriving at that time. The prisoners were in Polish uniforms. Transportation of the prisoners in the direction of Gniezdovo railway station lasted for 28 days.

Gregory Silvestrov saw the railway carriages arriving at Gniezdovo and men in uniforms being detrained. Their personal baggage would be taken away from them and thrown on lorries (trucks), whilst the prisoners themselves would be put into three prison buses and driven towards Katyn. Sometimes the prison buses repeated the journey between Gniezdovo railway station and the NKVD rest house ten times a day.

Ivan Andreyev saw trains arriving with the prisoners at Gniezdovo station in the months of March and April 1940. There were Polish soldiers in the trains; he recognized them by the shape of their caps. They were put into motor vehicles and driven towards Katyn.

Parfeon Kisselev said that for four to five weeks in the spring of 1940 prisoners were brought to Kosogory in three to four buses daily. From his house he heard shots and shouts. It was rumoured that 10,000 Poles were shot there. In 1942, several Polish workmen attached to the German Army came to his house and asked him to show them the place where the Polish officers were said to have been buried, and to lend them a shovel. Later these workmen told him that they had found the bodies of Polish officers.

This evidence, given here in summary, was published by the Germans together with verbatim reports, personal data, photographs of signatures and testimonies of each witness.

The Final Report of the German Police dated June 10th, 1943, read as follows:

'The work of exhuming, examining and identifying the bodies of Polish officers came to an end on June 7th, 1943. In the first place it must be stressed that the Kosogory forest was used as a place of execution of those sentenced to death by the NKVD or the Committee of "The Three", as early as in 1925. Preliminary excavations undertaken in various parts of the wooded area invariably led to the discovery of mass-graves "fraternal graves" in which the bodies of Russians of both sexes were found. Some of these bodies were carefully examined and it was proved that, without exception, death was caused by a shot in the back of the neck. From the documents found, it appeared that they were prisoners from the NKVD jail in Smolensk, the majority being political prisoners.

'The seven mass-graves of murdered Polish officers which have been cleared cover a relatively small area.

'Of 4,143 exhumed bodies, 2,815 have been definitely identified. Identification was based on identity cards, birth certificates, and award certificates found in their pockets together with their personal correspondence.

'In many cases identity cards, documents and considerable sums in zloty banknotes were sewn into the legs of their boots. Their clothes left no doubt as to their being Polish officers, for instance, the long cavalry boots of a shape normally worn by Polish officers.

'A large number of hitherto unidentified bodies will undoubtedly be identified by the Polish Red Cross.

'The number of officers of various ranks is given below:

Generals	2
Colonels	12
Lt.-Colonels	50
Majors	165
Captains	440
Lieutenants	542
2nd Lieutenants	930
Paymasters	2
Warrant Officers	8
Other NCOs	2
Identified as officers	101
Identified as 'in uniform'	1,440
Medical Officers	146
Veterinaries	10
Chaplains	1
Civilians	221
Names only identified	21
Unidentified	50
	4,143

'Bodies identified as "being in uniform" must also be regarded as officers, for corresponding epaulettes were often found in their pockets.

'After the identification (during which each body was given a serial number) and after the forensic medical examination, the bodies were buried in the newly-dug graves with the assistance of members of the Polish Red Cross. The new graves are numbered from 1 to 6 and the numbers can be found on the reverse side of the crosses. The two single graves of the generals were marked in a similar way.

'A name roll of all identified persons was made in order to facilitate meeting further inquiries from the families.

'From the translation of diaries, of memoirs and other notes found with the bodies, it was proved that the officers who had been taken prisoner by the Soviet Army in 1939, were sent to various camps: Kozielsk, Starobielsk, Ostashkov, Putiviel, Bolotov, Pavlishchev Bor, Shepyetovka, Gorodok. The majority of those killed in Katyn Forest had been in the Kozielsk camp (250 kilometres south-east of Smolensk on the railway-line Smolensk–Tambov). A few are known to have been brought from Starobielsk to Katyn through Kozielsk.

Corpse of a Polish major.

Bodies being selected from one of the
mass graves.

Aerial view of exhumed corpses laid
out in the forest.

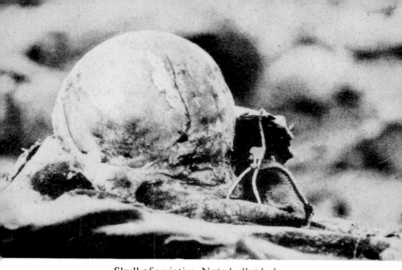

Skull of a victim. Note bullet hole
at base.

One of the disinterred victims. Note
hands tied behind back, greatcoat
pulled over head and, importantly,
wound from four-bladed bayonet.
Only the Russians had such bayonets.

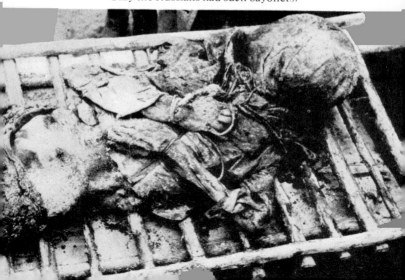

Two of the exhumed bodies. Note
flattened effect caused by mass burial.

A corpse being stripped of its clothing.
Note Professor Hajek examining
documents found in that clothing.

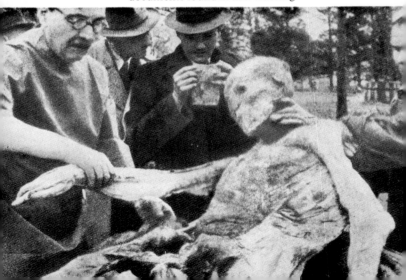

A Russian peasant from the immediate vicinity, questioned here by the Commission, told of Goat's Hill's reputation as a site of NKVD executions.

Stalin and Molotov explaining to Generals Sikorski and Anders (left) that the 'missing' officers will be found.

Własnoręczny podpis:

Exhibit 44. Identity card of Lieutenant Zbigniew Floriewicz.

Exhibit 66. Identity card of Franciszek Biernacki.

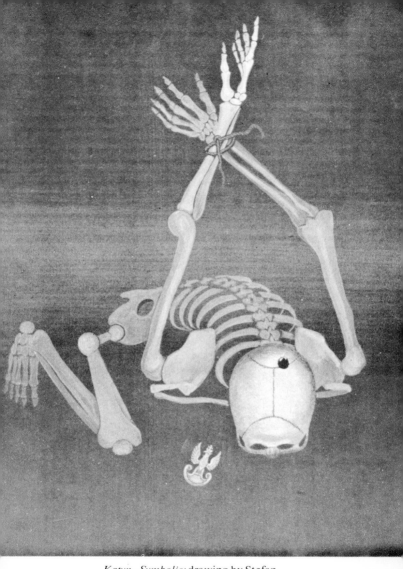

Katyn – Symbolic: drawing by Stefan Starzynski left as a testimony to the intense sufferings which he, and other Polish prisoners, experienced in Siberian slave labour camps.

The Katyn Memorial. Solemnly unveiled and dedicated in Kensington Cemetery, Gunnersbury, Hounslow, Middlesex, England on 18 September 1976 in honour of nearly 14,500 Polish prisoners of war massacred at Katyn and elsewhere in Russia in the spring of 1940 by the Soviet NKVD.

'From the end of March, until the first day of May 1940, the prisoners from Kozielsk arrived by rail. The exact dates cannot be established. A few short intervals apart, a batch left almost every day; the number of prisoners varied between 100 and 300 persons.

'... All trains were sent to Gniezdovo near Smolensk. Thence, in the early morning, the prisoners proceeded in special lorries (trucks) to the Katyn Forest, situated three kilometres west of Gniezdovo. There the officers were immediately shot, thrown into the waiting graves and buried, as may be seen from the evidence of witness Kisselev, who had seen the ditches being prepared.

'That the shooting took place immediately after the arrival of a batch of prisoners is proved by witnesses who heard shots after every such arrival. There was no accommodation in the forest apart from the rest house, which had a limited capacity. The notes of Major Solski merit attention: the translation of his diary is preserved with other documentary evidence of the crime. Major Solski made a few entries in his diary during the last hour of his life. (Not reported below.)

'A certain number of spent pistol cartridge-cases with the stamp "Geco 7.65 D" were found beyond the area of the graves; some single spent cases were found among the bodies in the graves. With a few exceptions, all the bodies show pistol-shots in the head; generally the place of entry of the bullet is below the protrusion on the back of the skull and the exit is in the forehead above the eye. (Cf. the report of the medical expert, Professor Dr. Buhtz, as well as the evidence of a Polish doctor, Wodziński.) In many instances the bullets had not left the skull. The calibre of the bullets found, 7.65 mm., would account for the damage to the skulls. The ammunition used was manufactured by the German firm of "Genschow". According to information given by the German High Command on May 31st, 1943 (Ch.H.Rüst und Befehlshaber des Ersatzheeres), ammunition for pistols of that calibre and actual pistols were supplied to Soviet Russia and Poland. It remains to be established whether the ammunition and pistols came from Russian dumps or from Polish equipment captured by the Russians when they overran the eastern part of Poland.

'From the position of the bodies it may be assumed that the majority were murdered outside the graves. The bodies were in a complete tangle, except in graves Nos. 1, 2 and 4, where some of them lay side by side or on top of each other. On some bodies spent cartridge cases were found between the collar of the victim's greatcoat and his neck, and there were holes in the collars of all the greatcoats. Every one of the collars was turned up. In other instances the bullets were found between the forehead and the inside of the cap. The number of persons shot in the graves totalled between 500 and 600.

'Very many of the dead men had their hands tied behind their back. In the case of a small number of bodies there was evidence that the head had been covered by the service dress or greatcoat and that a cord of the type used for hanging curtains had been tied round the neck.

'A few wedding rings and gold coins, etc., were the only valuables found in the victims' pockets. From the notes and the diaries of the murdered persons it was evident that all valuables had been taken away from them in the camps. If anybody still possessed something of that kind, he had to hand it over immediately before the execution. They were left with zloty banknotes and these were found in great quantities.

'In spite of repeated announcements and searches, no eye-witnesses of the murders could be traced. The only known name is that of the administrator of the rest house who lived there. The evidence of witnesses confirms that access to the forest was forbidden.

'Not all the bodies of the murdered officers had been exhumed when the work was interrupted, since a new grave of unknown capacity has recently been found. The possibility that further graves may come to light is not ruled out.

'The papers and personal effects were kept separately marked with the serial numbers of the victims and were always mentioned in routine reports.

Voss, Secretary of the Field Police.'

The Germans also included the report of Professor Dr. Gerhard Buhtz, Professor of Forensic Medicine and Criminology at Wroclaw (Breslau) University, whom they had invited to be in charge of forensic medical investigations. Here are some excerpts. 'On March 1st, 1943, I received for examination a report from the Secret Field Police dated February 28th, 1943, concerning the discovery in Katyn Forest of mass-graves of Polish officers shot in 1940 by NKVD personnel. Together with the representatives of the Secret Field Police I carried out a number of experimental exhumations and myself soon became convinced that the evidence collected during the interrogation of the inhabitants of a nearby village was confirmed by the facts. The frozen ground did not then allow the exhumation and examination of the bodies to be started.'

On the instructions of the German High Command the exhumation began on March 29th, 1943.

'Up to June 1st, 1943, seven mass-graves containing the bodies of officers of the Polish Army were found in the area of Katyn Forest. These graves were situated near each other in a clearing in the wood and had young pine trees planted on the top of them ...

'The seven graves occupied a total area of at least 478 square metres.

'The depth of the various graves was between 1.85 and 3.30 metres. The central sector of the longer arm of the L-shaped grave was the deepest place. The differences in the depth could be explained by the varying levels of the bottom of the graves. Thus, the depth of grave No. 6 at its north-eastern end was 2.10, at the south-western end only 1.74 metres.

'As a rule the graves were filled with bodies up to within 1.5 metres of the surface.

'Grave No. 8 was discovered in the south-western part of the marshy lowland on June 1st, 1943, about 100 metres from the area occupied by graves Nos. 1 to 7 ...

'In the woods north-east of the area of graves Nos. 1–7 on the other side of a forest track leading to the rest house, and to the south-east of grave No. 8, several experimental excavations were carried out. They led to the discovery of the graves of many Russian civilians; this definitely confirmed previous information received to the effect that the Katyn forest had been used for many years as a place of execution of the victims of the NKVD and of its predecessors, the Cheka and GPU.

'On June 3rd, 1943, the exhumation work had to be temporarily stopped by the sanitary police on account of the heat and the flies.

'Doctor Wodziński, from Cracow, a representative of the Polish Red Cross, was recently made responsible for the work of protecting the bodies, which service had previously been carried out by specially trained German personnel assisted by workmen recruited from among the local inhabitants.

'All bodies exhumed from the seven graves were duly buried in new graves situated to the north-west of the original grave area. Thirteen bodies of Polish Army personnel from the grave No. 8 were re-buried in the same grave after examination and the securing of proofs of identity.

'All the bodies from graves Nos. 1–7 wore winter clothing, for the most part military greatcoats, leather or fur jerkins, pullovers and sweaters. Only two of the bodies exhumed from grave No. 8 on June 1st, 1943, were in overcoats but not wearing warm underclothes; the remainder were in summer clothes (officers in service dress).

'We may deduce from this that the executions were carried out at different times of the year; this is corroborated by the various Russian and Polish newspapers, whole or fragmentary, found amongst the victims' personal papers. Whilst the newspapers found in graves Nos. 1–7 were dated March or the first half of April 1940 those found in grave No. 8 bore dates ranging from the latter part of April to the beginning of May 1940. For example, there were fragments of the Polish newspapers *Glos Radziecki* (edited in Kiev), dated April 26th and 28th, 1940, with an editorial headed "Catchwords for the First of May", as well as Russian newspapers dated May 1st and 6th, 1940.

'The uniforms in which the exhumed bodies were clothed were unquestionably those of the Polish Army, for with them were found the following articles: Polish eagles on the buttons, badges of rank, awards and medals, regimental badges, Polish type boots, field caps of officers and other ranks, belts with field flasks, aluminium cups, and markings on the linen. It must be pointed out that amonst the victims there were many officers of Marshal J. Pilsudski's First Cavalry Regiment. This is proved by shoulderstraps found in grave No. 8 with the letters "J.P.". It was a crack Polish Cavalry regiment.

'The highest awards for gallantry were found on many of the victims' uniforms; for instance, the Silver Cross, "Virtuti Militari" (corresponding to the German Knight's Cross), the Polish Cross of Merit, the Cross for Valour, etc.

'For the most part the uniforms were well cut and a good fit; the boots too were well-fitting. Often personal monograms were found on the underclothing. In all instances the uniforms and the underclothes were well-buttoned. Braces and belts were in good order. Apart from a few instances of damage by bayonets, the clothing had not been interfered with and there were no traces of violence.

'All these facts definitely lead to the conclusion that the victims were buried in the uniforms worn in captivity prior to their death, and that the bodies lay untouched until the opening of the graves. A theory, widely disseminated by the enemy, that the bodies were later dressed in Polish officers' uniforms is therefore without foundation. It is disproved by the results of the medical examination of the bodies; moreover, forensic medicine has taught us that it would be out of the question to remove the clothes of thousands of dead bodies and then, for the sake of camouflage, to clothe them in well-fitting linen and uniforms.

'No watches or rings were found on the bodies; detailed entries in the diaries of certain of the victims indicate, however, that they had their watches with them up to the last. On one of the bodies a well-concealed emerald ring of great value was found; several other bodies had valuables concealed on them, particularly silver cigarette-cases. The gold from teeth had not been removed. Crosses, gold chains, etc., were found under the shirts.

'Apart from small change (Polish paper money, nickel and copper coins), larger sums of money in zloty banknotes were found on the victims. In many instances wooden, hand-made cigarette-cases were found together with partly-filled tobacco pouches, cigarette holders engraved with mono-grams, inscriptions and the dates 1939 or 1940. Often the word "Kozielsk" was engraved on articles; this is the name of the camp, situated 250 kilometres south-west of Smolensk and 120 kilometres north of Orel, where the majority of the murdered officers had been held. There was also personal correspondence from relatives and friends addressed to Ko-zielsk. Documents found on the victims (identity cards – but not military passports – diaries, letters, postcards, calendars, photographs, drawings, etc.) gave the name, age, profession, origin and family relations of the victims. Pathetic entries in the diaries testify to the treatment of the victims by the NKVD. Letters and postcards from relatives in Upper Sil-esia, in the "General Government" and in the Russian-occu-pied zone, written, to judge the post-office stamps, between Autumn 1939 and March or April 1940, clearly point to the time of the crime (spring 1940).'

The summary of Professor Buhtz's Report ran as follows:

(1) As a result of the investigations in Katyn Forest 4,143 bodies of the members of the Polish Army were exhumed from the mass-graves. Out of this number 2,815 (67.9 per cent) were identified. On June 3rd, 1943, the exhumation had to be stopped for sanitary reasons (heat, flies). A lot more victims await exhumation, identification and forensic medi-cal examination.

(2) Besides two major-generals, the following victims were identified on the spot: 2,250 officers of various ranks, 156 medical and veterinary officers, 406 officers of unknown rank, warrant-officers and cadet-officers, and one chaplain. Identification of the remaining bodies continues, based on correspondence and other personal effects found upon them.

(3) On all the bodies were found small objects of a personal nature, including souvenirs, letters, documents, diaries. They wore well-fitting Polish uniforms on which the rank badges, award and medals could be recognized. In addition, many articles of military equipment were found on the bodies. The bodies from graves Nos. 1–7 were in winter clothing, those from grave No. 8 in summer clothing.

(4) Upon examination of the bodies, there was no suggestion that disease might have been the cause of death. With a few exceptions the usual bullet shot in the nape of the neck from a 7.65 mm. pistol was found. Corroboration is provided by corresponding spent cartridge-cases and bullets (some lodged in the bodies) and by one live cartridge found at the place of execution. In many instances the shots in the nape of the neck had passed through the raised collar of the great-coat. Up-to-date physical, chemical and optical methods of investigation showed that the shots were fired at extremely close range.

(5) The execution most probably took place outside the graves.

(6) A uniform method of binding the hands across the back had been used on a considerable number of the victims. Others (particularly those from grave No. 5) had greatcoats thrown over their heads and in some cases sawdust was found between the coat and the face of the victim. Forensic medical examination brought to light distinct signs of torture.

(7) Numerous stab-marks were found, undoubtedly inflicted prior to execution with a dagger-like weapon corresponding to the fluted Russian bayonet. No doubt these stabs were a means of urging the victims on their way to the place of execution.

(8) Broken jaws, obviously suffered by the victims when

135

they were still alive, prove that they were battered or beaten with rifle-butts prior to the murder.

(9) The uniform shot in the nape of the neck and the uniform method of tying the victim's hands and binding his head show that this was the work of skilled men.

(10) The bodies were in various stages of decay. In a few cases mummification of the uncovered parts had taken place (bodies from the upper layers), but generally the formation of adipocere had started with the fat penetrating into the clothing.

(11) Initially, the decomposition of the bodies was not affected by the ground, but after some time it was partly influenced by the acids in the soil (formation of adipocere and preservation of inner organs). On the other hand the products of the decomposition caused characteristic (chemical and structural) changes in the soil. These phenomena show that the bodies lay undisturbed for years in their original place.

(12) The material discovered in the graves (amongst others, documents found there) and the evidence of witnesses (Russian inhabitants of the neighbouring villages) prove that the bodies had lain in the graves for three years. The changes that had taken place, as ascertained during the post-mortem, and the other findings at the inquest, bear this out.

(13) The execution and the burial of the victims were carried out in a cool season, when there were no insects. The documents, correspondence, diaries and newspapers found on the bodies prove that the officers were murdered in March, April and May 1940.

Then follows the report of the International Medical Commission which the Germans invited to Katyn. This report is quoted in full in the following chapter.

Chapter II of the German book (pages 119–141) is devoted to published statements concerning the suggested examination of the Katyn murders by a representative of the International Red Cross. Amongst other statements, those of General Kukiel and of the Polish Government dated April 17th, 1943, are cited.

Chapter III (pages 142–166) contains notes, pronouncements and Press reports on the diplomatic and political attitudes adopted by the Allies towards the Katyn case, and deals particularly with the whole problem of the Polish–Soviet conflict to which the tragic discovery gave rise.

Chapter IV (pages 167–273) is entitled 'Description of the 4,143 bodies identified up to the seventh day of June 1943.' Actually, of this number, the Germans themselves stated in paragraph 1 of the 'Summary' that no more than 2,815 bodies had been identified and named. Detailed examination of the list, however showed that the number of bodies which were actually identified does not exceed 2,730. There were 464 bodies with documents containing insufficient information to establish the identity of the victims. The rest had no documents and were described for the most part just as 'in uniform'.

Chapter V (pages 274–330) contains photographs, taken at the scene of the crime, of the graves and the bodies, of persons working there and of others visiting Katyn Forest, as well as of documents and other objects found on the bodies or in the graves.

CHAPTER EIGHT

REPORT OF THE INTERNATIONAL MEDICAL COMMISSION

PREVENTED by the USSR from obtaining an investigation by the International Red Cross, the Germans gathered an international medical mission, composed of distinguished professors of forensic medicine from nine countries of German-occupied Europe, one neutral country (Switzerland) and her ally, Italy. There were no Germans on the commission. This International Medical Commission conducted an investigation into the mass-graves at Katyn Forest on the spot. In early May 1943 they published their report, which is given here in full.

1. Official communiqué

'A Commission consisting of the representatives from the Institutes of Forensic Medicine and Criminology of European Universities, as well as of other professors of medicine, conducted a scientific examination of the mass-graves of Polish officers in Katyn Forest near Smolensk, between April 28th and 30th, 1943.

The Commission was composed of the following members:

(1) Belgium	Speelers, M.D.	Professor of Ophthalmology, Ghent University.
(2) Bulgaria	Markov, M.D.	Reader in Forensic Medicine and Criminology, Sofia University.
(3) Denmark	Tramsen, M.D.	Assistant at the Institute of Forensic Medicine in Copenhagen.

(4) Finland	Saxén, M.D.	Professor of Pathological Anatomy, Helsinki University.
(5) Croatia (i.e. Yugoslavia)	Miloslavich, M.D.	Professor of Forensic Medicine and Criminology, Zagreb University.
(6) Italy	Palmieri, M.D.	Professor of Forensic Medicine and Criminology, Naples University.
(7) Holland	De Burlet, M.D.	Professor of Anatomy, Groningen University.
(8) Bohemia and Moravia (i.e. Czechoslovakia)	Hájek, M.D.	Professor of Forensic Medicine and Criminology, Prague University
(9) Rumania	Birkle, M.D.	Expert in Forensic Medicine of the Rumanian Ministry of Justice.
(10) Switzerland	Naville, M.D.	Professor of Forensic Medicine and Criminology, Geneva University.
(11) Slovakia (i.e. Czechoslovakia)	Subik, M.D.	Professor of Pathological Anatomy, Bratislava University.
(12) Hungary	Orsós, M.D.	Professor of Forensic Medicine and Criminology, Budapest University.

'Further, the investigations and meetings of the Commission were attended by:

(1) Buhtz, M.D.	Professor of Forensic Medicine and Criminology at Breslau (Wroclaw) University, entrusted with the exhumation work at Katyn by the German High Command.
(2) Costedoat	Medical Inspector, attending the work of the Commission on behalf of the Head of the French Government.

'The discovery of the mass-graves of Polish officers in Katyn Forest, near Smolensk, recently brought to the attention of the German authorities, induced Doctor Conti, the Head of the Reich Health Department, to ask the above-mentioned specialists from various European countries to investigate the Katyn discovery and thus to assist in elucidating this unique case.

'The Commission personally questioned a number of Russian witnesses from the vicinity who testified that in March and April 1940 large transports of Polish officers arrived almost daily at the railway station of Gniezdovo, near Katyn, where they were unloaded and sent in lorries (trucks) towards the Katyn Forest, never to be heard of again. The Commission also examined the discoveries and the results of previous investigations, as well as such evidence as had been collected. Up to April 30th, 1943, 982 bodies had been exhumed. Of these, about 70 per cent were gradually identified; documents found on the remaining victims could not be used for identification until they had been properly cleaned. All bodies exhumed prior to the arrival of the Commission had been examined and in most cases a post mortem had been carried out by Professor Buhtz and his colleagues. Up till now seven mass graves have been excavated. The largest contained the bodies of about 2,500 officers.

'The members of the Commission personally conducted a post mortem on nine of the bodies, and proceeded to establish the evidence in specially selected cases.

'All bodies so far exhumed show that death was caused by a shot in the head. These shots were without exception fired into the nape of the neck; generally one shot had been fired, in some instances two, and in one instance three. In every case the bullet had entered the lower part of the nape, piercing the occipital bone, close to the opening of the lower part of the skull; the point of exit was in the forehead, generally on the line of the hair-growth, in some rare cases in the lower part of the forehead. The shots were without exception those of a pistol with a calibre of less than eight millimetres.

'That the shots had been fired from a barrel touching the nape of the neck or at extremely close range is proved by the cracks in the skull, by traces of gunpowder on the base of the skull close to the entrance of the bullet, and by the similarity of the exit orifices caused by the bullet. This may also be deduced from the fact that, apart from a few isolated cases, the path of the bullet is identical. The striking uniformity of the injuries and the position of the bullet's entry, all within a very small circumference on the lower part of the skull, point to experienced hands having been at work. The wrists of a large number of victims were found to have been tied in exactly the same way and in a few cases light bayonet stabs were noticed in the skin and in the clothes. The way in which the hands of the victims were tied is similar to that observed in the case of corpses of Russian civilians, also ex-humed in Katyn Forest, but buried much earlier. Further, it has been established that the shots in the nape of the neck of these civilians had likewise been the work of experienced men.

'A stray bullet which had penetrated the head of a Polish officer previously killed by the usual shot in the nape of the neck, and which was wedged in the exterior part of the bone, proves that the bullet first killed another officer and then struck this officer who already lay dead in the pit. This fact warrants the assertion that shooting also took place in the pits themselves, in order to avoid transferring the corpses to the burial ground.

'The mass-graves are situated in clearings, which had been completely levelled and then planted with pine trees. According to personal examinations carried out by the members of the Commission and the statements of senior forestry inspector Von Herff, who had been summoned as an expert, the pine trees in question were at least five years old, rather stunted owing to their being in the shade of older trees, and had been planted in that area three years ago.

'The pits were dug in stepped terraces in a hilly area and in sandy soil. In places they penetrated to underground water.

'The bodies were almost without exception laid face down-wards, pressed together, fairly tidily around the sides of the pit but more irregularly in the centre. In almost all cases the legs were extended. It is clear that the bodies were arranged systematically. The Commission observed that the uniforms of the exhumed bodies, especially in respect of buttons, badges of rank, decorations, boots, marks on the underwear, etc., were typically Polish. The uniforms in question were winter ones. Fur coats, leather jackets, pullovers, officers' boots and caps customarily worn by Polish officers were frequently found. Only a few bodies of other ranks were discovered; the body of a priest was also found. All the uniforms were well-fitting despite the varying sizes of the wearers. The underclothes were buttoned up in the normal way; the braces of the trousers were properly adjusted. The Commission arrived at the conclusion that the victims were buried in the uniforms worn by them up to the moment of their death.

'No watches or rings were found on the bodies although, judging from the entries in the notebooks in which the exact time had been recorded, the officers must have been in possession of watches until the last moment. Valuable articles of metal were found concealed on a few bodies only. Banknotes were found in large quantities and quite often some small change. Boxes of matches and Polish cigarettes were also found, and in some cases tobacco pouches, and cigarette-cases bearing the inscription "Kozielsk" (the name of the last Russian POW camp where the majority of the murdered officers had been imprisoned). The documents found on the bodies (notebooks, letters, newspapers) bear the dates covering the period between the Autumn of 1939 and the months of April and March 1940. So far, the most recent date that has come to light is that on a Russian newspaper dated April 22nd, 1940.

'The stages of decay were found to vary in accordance with the position of the bodies in the pits. Whilst mummification had taken place on the top and at the sides of the mass of bodies, a humid process could be observed caused by the damp nearer the centre. Adjacent bodies were stuck together with a thick putrid liquid. The peculiar deformations due to pressure clearly show that the bodies remained in the position they had assumed when they were first thrown into the pits.

'Neither insects nor any traces of them, such as could have dated from the time of the burial, were found on the bodies. This proves that the shooting of the victims and their burial took place in the cold season, when there were no insects.

'Several skulls were examined with a view to seeing whether they showed a condition which, if present, constitutes, according to the experiments made by Professor Orsós, clear evidence regarding the date of death. This appears as a crust, formed of layers of necrotic structure, around the surface of the brain which is turned into a uniform clay, like pulp. Bodies that have been in graves less than three years do not show this condition. Amongst others, body No. 526, which was discovered on the surface of a big mass grave, bore distinct traces of this phenomenon.'

Then followed a brief summary, which contained the following paragraph.

'The death of all these victims was caused exclusively by a shot in the nape of the neck. From statements made by witnesses, as well as from letters, diaries, newspapers, etc., found on the bodies, it follows that the executions took place in March and April 1940. There is a complete conformity between the statements concerning the mass-graves and the results of the examination of single bodies of Polish officers.'

The whole report was signed by all members of the Commission.

Zusammenfassendes Gutachten:

Im Walde von Katyn wurden von der Kommission Massengräber von polnischen Offizieren untersucht, von denen bisher 7 geöffnet sind. Aus diesen wurden bisher 982 Leichen geborgen, untersucht, zum Teil obduziert und schon zu 70 Prozent identifiziert.

Die Leichen wiesen als Todesursache ausschließlich Genickschüsse auf. Aus den Zeugenaussagen, den bei den Leichen aufgefundenen Briefschaften, Tagebüchern, Zeitungen usw. ergibt sich, daß die Erschießungen in den Monaten März und April 1940 stattgefunden haben. Hiermit stehen in völliger Übereinstimmung die im Protokoll geschilderten Befunde an den Massengräbern und den einzelnen Leichen der polnischen Offiziere.

(Dr.Spaleeya)   (Dr.Markov)   (Dr. Tramsen)   (Dr.Saxén)

(Dr.Palmieri)   (Dr.Milosavich)   (Dr.de-Burlet)   (Dr.Hajek)

(Dr.Birkle)   (Dr.Naville)   (Dr.Subik)   (Dr.Orsós)

In 1944, after the Allied forces had captured Southern Italy – Professor Palmieri gave to the Polish military authorities in Naples, an account of how the Commission had been invited by the Germans and what method had been employed by the investigators.

The Commission was summoned after the refusal of the International Red Cross to participate in the investigation. As is known, the International Red Cross in Switzerland was obliged to refuse, because it had not received the necessary authorization from the Soviet Government. In view of the foregoing, the German Government decided to organize their own investigations, by entrusting the inquiry into the Katyn crime to the best-known European specialists in forensic medicine. A delegate of the Polish Government in London was invited to join the Commission, but he declined.

The thirteen delegates of various countries met in Berlin. German scientists did not partake in the work of the Commission; Doctor Buhtz, Professor of Forensic Medicine at the University of Breslau (Wroclaw), merely acted in a liaison capacity between the Commission and the German authorities.

From the very beginning, that is to say at the preliminary meeting of the Commission, it was unanimously decided that the investigations should be conducted on purely a scientific basis, excluding all political or polemic aspects. The Commission then proceeded to formulate the questions to which they would limit themselves, viz.:

(1) Identification of bodies.
(2) Ascertaining the cause of death.
(3) Establishing the time at which death occurred.

Dr. Palmieri stressed that during the entirely impartial investigations and the drawing-up of the well-known conclusions unanimously adopted, the Commission adhered strictly to the rules they had set themselves.

All members of the Commission enjoyed absolute freedom of movement and were provided with such technical means as might be of help to them. They were allowed to go to the graves in order to direct the exhumation in the places and under the conditions that they deemed suitable. A Commission of the Polish Red Cross which had arrived from Warsaw worked simultaneously but separately at Katyn and arrived at the same conclusions.

On their return to Berlin, the members of the Commission handed over their report to Doctor Conti, the Head of the Reich Health Department, and the Commission was then disbanded.

The work of the members of the Commission was entirely honorary. None of them received any salary or allowance, decoration or academic distinction, or any other compensation whatsoever. They merely received railway tickets and their hotel bills were settled on the spot.

The Bulgarian expert however, Dr. Markov, lecturer at the University of Sofia, subsequently revoked his signed statement, included in the report of the International Medical Commission. He did it for the first time in February 1945, when arraigned before the Court set up in Bulgaria under the Russian army of occupation, to try German war criminals. Accused of collaboration (evidently on the basis of his participation in the International Medical Commission) Markov knew he was on trial for his life. As soon as he revoked his statement the Communist Prosecutor withdrew the indictment against him.

At Nuremberg on July 1st, 1946, Markov repeated the evidence he had given before the People's Tribunal in Sofia. The Markov 'testimony' is discussed in Chapter Eleven.

CHAPTER NINE

PROFESSOR NAVILLE'S TESTIMONY

IN September 1946, when the Nuremberg Trial was nearing its end, a Communist member of the Swiss Grand Council, Mr. Vincent (Swiss Communists ostensibly belong to the 'Labour Party'), launched an attack against Professor François Naville on account of his participation in an International Medical Commission which in 1943 had conducted an investigation at Katyn and later published its well-known report. Mr. Vincent chose the form of an interpellation addressed to the Geneva Executive Body (State Council).

This interpellation had its repercussion at a sitting of the Geneva Legislative Body (Grand Council) in 1947, when Mr. Albert Picot, Head of the Cantonal Government, answered Mr. Vincent's case. A substantial part of this answer consisted in reading extracts from Professor Naville's report, presented by the latter to the Government, at their request, following the interpellation. The following is the substance of Mr. Albert Picot's statement.

At the meeting of the Grand Council of September 11th, 1946, Mr. Vincent asked the Council of State how they 'proposed to judge the case of Dr. Naville, Professor of Forensic Medicine, who had agreed to act as legal expert at the request of the German Government in April 1943, where the origin of the 10,000 corpses of Polish officers discovered in Katyn Forest near Smolensk was concerned.' Mr. Picot explained that Katyn was in Russia, in a region which the Russians had occupied since the beginning of the Polish–German war in 1939, and where the Germans had not arrived until the summer or autumn of 1941, after the first successes of their offensive in the direction of Smolensk.

If the killings took place in 1940 or the winter of 1940–41, then these men were executed by the Russians. If the corpses dated from the autumn of 1941 or from 1942, then the murderers were Germans.

Considering the climatic conditions, the question could be decided by the advanced state of decomposition of the bodies.

In its report the State Council would deal only with the following three points:

(1) The relations between Dr. Naville and the Swiss authorities (federal, cantonal and military) before his departure.

(2) Did Dr. Naville receive any reward from Germany?

(3) Did Dr. Naville agree to work under conditions of constraint, thus soiling the honour of a Swiss Professor?

On all these three questions Mr. Picot said, the State Council was in possession of a clear report from Dr. Naville, and he was happy to read them extracts from it:

1. *Preamble*

'I wish to state that in the present circumstances I have been obliged for the first time to abandon the restraint which I deliberately undertook to exercise for the last three years. I am not mixed up with politics. I consider that I did my duty by participating in the technical inquiry with a view to throwing some light on the matter concerned, and I have always refused to follow up the numerous requests addressed to me, either by Swiss or by foreigners, to make public my findings or my opinion. Rightly or wrongly, I considered that only the Poles, who had asked for an inquiry into the circumstances in which some ten thousand of their officers, prisoners-of-war, had been killed, could assume the responsibility of initiating a public discussion on the subject, of which the consequences could not be foretold.

'But the intervention of Mr. Vincent forces me to give certain information on the matter.

'I recall that after the Germans had uncovered the ditches containing several thousand Polish officers, killed, according to them, by Russian secret police, the Polish Government in London as well as the Polish and German Red Cross asked the International Committee of the Red Cross to conduct an investigation on the spot. As Russia seemed determined to veto such an inquiry, the German sanitary authorities in order to accede to the wishes of the Poles, decided to entrust the investigation to a committee of experts composed of one specialist in forensic medicine from almost every neutral country, that is, each country not directly interested in the matter.

'The Russians, considering that the demand for an impartial investigation submitted by the Poles was a hostile act on their part, severed diplomatic relations with the Polish Government on Monday, April 26th, 1943. This I was told by the Swiss envoy in Berlin, Mr. Fröhlicher, on whom I called immediately after my arrival in Berlin ...

'It was on the night of April 22nd, 1943, that Dr. Steiner, of Geneva, medical adviser to the German Consulate General there, asked me whether I could and would leave on April 26th to join the committee of experts concerned. May I add in this connection that I have never concealed from anybody my outspoken, and I may even say violent, hostility towards Germany after 1914, caused by their foreign policy which I always considered dangerous for Switzerland, and since 1933 by the attitude adopted by the Nazi bosses. I could give many proofs of this. It was well known to my students at the University, as even the late German Professor Askanasy occasionally protested to me about it. Your department can ascertain from Professor Liebeskind what I said after incidents provoked by one of his lectures to German students, and from the Dean of the Faculty of Law the way in which I intervened in connection with the affair of the German student-spies.

'Therefore I refused at first, and suggested some other Swiss experts in forensic medicine. In the meantime, however, I contacted other persons. They told me that this was not a matter of rendering a service to the Germans, but of responding to the legitimate wish of the Poles, who demanded that an impartial investigation be made, and that it should be established whether anything had been done to produce a nominal roll of the dead officers, to proceed with the identifications as far as possible, and to inform the next-of-kin. Here I must remind you that, contrary to the practice followed by all the other belligerents, the Russians always refused to supply lists of prisoners-of-war taken by them to the International Committee of the Red Cross, and that for a long time no news had been received of the 10,000 officers they had taken prisoners.

'When Dr. Steiner again invited me, therefore, I decided to accept; if I am not mistaken it was on Friday night. It seemed to me that it would be cowardly to refuse to co-operate in an inquiry whose object was to establish the truth, under the pretext that I would necessarily be dissatisfied with one or the other of the belligerents accused of a crime so particularly odious and contrary to the modern usages of war. At that time, moreover, I did not know what the composition of the committee of experts would be, or even what would be submitted to me for examination and inquiry.'

Professor Naville's report goes on to state that he was authorized to take part in the Medical Commission of Investigation both by the Swiss military authorities and by the Federal authorities (Political Department). In accordance with the regulations he advised the Dean of his Faculty, who neither at that time nor at any later period, raised any objection. Next, the report deals with the question of the fees which the Germans were supposed to have paid to the members of the Commission:

'Mr. Vincent seems to be under the impression that I received a considerable amount of German gold. He can be relieved of his anxiety. I was certainly entitled to ask for a fee for such complicated work of such importance, on which I spent one month of my time carrying out various researches, after a journey taking eight days. But from the very beginning I decided to refuse it, on moral grounds. I did not want to obtain money either from the Poles or from the Germans. I do not know who paid the expenses of the journey of our committee of experts, but I personally never asked for nor received from anyone any gold, money, gifts, rewards, assets, or promises of any kind. If, at a time when it is being mauled simultaneously by the armies of two mighty neighbours, a country learns of the massacre of nearly 10,000 of its officers, prisoners-of-war, who committed no crime other than to fight in its defence, and when that country tries to find out how this came about, a decent man cannot demand fees for going to the place and trying to lift the hem of the veil which concealed, and still conceals, the circumstances in which this act of odious cowardice, so contrary to the usages of war, was committed.

'Mr. Vincent asserts that I was acting under constant pressure from the Gestapo, which prevented us from having a free hand. This is absolutely untrue. I do not know whether the police were represented amongst those who received and accompanied us (doctors and guides), but I can definitely state that we were able to proceed undisturbed with our work as experts. I did not notice any signs of pressure being exerted on myself or on any of my colleagues. We were always able to discuss all matters freely amongst ourselves without the Germans being present. On many occasions I told my co-experts and the Germans who received us certain "truths" which they considered rather outspoken. They seemed dumbfounded, but no one ever molested me. I did not conceal what I thought of the moral responsibility of the Germans in this matter, as it was they who went to war and invaded Poland, even if our conclusion should establish their innocence in the matter of the death of the officers.

'We spent two days and three nights at Smolensk, about 50 km. from the Russian lines. I moved about quite freely at Smolensk, as in Berlin, without being in any way accompanied or shadowed. As two of us could speak Russian, we were on several occasions able to talk to the peasants and

Russian prisoners-of-war. We also contacted the medical personnel of the Polish Red Cross, who co-operated at the exhumation, and were specially detailed to identify the bodies, make nominal rolls and inform the next-of-kin. We assured ourselves that everything possible was being done in that respect.

'We freely carried out about ten post-mortem examinations of bodies which we had had taken, in our presence, from the lower layers of the unexplored common graves. Undisturbed, we dictated reports on the post-mortem examinations, without any intervention from the German medical personnel. We examined, superficially but quite freely, about one hundred corpses which had been disinterred in our presence. I, myself, found in the clothes of one of them a wooden cigarette-holder engraved with the name "Kozielsk" (one of the three camps from which the doomed officers had come), and in the uniform of another I found a box of matches from a Russian factory in the Province of Orel, the region where the three camps concerned were situated.*

'At the examinations, being concerned with the forensic medicine aspect, we paid particular attention to the transformation of the fatty substances of the skin and internal organs, to changes in the bones, to the destruction of joint tendons, to changes and atrophies of various parts of the body, and also to all other signs which would testify to the time of death.

'Examination of the skull of a lieutenant, undertaken specifically by Professor Orsós from Budapest, at which I was present, brought to light a condition that virtually excluded the possibility of death having occurred less than three years previously, according to scientific works already published on that kind of mutilation ...

'We experts were also at liberty to discuss amongst ourselves all our findings as well as the wording of our report.

* Only Kozielsk was in fact situated in the region of Orel.

After having examined the graves and the corpses on Thursday and Friday, April 29th and 30th, all the experts met on Friday afternoon to discuss and decide on the composition of the report. Only medical personnel took part in that discussion, but without any interference. Some of us made a draft of the final report, and it was submitted to me for signature on Saturday, May 1st, at 3 a.m. I offered several comments and asked for some changes and additions, which were immediately made. I do not know whether the same consideration was given to the observations and criticisms made by Dr. Markov of Bulgaria; I do not remember whether he intervened during our discussion at the meeting, but I was present when he signed the report on May 1st about noon, and I can state that he did not then make any objections or protests. I do not know whether he was subject to any constraint by the authorities of his own country, either before the journey to Katyn or at the time he revoked his signature, on being charged with collaboration and when he declared that he had acted under pressure; but he was certainly not under any pressure or constraint while the committee of which he was a member was at work. In any case, he made in our presence a post mortem of one corpse and quite freely dictated the report on it, of which I have a copy . . .

'By joining the twelve other experts in signing our report of 1943, I by no means wished to serve the Germans, but only the Poles and the Truth. The report, by the way, occupies only five pages in the thick illustrated volume of 331 pages which the Germans published about Katyn, which I possess, and which I was told is also in the possession of the public library in Geneva.

'Mr. Vincent is a solicitor in Geneva. He knows that even in our country, in matters where a public confession or substantial evidence have not entirely clarified matters, the parties concerned try to take advantage of all the obscure points. He also knows that not everywhere in Europe are the rights of man and the truth unsullied by the ideological and political trends of the day respected as they are, happily, in Switzerland.

'As for us, the forensic medicine experts, it is our right and our duty in our modest sphere to seek above all to serve the truth in conflicts where the parties sometimes serve other masters; it is the tradition and the pride of our profession, an honour sometimes dangerous. We must do this without yielding to pressure, from whatever quarter it may come, without regard for the criticism and hostility of those who may be put into an awkward position by our unbiased impartiality. May our motto always remain that which honours certain tombs: *Vitam impendere vero.*

'Here, Mr. President, is the report you asked me to submit in justification of my actions. I leave it to you to decide whether it would be appropriate to contact the Federal Political Department, with whose consent I took part in the experts' examination in question, before you submit the text or its gist to the Grand Council, which might have political consequences I cannot foresee.

(signed) F. Naville.'

Mr. Picot's statement

Those, continued Mr. Picot, were the parts of the report submitted by Dr. Naville that concerned them most. On behalf of the State Council he concluded:

'The State Council considers that there is nothing with which to reproach Dr. François Naville, distinguished man of science, excellent forensic medicine expert, who acted on his own responsibility and who did nothing to infringe any rule of professional conduct or of the code of honour. Dr. Naville's report contains a statement justifying the conclusions of his original report of 1943. He may publish it when he wishes. The Grand Council is not entitled to make any pronouncement on this matter.

'On the other hand, the Grand Council agrees with us that it is in accordance with the ideal of science and the moral principles of our country that a scientist should seek the truth by means of thorough investigation.'

CHAPTER TEN

THE RUSSIAN 'INVESTIGATION'

WE come now to the evidence offered by Soviet Russia.

Within a few weeks of the publication of the *Amtliches Material* in mid-1943, the German Army was driven from the Smolensk region. After unusually heavy fighting the attacks launched by General Sokolowski's Army on Jartsevo and by General Jermienko's Army on Duchovshtchizna on September 15th, 1943, led to the capture of Smolensk by the Soviet armies on September 25th. Soon afterwards they also retook the region of the Katyn graves, with the result that the 'resumption' of the exhumations which the Germans had declared would take place in the autumn became impossible.

The publication of the *Amtliches Material* was therefore the 'swan song' of German propaganda about the Katyn affair. For some months the Germans had used it to shock public opinion in Europe and the world; but by October 1943 almost nothing was heard of it.

It was, however, swiftly taken up by the Russians when their forces re-occupied the area in the autumn of 1943.

By a Decree of the Supreme Council of the USSR dated November 2nd, 1943, an 'Extraordinary State Commission for Ascertaining and Investigating the Crimes committed by the German Fascist Invaders and their Associates' was set up. The Extraordinary Commission set up a 'Special Commission for Ascertaining and Investigating the Circumstances of the Shooting of Polish Officer Prisoners by the German Fascist Invaders in the Katyn Wood'. The first mention of this 'Special Commission' was made in Moscow on January 17th, 1944.

The composition of this Special Commission was as follows:

Chairman:
   M. N. Burdenko – surgeon and Academician.

Members:
   A. N. Tolstoy – Academician – Author;
   Nikolai – Metropolitan of Kiev and Halich;
   Lt.-Gen. Gundurov – President of the All-Slav Committee;
   S. Kolesnikov – Chairman of the Executive Committee of the Union of Red Cross and Red Crescent Societies;
   W. Potemkin – Peoples' Commissar of Education of the Russian SFSR, Academician;
   Col.-Gen. E. Smirnov – Chief of the Central Medical Administration of the Red Army;
   B. Mielnikov – Chairman of the Smolensk Regional Executive Committee.

It appears from the Report of the Special Commission that a member of the Extraordinary State Commission, M. N. Burdenko, together with his collaborators and medico-legal experts (none of whom are named in the Report), proceeded to Smolensk on October 26th, 1943, that is on the day following the Capture of that city by the Red Army, and for a period of nearly four months 'carried out preliminary study and investigation of the circumstances of all the crimes perpetrated by the Germans'.

The vast amount of material collected in those four months defined as 'study and investigation' in the Report, was then put at the disposal of the Special Commission, operating under the Chairmanship of the same Burdenko. By January 24th, 1944, the Report of the Special Commission was ready.

The Report opened with the statement that 'The Katyn forest had for long been the favourite resort of Smolensk people, where they used to rest on holidays. The population of the neighbourhood grazed cattle and gathered fuel in the Katyn forest. Access to the Katyn forest was not banned or restricted in any way.'

The Special Commission recalled as a proof of this statement the fact that even in the summer of 1941 there was a Young Pioneers camp of the 'Industrial Insurance Board' in this forest, and it was not liquidated until July 1941. But the Report said nothing of the site of that Pioneers camp in Katyn wood which extended over a fairly large area and consisted of different parts, some of them bearing separate names, except the possibility of other parts being used for different purposes. The fact that the various parts of the Katyn wood were called by different names was confirmed in the last paragraph of Chapter One of the Report, which said that 'the part of the Katyn forest named Kozy Gory was guarded particularly strictly' by the Germans. The Report of the Special Commission definitely failed to mention how far that Pioneers camp lay from the 'rest house of the Smolensk Administration of the Peoples' Commissariat of International Affairs'. (NKVD.)

The Report went on to refer to the Polish prisoners who were alleged to have been in the Smolensk area when it was taken by the Germans in 1941. Except however for a vague reference in the testimony of one of the witnesses (Savatiexev – see below) to the fact that those prisoners were brought to the region of Smolensk in the spring of 1940 and were disembarked at the Gniezdovo station, it confined itself to stating that 'Polish war prisoners, officers and men, worked in the Western district of the Region, building and repairing roads' and that they were 'quartered in three special camps named: Camp No. 1 O.N., Camp No. 2 O.N. and Camp No. 3 O.N. These camps were located 25–45 kilometres (about 15½–28 miles) West of Smolensk'.

Unfortunately the Report made no mention of such important and essential points as:

1. the general number of Polish prisoners who were supposed to have been in that region in 1941;
2. the number of prisoners in each of the three camps;
3. the Polish military ranks of the prisoners, which should have presented no difficulty to the Soviet authorities in view of the detailed records made in the camps;

157

4. the actual site of each of those camps, which could have been named after the geographical names of the places in which they were supposed to have been situated instead of being referred to only by numbers.

The report also did not explain why those particular POW camps for Polish officers and soldiers near Smolensk were called 'special' camps, nor did it give any indication of specialized features that might have distinguished them from other 'ordinary' POW camps.

In general there was no answer to be found in the Report to the many questions which naturally arose if, as the Soviets maintained, the Polish POWs from Kozielsk, Starobielsk and Ostashkov had been moved to 'special camps' in the Smolensk area:

1. Why, in 1940 and 1941, 97 per cent of Polish officers captured by the Soviets were detained in the special camps Nos. 1 O.N., 2 O.N. and 3 O.N., and engaged in 'building and repairing roads', while the remaining 3 per cent, at that time in the camp at Pavlishchev-Bor and subsequently at Griazovietz, were exempt from all forced labour?

2. Why – as appears from an article by Warrant Officer Marian Klimczak entitled 'I was a prisoner in the Katyn Forest', published in No. 7/48 of the Moscow 'Wolna Polska' of February 24th, 1944 – were the prisoners in camp No. 2 O.N. (in which the author of the article is supposed to have passed 'a certain time' in 1941 with 'a group of 300 persons') kept on normal rations for Soviet correctional labour camps which depended on the results of their work, while those in the camps of Pavlishchev-Bor and Griazovietz were receiving full rations regardless of the fact that they did no work?

3. Why did families in Poland receive no news for eighteen months from Polish prisoners-of-war in special camps No. 1 O.N., 2 O.N. and 3 O.N., while they were able to correspond comparatively freely with prisoners of war at Griazovietz?

4. Why, in camps No. 1 O.N., 2 O.N. and 3 O.N., did Gen-

erals and staff officers have to work at 'building and repairing roads' while in other camps such officers were not only
exempt from all work but had batmen and even adjutants
assigned to them?

5. Why and for what purpose were even invalids and
people with artificial arms and legs transferred from Kozielsk to these 'special' camps? And why were prisoners sent
to these special camps for building roads without regard to
their age or state of health, among them people over 60 years
of age, while from the camp for internees at Kozielsk (Kozielsk III) only those pronounced fit for work by the medical
commission were sent to labour camps?

6. Why, if, in the period from October 1940, when in the
POW camp of Griazovietz and the camp for internees at
Kozielsk the Soviet authorities were taking steps to find
people to organize the already planned 'Polish Division' of
the Army were similar steps not taken in 'special camps Nos.
1 O.N., 2 O.N. and 3 O.N.' which contained 97 per cent of
Polish officer prisoners-of-war?

7. Why, finally, were such large numbers (over 10,000) of
Polish prisoners-of-war, particularly officers, concentrated for
the work of 'building and repairing roads' in the Western
district of the Smolensk region, when – as is stated in the
Short Soviet Encyclopaedia, pub. 1941, vol. IX p. 810 – the
lines of communication in the region of Smolensk, were as
fully developed as in any place in the whole Soviet Union?

The Report of the Special Commission went on to explain
why Polish prisoners-of-war from the three 'special' camps in
the Western areas of the Smolensk region had not been
evacuated before the German advance. It stated that: 'Testimony of witnesses and documentary evidence establish
that after the outbreak of hostilities, in view of the situation
that arose, the camps could not be evacuated in time and all
the Polish war prisoners, as well as some members of the
guard and staff of the camps fell prisoner to the Germans.'

The 'documentary evidence' mentioned in the foregoing
paragraph was neither quoted in the Report of the Special
Commission, nor discussed in any detail, so that we know

nothing about it. As far as statements of witnesses in this matter are concerned, the Report quoted two of the depositions:

'The former Chief of Camp No. 1 O.N. Major of State Security Vetoshnikov interrogated by the Special Commission testified:

' "I was waiting for the order on the removal of the camp, but communication with Smolensk was cut. Then I myself with several staff members went to Smolensk to clarify the situation. In Smolensk I found a tense situation. I applied to the chief of traffic of the Smolensk section of the Western Railway, Ivanov, asking him to provide the camp with railway cars for evacuation of the Polish war prisoners. But Ivanov answered that I could not count on receiving cars. I also tried to get in touch with Moscow, to obtain permission to set out on foot, but I failed. By this time Smolensk was already cut off from the camp by the Germans, and I did not know what happened to the Polish war prisoners and guards who remained in the camp."

'Engineer Ivanov, who in July 1941 was acting Chief of Traffic of the Smolensk Section of the Western Railway, testified before the Special Commission:

' "The Administration of the Polish War Prisoners' camps applied to my office for cars for evacuation of the Poles, but we had none to spare. Besides, we could not send cars to the Gussino line, where the majority of the Polish war prisoners were, since that line was already under fire. Therefore, we could not comply with the request of the Camps Administration. Thus the Polish war prisoners remained in the Smolensk region." '

The report did not mention if both these witnesses were interrogated during the public session of the Special Commission. Jerzy Borejsza, special correspondent of the 'Wolna Polska' mentioned in his report 'On the trail of crime' only Ivanov's depositions and he quoted from it extremely important and essential factual details, which were entirely omitted in the report of the Special Commission.

'The former stationmaster of Gniezdovo (the Report of the Special Commission referred to Ivanov as the acting Chief of

Traffic of the Smolensk Station) Ivanov, a precise, neat old man, recalled the circumstances of the evacuation of Smolensk. On July 12th, 1941, he was asked by the Chief of one of the Polish war prisoner camps to extend to him facilities to evacuate the war prisoners. But the German offensive was so rapid that it was impossible even to evacuate certain factories and some of the workers. "How many wagons were you asked to provide for the prisoners" – I asked. "I was asked for at least 40 wagons" – replied Ivanov . . .'

This quotation shows that the Soviet journalist succeeded in recording a very important detail from the testimony of the witness Ivanov – a detail completely ignored in the report of the Special Commission – namely the *date* on which he was supposed to have been approached by the chief of the War Prisoner Camp with the request for wagons.

The brief German communiqué of August 7th, 1941, states that 'on July 11th we captured Vitebsk'.

On the next day flying columns attacked on a far-flung front East of the Orsha–Smolensk road.

This attack cannot have been very successful and could not have advanced very rapidly, since it was not until July 15th that the German communiqué stated that 'the last fort on the Eastern-most point of the Stalin Line in the Vitebsk region has been captured'. This is also borne out by Soviet communiqués of July 13th, 14th and 15th, which spoke of stubborn fighting 'in the direction of' or 'in the sector of' Vitebsk and the Soviet communiqué of July 16th stated that 'near Vitebsk enemy attempts to penetrate this region have failed completely'.

In the light of the communiqués by both combatants the situation on July 15th, 1941, appeared to have been as follows: stubborn fighting was going on in the region of Vitebsk on Orsha, while pressure of the German forces to the East was – according to the Soviet communiqué of July 16th – being successfully held or, at least, delayed.

If at the same time we bear in mind the fact that according to the Soviet version the three 'special' Polish war prisoner camps were supposed to have been situated at a distance of 15–28 miles West of Smolensk, i.e. 50–62 miles

East of Vitebsk, we cannot but conclude that it would have been possible to evacuate these camps as late as July 15th, 1941.

The German communiqué of July 17th speaks of the capture of Smolensk but the Soviet communiqué of July 23rd states that 'Smolensk continues to be held, German formations which had reached it several days previously, have been ejected'. It may be assumed, therefore, that the German communiqué of July 17th was not quite accurate and that on July 16th only some light German units had reached Smolensk and had possibly entered the outskirts of the city – a fact which supplied the Germans with a foundation for the communiqué about the capture of the city. This hypothesis is confirmed by the historians W. E. D. Allen and P. Muratov, who say that German units were in the region of Smolensk as early as July 17th, but remark that 'it was not the end but only the beginning of the battle of Smolensk'. The battle of Smolensk, during which there were no major moves by either army, continued for two weeks.

As late as July 28th the German communiqué states:

'The battle of Smolensk is nearing a favourable conclusion' but it was not until August 6th that the Germans published a special communiqué announcing the completion of this operation and describing its course.

This short summary of the military operations in the sector of Smolensk suggests without any doubt that, not only on July 12th, but even on the 13th, 14th and probably also on the 15th the 'special' camps might have been evacuated on foot, without any difficulty. These camps could easily have been transferred in one day to the city of Smolensk, some 15½–28 miles distant, after which there would have been two weeks in which to evacuate them further, no matter how slowly, under cover of the armies fighting in the battle of Smolensk. During that fortnight they might have easily marched to some railway station which was still functioning, or even gone on foot to Moscow, which was only about 187 miles away. In any case such a march would have been much shorter and less exhausting than the long marches, lasting many weeks and covering distances of several hundred miles, done by other Polish prisoners-of-war, such as the march from Brody to Ztotonosz.

The question arises, therefore, why the commandant of the Special Camp No. 1 O.N., major of the NKVD Vetoshni-kov, who on an unspecified date left 'together with several staff members' the camp entrusted to his care and made attempts in Smolensk on July 12th to secure wagons, did not return during the period of three, four or more days between July 12th and the capture of Smolensk by the Germans. The assertions of Vetoshnikov that he had unsuccessfully tried to get in touch with Moscow in order to receive from the Central Authorities 'permission to start on foot' are not convincing. In the face of the enemy and in direct danger one would expect a senior officer to show initiative and not to wait passively for orders or 'permission' from his superiors, especially in this case since the railway network in the Smolensk region was particularly well developed.

It is extremely odd that such ill luck should have haunted the three 'special' camps of the Polish officer prisoners-of-war. Situated on the most important sector from an operational point of view, distant only by 200 miles from the chief dispositional centre, Moscow, and by more than 350 miles from the boundary of 'Soviet–German interests' in a region which was captured by the enemy at the earliest on the 24th day of the war – it was still not possible to evacuate them. The senior authorities, of whom very many were stationed in this important sector, forgot all about them, and their immediate superiors proved criminally negligent. Silently, entirely without publicity, all of them apparently fell into German hands and no trace was ever found of them until the discovery of the bodies in the Katyn graves.

This particular misfortune becomes even more amazing when one recalls the fate of other Polish prisoner-of-war camps. The Sknilow Camp near Lwów, 40 miles from the Soviet–German frontier, situated in a region which the Germans captured a few days after the outbreak of the war, was successfully evacuated on foot to Zolotonosha on the Dnieper and thence by rail; it was not forgotten by the superior authorities in spite of the fact that it was some 800 miles distant from Moscow. The Brody Camp, in a region which the Germans reached on July 2nd (and distant by 65 miles from the Soviet–German frontier) also was successfully evacuated to Zolotonosha, although it was situated right off the beaten track, far from any large town or the GHQ of senior authorities.

More such examples could be given, but taking these two alone into consideration the fate of the three 'special' camps near Smolensk becomes so improbable that the question whether these camps really existed spontaneously arises, especially since, up to the time of the publication of the Soviet communiqué of April 15th, 1943, no one was aware of the presence of special Officers' camps in these regions.

The Special Commission evidently realized that such a doubt must of necessity arise in the minds of critical observers, and, therefore, after quoting the statements of the two witnesses, given above, to the effect that it was not possible to evacuate the Polish prisoners-of-war from Smolensk after it was captured by the Germans. The 'proofs' are limited to the statement made by a certain Sashneva who sheltered one of the prisoners for one night, and to the statement of one Danilenkov who 'in August and September 1941 saw groups of Poles of 15–20 men working on the roads'. A fact confirmed by a further twelve witnesses who made 'similar statements'.

It is impossible not to wonder that so very large a group of Polish prisoners-of-war – numbering more than 10,000 officers and men, for the most part, young and healthy – were inefficient and indolent in escaping in such circumstances.

During the Second World War, Poles have achieved a certain measure of renown for their skill in slipping across frontiers, for moving about in enemy-occupied territory, and for escaping from prisons and camps. Those abilities of the Poles in this respect have even been confirmed by Stalin, who in his conversation with General Sikorski on December 3rd, 1941, expressed his supposition that several thousand of the Polish officers searched for in the Northernmost parts of the USSR had probably succeeded, after their release from Soviet camps, in escaping to Manchuria without the knowledge of the local authorities.

Therefore the fact that out of several thousand Polish prisoners-of-war not a single one managed to make his way to Poland, neither during work on road constructions under Soviet or German supervision, nor in the chaos caused by the capture of the camps by the Germans, coupled with the fact that those who escaped did not succeed, in spite of the most favourable conditions, present such an improbable picture, as to be wholly unbelievable. Inevitably the critical inquirer is inclined to doubt whether the three 'special' camps from which no sign of life was given and about the existence of which the world was wholly unaware until the publication of the Soviet communiqué of April 15th, 1943 – had ever really existed at all.

In the Report the signatures of the medico-legal experts were placed at the end of their Conclusions and after them the Report listed the documents found by them on the bodies, which it considered were deserving of 'special attention'.

Of these there were nine in all, found on six bodies which were not identified by the Commission but only numbered.

By a strange coincidence although in all 925 bodies had been exhumed, according to the Report, the body bearing the highest number on which such documents had been found was No. 101. It may of course have been the case that all the important documents from the Commission's point of view had been found in the hundred or so bodies lying in the upper layers of the graves.

These revealing documents were not listed in the Report in any particular order nor were they given as one might have expected, in the order of the numbers of the bodies on which they were found. Those body numbers were not listed in numerical order and, where more than one document had been found on the same body, it was listed as a separate item and not grouped with the other documents from the body, so that the same body number appeared several times in the list. This arrangement naturally makes the analysis of the documents unnecessarily difficult.

The analysis, however, of the contents of the documents as given in the Report is very interesting. They fall into three groups:

1. Letters
2. Receipts
3. An ikon

1. Three letters were said to have been found:

(a) A postcard stamped at Tarnopol on November 12th, 1940, bearing no text or address ('written text and address are discoloured'). Found on body No. 4.

(b) A letter from Warsaw dated September 12th, 1940, addressed to the Central War Prisoners Bureau of the Red Cross, Moscow, and written by the wife of one Tomasz Zigon, inquiring after his whereabouts. This letter bore the stamp of Central Post Office, Moscow, and an anonymous inscription in Russian: 'Ascertain and forward for delivery, November 15th, 1940.' Found on body No. 92.

(c) An unmailed post card addressed to Warsaw by one Stanislaw Kuczinski and dated June 20th, 1941. Found on body No. 53.

2. Five receipts were found made out to two people and given by the Soviet Authorities.

(a) Three were made out to one Araszkevicz. The first dated December 16th, 1939, for a gold watch, had been issued at Starobielsk camp. On the back it bore a note dated March 25th, 1941, stating that the watch had been sold to the Jewellery Trading Trust. It was not said whether this note had been signed.

The second was dated April 6th, 1941, issued at Camp 1 O.N., for an unknown sum of roubles. (In the edition of the Report published in Polish the sum is given as 226 roubles.)

The third was dated May 5th, 1941, issued at Camp 1 O.N. for 102 roubles.

All three documents said to have been found on the same body, No. 46, were numbered on the list given in the Report as 4, 6 and 7.

(b) Two receipts said to have been found on body No. 101 were made out to one Lewandowski. The first dated December 19th, 1939, issued at Kozielsk camp, was for a gold watch and bore a similar inscription on the back about the watch, having been sold to the Jewellery Trading Trust dated March 14th, 1941.

The second issued at Camp 1 O.N. on May 15th, 1941, was made out for 175 roubles. On the list these documents were numbered 3 and 8.

3. The paper 'ikon'.

The paper 'ikon', with the image of Christ was said to have been found on body No. 71. This body was not identified in the Report, although care was taken to point out that the picture was found 'between pages 144 and 145 of a Catholic prayer book'. This 'ikon' was said to have borne the inscription 'Jadwiga' and the date April 4th, 1941. This date found on the paper 'ikon' unrelated to anything except a woman's name and therefore establishing nothing as to the date of death of the owner, hardly seems to have deserved the 'special attention' accorded to it by the Commission.

In considering the list of documents as a whole, the following reflections spring to mind. The Soviet reaction to the Katyn Revelations was much concerned from first to last with the documents found on the bodies in the graves. Very early on they asserted that the documents which the Germans declared had been found in the graves had, in reality, been taken from the archives of the Gestapo and placed on the bodies by the Germans themselves.

The same accusation was brought against the Germans in the report of the Special Commission, namely in the testimony of Moskovskaya when she related how Yegorev had told her that 'the Germans made the prisoners put into the pockets of the Polish officers some papers which they took from cases and suitcases (I don't remember exactly) which they had brought along'.

By giving so much prominence to the whole question of the documents found with the bodies, and stressing their belief that they had been planted by the Germans, the Russians to some extent, laid themselves open to the possibility of similar accusations begin brought against themselves. In this connection it might well be pointed out that the documents found in the spring of 1943 and inspected by the Polish professional team, the 'International Commission' and many journalists and visitors, were mostly personal papers, photographs of which were published throughout the world. Those described by the Russians medico-legal experts were in no case personal documents and all but one (the 'ikon') had either been issued by the Russian authorities themselves or had passed through their hands. They were moreover only made known to the public by the vague description of them found in the Report itself.

CHAPTER ELEVEN

DR. MARKOV'S REVOCATION

DR. M. D. MARKOV, the Bulgarian Reader in Forensic Medicine and Criminology at Sofia University, one of the signatories of the Report of the International Medical Commission called in by the Germans in 1943 (see Chapter Eight) provided the Russians with the only endorsement they achieved for their otherwise untenable, if elaborate, proposition that the Germans were responsible for the crime.

The day after the Russian forces invaded Bulgaria on September 8th, 1944, they swept away the interim democratic non-Communist government of Muraviev and set up a Communist 'Fatherland Front' headed by Kimon Gheorghiyev. On October 2nd, 1944, the Bulgarian Radio announced a proclamation that the Bulgarian Government was committing for trial all those who had evidenced an attitude openly hostile to the USSR. As a signatory of the Commission's report implicating the USSR, Dr. Marov was immediately arrested and imprisoned for over three months before he appeared before a 'People's Tribunal'. On January 26th, 1945, the Bulgarian Radio announced that the Third Section of the Supreme People's Tribunal would start a trial of those accused of having participated in 'the monstrous German imposture of Katyn'.

On February 19th, 1945, the Bulgarian Radio announced: 'The first of the accused, Dr. Markov, has declared: "I am guilty before the Bulgarian People, before their liberator, Russia, and before civilized humanity. My crime is that during the tyrannical government of Ficov* I succumbed to strong pressures to take part in the so-called inquiry at

* President of the Council of Ministers in Bulgaria, 1943.

169

Katyn, and to not having found sufficient strength to resist and to support those more courageous Bulgars – enemies of that political government – who found themselves in prisons and concentration camps".' The communiqué went on to state that Dr. Markov had declared that he had no intention of helping German propaganda; that in his opinion the bodies had not been buried three years previously 'as affirmed by the Germans' but later, and that it was materially impossible for the Russians to have committed the crime. 'In these circumstances,' ended the Bulgarian Radio statement, 'the Prosecutor had dropped his charges against Dr. Markov.'

On February 23rd, 1945, the Bulgarian Radio announced that Dr. Markov, having been judged not guilty, was acquitted.

These 'People's Courts' had sweeping powers, including the imposition of the death penalty and the condemning of guilty parties to terms of forced labour for ten years and more. Despite the fact that there is no evidence to show that Dr. Markov signed the Protocol of the International Medical Commission under any kind of duress and that Professor Naville, an unquestionably impartial witness, stated in Geneva that he carried out a post-mortem in Markov's presence, Dr. Markov recanted. He revoked his earlier statements, and there can be no reason for that other than fear of Soviet reprisals against his own person or family.

After the defeat of Germany the Allied Powers set up the Tribunal at Nuremberg to try alleged German War Criminals, and to investigate the responsibility for German war crimes. The Russians having taken the position they did on the Katyn massacre, it was inescapable that Katyn itself should take its place in the proceedings of the Tribunal. It was the Russian prosecutor, Colonel L. N. Smirnoff, who was responsible for calling Dr. Markov once more.

Markov spoke of the 'psychological pressure' exerted on the members of the International Commission. He claimed that the Commission had not been shown the document in Smolensk, but had been taken out to the 'isolated airfield at Bela' to sign it.

Colonel Smirnoff extracted most of this testimony by giving leading questions – to such an extent that Lord Justice Lawrence had to intervene: 'I don't think it is proper for you to put leading questions to him.'

It will be recalled that in his report of 1946, Professor Naville stated that '... Dr. Markov ... was certainly not under any pressure or constraint while the committee of which he was a member was at work. In any case, he made in our presence, a post-mortem of one corpse and quite freely dictated the report on it, of which I have a copy ...' Markov himself spoke no German, and so when dictating his report, referred to by Professor Naville, he had to use the services of an interpreter. That interpreter, obviously a vital witness, was never asked by the Russian prosecutor to be produced at Nuremberg.

The Russians produced a certain Boris Basilevsky, who was Deputy Mayor of Smolensk during the German occupation. His evidence consisted of a statement that the Katyn wood was not reserved as a special territory and that there had been a camp of the Pioneer Youth Movement in the vicinity before the war. Two other witnesses were called who claimed to have seen Polish prisoners working on the road in the general area in September 1941, after the Germans had occupied the region.

The German officer, Colonel Ahrens, named in the Soviet report as having been in charge of the massacre, volunteered to testify. For a week he stood up to a barrage of Soviet questions. When it was proved beyond doubt he was not present at the alleged time of the massacre, nor was the commander of the unit accused, the Russians claimed that his predecessor, Colonel Bedenk, was responsible. When Bedenk was produced by the German defence, the Russians dropped the case.

Later, Dr. Hans Laternser, counsel for the German General Staff and High Command, asked: 'Who is to be made responsible for the Katyn case?' To which Lawrence retorted: 'I do not propose to answer questions of that sort.' Katyn never appeared in the final verdicts. As for Markov, nothing more has been heard of him.

It may also be pointed out here that the Germans allowed a team from the Polish Red Cross to carry out investigations at Katyn through the medium of a 'Technical Commission' (known as TC-PRC – Technical Commission of the Polish Red Cross). A member of that Polish Commission was Dr. Marian Wodzinski, an expert in forensic medicine, who started work at Katyn on April 29th, 1943, and continued until mid-May of that year. In his report, which contains perhaps the most impressive and entirely credible evidence of the absence of German 'pressure', Dr. Wodzinski states that although constantly under the supervision of the Germans, no restrictions or limitations were set upon the personal freedom of members of his Commission. Members of the Commission wore Red Cross brassards, and had complete freedom to come and go to their quarters outside the forest at any time they chose. Dr. Wodzinski states that the work of the Commission was never impeded or hampered by the Germans, who merely watched what was being done. He even added that Dr. Buhtz, the German member of the International Medical Commission, came into occasional conflict with German propaganda experts when the latter tried (but failed) to interrupt his work which he approached from a purely scientific angle. The assistant to the head of German propaganda at Katyn was a Lt. Sloventzyk, a journalist from Vienna; but neither Lt. Sloventzyk nor Lt. Voss of the *Geheime Feldpolizei* ever interfered with Dr. Wodzinski or his work. The absence in Dr. Wodzinski's report of any mention of coercion by the Germans is directly contrary to the allegations made by Dr. Markov in his recantations of 1945 and 1946.

Dr. Wodzinski recognized among the disinterred corpses two former medical colleagues, Dr. Kalicinski and Professor Pienkowski, of Cracow University. Another member of the TC-PRC, W. Kasur, also identified another body as that of Colonel Dr. Steganowski.

None of this in any way corroborates the statements made by Dr. Markov, although in his recantation, Markov limited himself to answering points put forward by the Soviets, and did not comment on their allegations that the Germans had interfered with the corpses for the purpose of removing from them any document or evidence dated later than May 1940. It is however quite evident from what Dr. Wodzinski said, that such 'interference' with the corpses for the purpose alleged by the Soviets would have been physically impossible.

Dr. Markov, as Professor Naville testified, freely carried out examinations while a member of the International Medical Commission in 1943. At that time of German victory, Markov had no reason to believe that the bodies would again be disinterred by the returning Soviets, neither did he have any reason to think that he would, in Sofia, find himself in the hands of the Communists or be arraigned before a 'People's Court'. We have referred to the extreme penalties which such a court could impose, and there is no other possible reason for Markov's revocation in 1945 than fear of those penalties or fear for his family. At Nuremberg in 1946, Markov, who still lived in the Soviet sphere of influence, had no course open to him but to repeat his earlier revocation.

CHAPTER TWELVE

SUMMING UP

POLAND, unprepared at the request of the Western Allies, was attacked from the West by Nazi Germany on September 1st, 1939. The Germans had been preparing for this moment for years, and were in any case technically much better equipped for a conflict than Poland. It is not therefore surprising that in the first two weeks the Poles fell back, although fighting grimly for every inch of ground as they retreated. The Blitzkrieg was something quite new, and its impact upon Poland was traumatic. However, after the first stunning blow, the Poles recovered sufficiently to slow the German advance, and at Lwów General Langner halted their progress completely. It was at just this moment that Soviet Russia, on September 17th, invaded Poland from the East. Caught between these two mighty armies, Poland collapsed, and on September 28th the Ribbentrop–Molotov Treaty came into effect, dividing Poland almost equally between the two invaders, presumably for ever.

The Russians then started upon a systematic destruction of Poland, a country they had hated for centuries, and which to the Communist mind presented a bourgeois régime, the very opposite to their proclaimed ideals. Short of destroying the entire population, a well-nigh impossible task, the next best method of reducing Poland for good was to remove all those in a position of leadership, military or intellectual.

Of the many hundreds of thousands of Poles deported into Russia, some 15,000 Service, Police and Frontier Guard Officers were skimmed off including a large number of intellectuals, lawyers and similar potentially influential people.

These 15,000 were separated into three groups of between

4,000 and 6,000 each, and taken to three special camps at Kozielsk, Starobielsk and Ostashkov. All three were desecrated monasteries in isolated spots, and from any of them there could be no escape. The Russians had not only broken all their treaties with Poland, but they ignored the humanitarian principles which are accepted by the Geneva Convention and international consent as to the treatment of prisoners-of-war. Conditions in the three camps were appalling, and the inmates lived only just above subsistence level.

The Russians then made an appraisal of the leadership potential of their 15,000 captives, and in October 1939 they started an intensive interrogation in all three camps simultaneously. This grilling went on for six months until March 1940, and during all that time hints that the Poles would soon be released or sent to join the Western Allies were constantly let drop. False rumours were started, and in a short time the Poles were completely confused, although their optimistic natures refused to allow them to give way to despair. Never, however, did they suspect the fate which awaited them. Some 400 were filtered out of the camps as being of possible use to the Russians in other circumstances.

The similarity of what happened in all the camps at the same time shows that this extermination was planned centrally and at the highest level. Clearance of the camps began in March 1940, and after May of that year nothing further was ever heard from the condemned 14,500.

It is not possible to say with certainty what happened to the 4,000 from Starobielsk, nor to the 6,500 at Ostashkov, but the fate of the 4,500 at Kozielsk Camp was later only too plainly revealed.

The inmates of Kozielsk Camp, some 4,350 of them, were taken away daily in batches of up to 300, and shot dead individually in the back of the head in the forest of Katyn near Smolensk, as they lay in the mass graves, previously dug. When the graves were full, they were covered over with earth which was planted with young trees. Unchallenged documents and other items found on the bodies, proving the victims had been transported directly from Kozielsk, included the diary of Lt. Solski which related his batch's transportation to Gniezdovo railway station and into the neighbouring (Katyn) woods to a dacha (beside which the graves were found).

At this time Russia and Germany were allies, and so there was no reason for the Soviets to suppose that any intruder would ever set foot in Katyn forest, much less start digging in its soil. For that reason, and to avoid evidence of the existence of these Polish Officer prisoners-of-war, all possessions (other than valuables) were left on the bodies. To the Soviets, this must have seemed an excellent plan, for not only had they effectively disposed of these men, but nothing remained of them elsewhere to testify to their ever having existed.

Nothing further happened until June 22nd, 1941, when Germany attacked Russia. The Germans were still fresh and ready to fight, and they were further invigorated by their successes in Western Europe. The Wehrmacht launched another of their by then well-tried Blitzkriegs on the Russians, and advanced at an alarming pace, penetrating close to Moscow. Among the millions of square miles overrun was the area of Katyn forest.

Katyn looked like any other forest, and there was no reason to suspect that it contained a secret of any kind. However, occupation troops become idle, they fraternize with the local population, they listen to gossip. In this way the Germans came to hear stories of Polish officers murdered and buried in the Katyn wood, at a place called Kozy Gory. In their methodical way, they felt this should be investigated. They started digging.

On April 13th, 1943, the Germans broadcast their discovery of thousands of bodies of Polish officers, all shot in the back of the head, and many with their hands tied behind their backs, some with bayonet wounds in their flesh.

This shattering announcement came upon the world after three and a half years of war. It was received at first with disbelief and then with scepticism. Dr. Goebbels, that expert propagandist, had said many things over the years, and the minds of the people in many lands felt this discovery at

Katyn might be just another 'stunt' to turn opinion against Germany's largest enemy, Russia. But the Germans frustrated this by inviting the International Committee of the Red Cross to investigate the find, and this request was backed up by the Polish Government in London.

How did the Soviets react to that proposal? First of all they said the Germans had found an historic burial ground, and then they furiously attacked the Poles for collaborating with the Germans and cut off relations with them – up till then their allies. In all this furore they also refused their (necessary) consent to the intervention of the International Red Cross – a fact that was not lost on the waiting world.

Deprived of the impartiality of the Red Cross, the Germans then mustered an impressive team of forensic experts, which they called the International Medical Commission, and which included the well-known Swiss Professor François Naville, a known anti-Nazi. Simultaneously, they invited a Technical Commission of the Polish Red Cross to attend at the work being done at Katyn. It is difficult to see what more the Germans could have done to have the matter investigated as impartially as possible. After examining over 900 of the 4,250 corpses, the International Medical Commission – which also included a Bulgarian, Dr. Markov – unanimously came to the conclusion that the crime was committed not later than April or May 1940 (at a time when the Russians physically controlled the area and were at peace with Germany). They all signed a protocol to that effect. Owing to the fact that the Russians had left all papers and valueless personal possessions on the bodies, some 70 per cent of the victims were positively identified by name, and by rank as the well-fitting uniforms had not been tampered with in any way except when greatcoats were pulled over the victims' heads to prevent them shouting out just prior to death.

But the tide of war was turning, and in the summer Germany reached the peak of her conquest in Russia. By the autumn the Russians were advancing westwards, and the Germans fell back so that once again the Katyn area came under Soviet control. The Russians were only too alive to the general knowledge of the massacre, so widely publicized by the Nazis, and they took immediate steps to nullify, or at least to smudge, the evidence, and, as it were, smother those Polish prisoners again and for the last time. Like the Germans, they set about forming an 'investigatory' commission but there the likeness ended. First, the Russian team was composed entirely of men from within the Communist world. Secondly, this commission performed no first-hand investigation of its own but judgements were pronounced on 'evidence' produced for it by an unnamed group working at the site.

Once again the bodies were dug up, dragged out for propaganda purposes, and probed by surgeons. They could have looked little different from when the Germans re-buried them in May of that same year. However, the Russians produced newspapers and other documents – none of them handwritten – dating from 1941, which they said they had found on the bodies. Kisselev, the old peasant who lived in the forest and who had given evidence to the Germans, was again found, but had suddenly become deaf. The Russian team gave it as their opinion that the murdered men were indeed Polish officers, but that they had been massacred by the Germans in the late summer and autumn of 1941. When asked by the daughter of Averill Harriman, who was among Allied journalists in Moscow invited to look at the bodies, why they were clad in greatcoats and winter underclothing, the Russians gave the absurd response that the climate varied greatly in the area from year to year, and that it must have been a cold summer.

Russia was an ally of the Western Powers, jointly fighting to overcome the Third Reich. It was not in the interest of the allies to query or even overtly consider the Russian story. If it was difficult to accept the fabrication, they could at least ignore it. This they did.

And so the war came to an end, and the Allies set up an apparatus of 'justice' at Nuremberg to try and punish the major German war criminals. Having taken the stand they did, the Russians had no alternative but to list Katyn as a Nazi war crime. Unwisely, they pinned the Katyn massacre on to the person of Herman Goering, and thus it appeared in the indictment. Meanwhile Dr. Markov, the Bulgarian member of the International Medical Commission had been tried in Sofia for his life for anti-Soviet activities and had revoked his statement that the murder must have been committed not later than 1940 (i.e. that it was committed by the Soviets). Dr. Markov repeated his revocation at Nuremberg, and there were other apparent witnesses produced. But after a few hearings the Soviet prosecution itself dropped the indictment.

After the war Russia greatly increased its strength, its territorial possessions and its potential danger to the other powers in Europe. It would have seemed, and still does appear, imprudent to irritate or provoke so powerful a country, and further mention of Katyn would have done just that. So a conspiracy of silence descended on the matter, and various efforts, presented as appendices to this book, have failed to produce a clear and positive international proclamation of the truth.

President Roosevelt, shortly before his death in 1945, played an important and curious part in suppressing the truth. Three reports were made available to him demonstrating Soviet guilt. George H. Earle, a former U.S. Minister to Bulgaria and to Austria, who also held a Naval rank, went to see Roosevelt personally about information he (Earle) had received. 'George,' said Roosevelt, 'this is entirely German propaganda and a German plot. I am absolutely convinced the Russians did not do this.' A few days later, on March 24th, 1945 (less than three weeks before his death), Roosevelt wrote to Earle, 'I have noted with concern your plan to publish your unfavourable opinion of one of our allies ... I not only do not wish it, but I specifically forbid you to publish any information or opinion about an ally that you might have acquired while in office or in the service of the U.S. Navy.' Earle was promptly transferred to Samoa.

One of the few Allied prisoners-of-war taken to Katyn by the Germans was an American, Lt.-Col. John H. Van Vliet. With Captain Donald B. Stewart, he witnessed the exhumations, and – on release – at once wrote a full report to his superior, General Birrell. The General ordered Van Vliet 'to remain silent on this matter'; and the official copy of the report disappeared.

But who would make the best witness in an international trial on this matter? Joseph Stalin, I suggest, who is dead. His daughter, however, Svetlana Alleluyeva, published a book entitled *Only One Year*,* in which we read the following on page 367:

'I think that my father also found something personal in his favourite opera, *Boris Godunov*, which in his last years he often went to see, usually sitting alone in his box. But once he took me with him, and I felt shivers down my spine during Boris's monologue and the recitative plaint of the Fool in Christ's Name. To glance over my shoulder at my father would have been too frightening – maybe he, too, at that moment had "bloodstained little boys before his eyes"? Why of all operas did he constantly choose this one, when in general his tastes tended towards what was gay, the folk story of *Sadko* or *Snegurochka* (*the Snow Maiden*)? We also went to see *Ivan Susanin*, but only for the sake of the scene in the forest, after which my father would go home.

'This forest scene is very dramatic. Ivan Susanin, an old Russian peasant, leads the Polish Army into a dense winter forest near Smolensk, into its very heart, from which there is no way out. He is killed, but the Polish Army also remains there forever, frozen to death. After this scene my father used to leave, never remaining for the next act with its lovely ballet – a mazurka and a polonaise. What did he find in this destruction of Poles in a forest? Perhaps it reminded him of the ten thousand Polish officers, prisoners-of-war, secretly shot by the Soviets in the Katyn woods near Smolensk in 1940.'

* By courtesy of Harper and Row, Inc., New York

CHAPTER THIRTEEN

POSTSCRIPT

MUCH has happened since April 1971 when this book was originally published, timed to coincide with a 'documentary' film on BBC 2 entitled *The Issue should be avoided* (themselves words used by the late Winston Churchill when speaking of Katyn). Professor Zawodny had, in January 1971, already re-published a book he wrote in 1962 entitled *Death in the Forest* and this aroused public interest which was greatly increased by both my own book and the BBC film. Within a few days, also in April 1971, Mr. Airey Neave, MP, tabled a motion in the House of Commons calling for a further investigation of the massacre which, if shown to be conclusive, should be followed by a condemnation of the culprits. No time was found for a debate on this question so that on June 17th, 1971, Lord Barnby initiated a debate in the House of Lords in the hope that the British Government would make some statement. He was joined by twelve other peers of all parties and the event was unique in that it was the first time that Katyn had ever been discussed in the Upper House. The debate lasted over two hours, and despite an attempt to 'white-wash' the actions of the Foreign Office, the strength of opinion was clear for all to see. However, once again, the Government of the day did not have the stomach to tackle the point and no further action could be foreseen. Nevertheless echoes of the debate reached far and wide and made a special impact in America where some six million people of Polish descent now live.

All this was greatly stimulating to the Poles in England and they were encouraged to write to the BBC requesting a further showing of the documentary film. This effort was successful and the film was shown again in October 1971 and reached an audience of over five million people. It is interesting to note that the Soviet Government brought considerable pressure to bear in an attempt to stop the film, but when its representatives were politely informed that in a free society it was not possible to curtail such activities, an invitation to the Head of the BBC to visit Poland was abruptly cancelled.

After the hail of letters which greeted Soviet attempts to blame Katyn on the Germans in the British press, the Russians wisely remained silent. But by October it must all have been too much for them, and in October also they published an article in the officially-sponsored magazine *Soviet Weekly*. They had nothing new to say. They simply contented themselves by repeating their threadbare story of German guilt and trotted out the fact that in 1952 the Polish Government had also affixed the blame on to the Germans. This, if nothing else, proved the extent to which they had oppressed the countries so shamefully handed to them at Yalta.

As has been said, the events of 1971 reverberated throughout the world, and articles about Katyn appeared in newspapers as widely dispersed as Brazil, Germany, New Zealand, South Africa, Australia, Switzerland and America. It was from South Africa, again in October 1971, that an inspired suggestion arrived in the author's hands. A Polish exile, who wished to remain anonymous, sent a donation of some £30 to help relatives of the massacre victims who might be in distress, and almost as an afterthought he added the idea that a monument or memorial be erected in honour of those victims in '... some free country of the West, until it might be possible to build such a memorial in a freed Poland ...'. This suggestion came at a most interesting time, and at one when it seemed nothing much further could be done about Katyn. The idea was immediately put to the leading personalities amongst the exiled Polish community in England and after some thought, it was welcomed with enthusiasm. As a natural consequence, those who had helped so much during the year were asked to take part, and thus it was that by November the Katyn Memorial Fund had come into being, the author being honoured by the post of Honorary Secretary to the Fund's committee. The Fund, chaired by Lord Barnby, set itself three tasks: to design a suitable memorial; to find a site in London where it could be erected and finally to attract sufficient money with which to complete the project. It was a challenge of considerable magnitude for it had been at once decided that this monument would bear within an inscription the fateful date '1940', which is tantamount to a direct accusation of the Soviet Union. In all, 1971 had been a year of surprising and enormous achievement about Katyn, a subject, it will be recalled, which had been forcibly stifled for nearly twenty years.

1972 was heralded by another surprise: the Foreign Office Public Records Office decided, quite arbitrarily, to release a bunch of hitherto secret documents which would not normally have seen the light of day until thirty years after their inception. Amongst these were two vital reports written in 1943 and 1944 by the then Mr. Owen O'Malley, wartime British Ambassador to the Polish Government. They were written immediately subsequent to the publication of the German findings and reports in Katyn forest of 1943 and the report of the so-called Russian 'Commission of Investigation' of 1944.

In both reports Mr. O'Malley chased away any doubts that it could have been any country other than Soviet Russia who was responsible for the Katyn massacre. His reports caused consternation in the British Foreign Office, and only a very limited circulation was given to them before they were buried in the archives, and thus hidden from official and public sight. But they were there, and were known to the Foreign Office when it strenuously denied knowledge of the case during the Lords debate of June 1971.

By early 1972 another 'Katyn Committee' had been created in America as a Commission of the powerful Polish American Congress, and that Commission immediately reprinted both reports in Polish and circulated them over a wide area. Similarly in England, the reports received a

183

special publication and became known to many for the first time. I was able to incorporate both in a further small book I wrote about the 1971 events and entitled: *The Katyn Cover-up*. Early in 1972 the Katyn Memorial Fund set about its determined tasks, and a search for a site proved interesting but at first abortive. Eventually, with the help of Sir Malby Crofton, Leader of the Kensington and Chelsea Council, a place for the memorial was found in St. Luke's Gardens, Chelsea. The gardens were central and quiet and seemed to the Fund to be entirely suitable. Next a competition amongst Polish artists was started to find a design for the monument, and this too brought many distinguished suggestions. But there is a difference between the British and the Polish (Slavonic) concept of such a subject, and although many of the Polish ideas had great merit, they were not such as would recommend themselves to British people and certainly not to a Local Authority Planning Committee.

Eventually it was decided that a simple obelisk could not be objectionable to anyone and a design was submitted which received the necessary planning permission, being a needle in black granite some twenty feet high rising from white stone steps, the lowest of which would be some 20 feet square at the base. The third task, that of raising money was also tackled, and with so much success that by the autumn of 1972 a sum exceeding £10,000 had been raised, with a similar action being taken in America by the Katyn Memorial Fund Commission based on Chicago.

At this point, and feeling that all obstacles had been overcome, I felt free to accept an offer by the United Nations and proceed to the Sudan in charge of an emergency refugee relief programme. It was a different life indeed from London, and apart possibly from the tomb of the Mahdi at Omdurman, there was little to remind me of the Katyn Memorial except through letters from England. These were optimistic at first, but gradually I detected a growing unease caused, it seemed, by some unexpected opposition from the Church authorities. But these appeared purely technical, as who would suppose for a moment that any church would oppose a concept as humanitarian as that of seeking to honour the dead? – dead, in this case from a country for which we allegedly went to war in 1939; dead indeed from a people who gave of their very lives for *our* freedom. No; it could not be that the Church could do anything but welcome such a project in the spirit of Christian Charity about which it so often preaches. Thus both the Fund and I were most disagreeably surprised when we found it to be quite otherwise.

The gardens of St. Luke's had formerly been a graveyard, although that use had ceased over a hundred years before when the land was obtained by the Local Authority and laid out as an open space for the enjoyment of residents and passers-by. Now the Disused Burial Grounds Act of 1884 requires that before anything is put into or taken out of such a disused graveyard a 'faculty' must be obtained. It was upon this technicality that the Church fastened in its subvert attempt to thwart the whole plan. At first the Diocesan Advisory Committee objected to the Memorial on purely aesthetic grounds, and delays were manufactured by which it was probably hoped that the Katyn Memorial Fund would tire and go elsewhere. But the site was the offer of the Royal Borough, and at first this sinister purpose was not fully perceived nor understood. Query was answered with explanation throughout 1973, in the latter part of which I again became Honorary Secretary of the Fund on my return from Africa. But as the year dragged on it became increasingly obvious that the Church's purpose was entirely suspect and indeed that its opposition was hardening. Far from causing the Fund dismay, it served only to increase determination until no other course was open but to fight the case in the Diocesan Consistory Court.

Counsel were briefed, conferences took place, typewriters clicked, letters were written and both sides prepared for the legal tussle to come. The 'battle' opened in St. Paul's Church, Covent Garden, where the consistory court chose to sit, in the summer of 1974. After only half one day's hearing it became obvious that irrespective of legal arguments, there was something else, something hidden, which was causing the Church to behave in this extraordinary and grossly uncharitable manner. But that mystery was soon resolved: I was approached with a message from the 'Other side' to the effect that the date '1940' be removed out of the proposed inscription and that it be replaced with a 'looser expression' such as '. . . in the early years of the war . . .'

So this was it – a deliberate attempt to run from the truth and smudge the facts in a manner which could include both 1940 and 1941 (the year when the Soviets alleged the Katyn crime was committed by the Germans). Realization came as a shock, for the implications of what the Church was about were considerable and most disturbing. In effect, that authority was hell-bent on avoiding an accusation in stone against the perpetrators of this foul mass-murder, and thus it could only be siding with them by protecting their name.

This became more evident as time went by, and it was meant to go by slowly, very slowly. The Church caused one delay after another until the year ended and the judgement was awaited. In January 1975 everyone concerned assembled in St. Luke's Church to hear that judgement. The obelisk was duly pronounced to be a 'building' within the meaning of the Act, and the Royal Borough was duly said to be in breach of its trust by giving planning permission for it to be placed in the gardens. This much might have been expected; indeed it had been plain from the outset, together with much else concerning the scale of the monument and even the trumped up 'feelings of local residents'. But the Worshipful Chancellor went further, far further than he should: he said that the Memorial was 'intended to be political and to be politically controversial'. He added that it would 'help to perpetuate bitter feelings in the years ahead' and he said that he 'made no finding of the truth or otherwise of the date "1940",' and he wound up with this astonishing statement:

'For the present purpose the critical point is that the Petitioners say "1940" is essential: that is, the monument is intended to make and to perpetuate in stone a specific accusation. In my judgement it is no part of the duty of the Courts of the Church of England to allow land under its jurisdiction to be used to advertise accusations of crime. I do not recall ever having been asked to sanction an inscription naming the murderer on a tombstone of a murdered person, and I should be most unwilling to allow any such thing in an ordinary churchyard.'

It will be recalled that the Chancellor expressly set to one side the question of the inscription and yet, in his judgement, he pronounced upon it without ever having called the evidence to be adduced on this point. But one thing did stand out clear and plain: it was, after all, the date on the memorial which lay at the root of all the Church's objections, while all the other legal arguments were mere camouflage. In a dictum of 1949, Pope Pius XII said: '... it is inconsistent to seek to sit at the table of God and that of His enemies ...' No worse example of that seeking could be found than the behaviour of the London Diocese in this matter.

There was, of course, an option to appeal against this vicious judgement, but it was by then quite obvious that the law itself was being twisted to an unholy purpose and it seemed that to appeal would be only to fall further into the hands of an unscrupulous enemy and to fritter away the falling resources of the Fund in time and money. That a decision not to appeal was right was amply proved in a small incident which took place when the idea of appealing was still being pursued. The Borough was given the impression that it had plenty of time in which to prepare an appeal, but suddenly this 'gentlemen's agreement' was broken and it was said to be 'out of time'. Even to rectify that took further weeks, and in the doing quite convinced the Fund that it was literally wasting its time. Further, the wilful murder of so many thousands is not a subject to be brought down to a petty lawyer's wrangle, nor was a consistory court the right place in which to argue the guilt for so massive a crime – the proper place for that was at the highest international tribunal. Thus the Fund withdrew noting that ironically the Church had caused its friends more harm than good, for the protracted proceedings had brought much publicity, itself as unwelcome to the Soviets as the monument itself. Further, the delays had also produced interest at the bank on the sum originally donated, and these almost exactly paid the cost of this legal struggle. At the end of the day the Fund had lost nothing, but proved much.

The Royal Borough had never faltered in its loyalty, and it offered an alternative site at Gunnersbury Cemetery; an unconsecrated graveyard it owns in the Borough of Hounslow and in which many Poles and other exiles are buried (including General Bor-Komorowski, hero of the Warsaw Uprising of 1944). Here was a place free from meddling by the Church, beautifully tended and suitable in every way. The Fund accepted this site and was glad to wash its hands of St. Luke's and the shabbiness of the whole episode. But if to this day St. Luke's Gardens seem empty it is as a reflection only of the empty morals and hearts of those too small in stature to grasp an opportunity to extend the hand of friendship to ageing and exiled people already bereft of so much else.

The Fund lost no time in furthering its purpose and immediately the work was put out to tender. Early in 1976 a suitable price was selected and in reporting it, the Fund's expert consultant also stated that he had saved £6,000 on the foundations, the land below the new site being much more suitable than that of St. Luke's Gardens. More suitable, it would appear, in several ways. But news of the acceptance of the site at Gunnersbury triggered off the KGB and, probably acting on instructions, the Communist Polish Embassy approached the Borough, saying that the Memorial was not wanted!

In a letter dated January 20th, 1976, Mr. A. Starewicz, the Polish ambassador, wrote very politely about Poland's sacrifices during the war, but half-way through his letter shifted his sentiments in favour of the Soviet Union declaring that to single out the Katyn victims was inappropriate. He went on to quote Dr. Goebbels' diary out of context on the subject of 'the German bullets' and referred to a totally false argument put forward by the late D. N. Pritt, QC, in a letter to the *Daily Telegraph* of April 15th, 1971. Seeking to reinforce his arguments (and how much pain must it have caused him?) he referred to the judgement given in the London Diocesan Consistory Court, urging the

Royal Borough to take note of it. He ended his letter by invoking the dangers which might accrue in 'upsetting friendly relations among nations'. Reading Mr. Starewicz's letter can bring to the reader only sadness and pity for a diplomat forced by a brutal master to write something completely false and against his own country. That Great Britain had a hand in the Yalta Agreement must also, in this moment, cause a second of silence. No doubt the Communist Poles reported back to the Soviet embassy that the effort had been fruitless, and the Soviets themselves felt the time had come to apply their own heavy methods.

On February 10th, Mr. V. Semenov, Minister-Counsellor at the embassy of the USSR, penned another letter to the Mayor of Kensington and Chelsea following a call, on January 23rd, made by a personal representative. This was a very different communication, couched not in the polite language used by the Poles, but in stark terms such as Russians so often use. He said:

'... you are well aware of the provocative purposes pursued by the organizers of the "memorial project" who attempt to revive a vicious lie of the Goebbels propaganda concocted to cover-up the crimes committed by Nazis. The inscription on the "memorial" which the Council, as you say, have approved, is wholly slanderous because it tends, following in the footsteps of the Goebbels lie against Britain's ally in the second world war, to put on the Soviet Union the blame for the victims of Katyn. Having full knowledge of these facts, the Council thus assumes entire responsibility for this provocation which is bound to raise indignation in the people of our country ... We would like to expect that since the "project" has not yet been realized the Council will find a way to prevent it.'

This was not a suggestion; it amounted almost to an instruction and is breath-taking in its effrontery. In effect it meant that a foreign power was making a direct attempt to alter the decision of a British Local Authority, thereby flouting not only normal diplomatic usage but also infringing that hospitality which allows embassies to exist on British soil.

Events followed swiftly. On March 17th, Lord Hankey sought to dismiss the circumstances contained in Lord Bethell's book: *The Last Secret* in which the whole shameful story was told of how we gave up to the USSR those Cossacks and Caucasians who had sought refuge in the German Army as their only escape from Stalin's death-like grip. We also handed over their families and even German officers (General von Pannwitz) to certain death at the hands of the NKVD. The debate in the Upper House was notable for the white-washing that took place, challenged only by Lord St. Oswald who included in his full-blooded speech the subject of Katyn. Referring to the memorial he said:

'... Now, my Lords, at this stage, the Soviet Embassy is having the effrontery to write bullying, almost threatening letters to the officers of the Royal Borough. Here is interference by a foreign Power in the affairs of local government of this country, of this capital. With the British Foreign Office and the Soviet Foreign Ministry against us, it will be something of a triumph over odds when the memorial is erected in Gunnersbury Park in September.'

One would have thought that other peers present would immediately have taken up this point; they did not, many of them being content to brush aside the matter as they had in 1971.

However, in the Commons, Sir Frederic Bennett, MP, took the opportunity to table a motion in these terms:

'That this House deplores as totally unacceptable the attempted Soviet intervention in a matter solely and wholly within the purview of responsibility of appropriate authorities within the United Kingdom, namely the erection of a Monument dedicated to the memory of 14,471 Polish officers and men massacred at Katyn in 1940, and is confident the Royal Borough of Kensington and Chelsea will resist pressures from any source to vary their free and democratic decision to permit the erection of such a memorial.'

It is indeed interesting to note that in March 1976 Great Britain was having its attention drawn to Alexander Solzhenitsyn and his timely warnings against the dangers of 'detente'. In his *magnum opus*, 'Gulag Archipelago' Solzhenitsyn mentions Katyn in Volume 1 on page 77 and in Volume 2 in the notes at the foot of page 39 – both showing that the USSR was responsible for the massacre. Solzhenitsyn is, to my mind, the 'biggest' man in the world today; a man of immense courage; of prophetic vision; of infinite perception and a being who has survived the hell of Siberia and is now desperately trying to tell us what is what. Needless to say he has been denigrated by those too shallow to comprehend his stature and by those who so expertly imitate the ostrich.

Sir Frederic's motion gathered signatures over the turn of the month, and by the end of March 1976 had attracted no less than 68 supporters – of whom only one was a Labour Member (Sir Geoffrey de Freitas). The question naturally arises: was there some subvert 'instruction' to the Left to shun this motion? It is a point worthy of consideration. Not content with his motion, Sir Frederic Bennett asked a number of Parliamentary questions, seeking details of what action the Foreign and Commonwealth Office had or was taking to tell the Soviets that they are not to interfere with local government business in this country, and whether the matter of the Katyn memorial was discussed with Mr. Gromyko during his visit to Britain at the end of March. The replies were far from satisfactory and echoed what Lord Bethell said in his book *The Last Secret*: '. . . the discussions which followed the discovery of the Katyn forest massacre in April 1943 had shown that in any such dispute the Western Allies could be relied upon to take the Soviet side . . .'

One event stands out as a milestone in this saga, and that was the signing on March 29th of the contract for the physical building of the memorial. This took place at 9.30 a.m. in London, and Lord St. Oswald joined me in completing a document which spelled a legal obligation upon the builders to erect the monument in return for a fixed price of £21,515.75. It was an almost supreme moment when, for the first time on paper, the Katyn memorial appeared not as a dream but as a factual engineering project protected on all sides by the legal implications of the contract. Preparations for the ceremonial unveiling of the monument were proceeding and were given great impetus by the acceptance of Bishop Rubin, Delegate of the Cardinal Primate of Poland at the Vatican, to lead the prayers for the dead on September 18th – the date decided for the birth of the obelisk.

Thus, again, in the spring of 1976, Katyn appeared as a case by no means dead but very much alive; as a matter standing like a wall between those with integrity and those without it.

Above all, Truth had emerged victorious in a struggle against deceit, hypocrisy and, perhaps worst, cowardice. The murdered Poles will regain their place in history and, in that the Katyn Memorial stands proud on British soil, perhaps some part of the debt we owe to that unhappy nation is repaid.

A DARKENED VISION –
SIR OWEN O'MALLEY REPORTS OF
1943 AND 1944

THE full extent of the information on the Katyn murder available to the 1943 Government has never been generally known. During the debate in the House of Lords, Lord Shinwell suggested that 'the Foreign Office at that time must undoubtedly have been aware of what happened'. The Earl of Dundee, with the support of several Lords claimed that 'nobody in Parliament had the slightest doubt that the Russian version of the affair was a totally false fabrication', and the Earl of Arran followed by asserting that 'it is and always has been common knowledge in the FO that Katyn was the act of the Russians and not the Germans'.

On January 1st, 1972, however, some six months after the debate, the full details of this knowledge were for the first time made public by the general release of two reports sent to the Foreign Office by the late Sir Owen O'Malley, then Ambassador to Poland. The first report deals with the German revelations, the second with the Russian investigations. Both these important and brilliant reports are given here in full.

The minutes attached to the first report are also reproduced, giving as they do, such a clear indication of the initial attitudes of the Foreign Office – attitudes which persist to this day.

Sir – My dispatch No. 43 of April 30th, dwelt on the probability that no confederation in Eastern Europe could play an effective part in European politics unless it were affiliated to the Soviet Government, and suggested that so long as the policy of this Government was as enigmatic as it now is, it would be inconsistent with British interests that Russia should enjoy a sphere of influence extending from Danzig to the Aegean and Adriatic Seas. The suppression of the Comintern on May 20th may be considered to have brought to an end what was in the past the most objectionable phase of Soviet foreign policy and to entitle the Soviet Government to be regarded less distrustfully than formerly. It is not, then, without hesitation that I address this further dispatch to you which also gives grounds for misgivings about the character and policy of the present rulers in Russia.

2. We do not know for certain who murdered a lot of Polish officers in the forest of Katyn in April and May 1940, but this at least is already clear that it was the scene of terrible events which will live long in the memory of the Polish nation. Accordingly I shall try to describe how this affair looks to my Polish friends and acquaintances of whom many had brothers and sons and lovers among those known to have been taken off just three years ago from the prison camps at Kozielsk, Starobielsk and Ostashkov to an uncertain destination; how it looks, for instance, to General Sikorski who there lost Captain Fuhrman, his former ADC and close personal friend; to Monsieur Morawski who lost a brother-in-law called Zoltowski and a nephew; or to Monsieur Zaleski who lost a brother and two cousins.

3. The number of Polish prisoners taken by the Russian armies when they invaded Poland in September 1939 was about 180,000, including police and gendarmerie and a certain number of civilian officials. The total number of army officers was round about 15,000. At the beginning of 1940 there were in the three camps named above round about nine or ten thousand officers and six thousand other ranks, policemen and civil officials. Less public reference has been made to these 6,000 than to the 10,000 officers, not because the Polish Government are less indignant about the disappearance of other ranks than about the disappearance of officers or were less insistent in inquiries for them, but because the need of officers to command the Polish troops re-

cruited in Russia was more urgent than the need to increase the total ration strength of the Polish Army. There is no reason to suppose that these 6,000 other ranks and the police and the civilians were treated by the Soviet Government differently to the officers, and mystery covers the fate of all. For the sake of simplicity, however, I shall write in this dispatch only of the missing officers without specific reference to other ranks, to police prisoners or to civilians. Of the 10,000 officers only some 3 or 4,000 were regular officers. The remainder were reserve officers who in peace time earned their living, many with distinction, in the professions, in business and so on.

4. In March 1940 word went round the camps at Kozielsk, Starobielsk and Ostashkov that under orders from Moscow the prisoners were to be moved to camps where conditions would be more agreeable, and that they might look forward to eventual release. All were cheered by the prospect of change from the rigours which prisoners must endure to the hazards and vicissitudes of relative freedom in Soviet or German territory. Even their captors seemed to wish the prisoners well who were now daily entrained in parties of 50 to 350 for the place at which, so they hoped, the formalities of their discharge would be completed. As each prisoner was listed for transfer, all the usual particulars about him were re-checked and re-registered. Fresh finger-prints were taken. The prisoners were inoculated afresh and certificates of inoculation furnished to them. Sometimes the prisoners Polish documents were taken away, but in many such cases these were returned before departure. All were furnished with rations for the journey and, as a mark of special regard, the sandwiches furnished to senior officers were wrapped in clean white paper – a commodity seldom seen anywhere in Russia. Anticipations of a better future were clouded only by the fact that 400 or 500 Poles had been listed for further detention first at Pavlishchev-Bor and eventually at Griazovietz. These were, as it turned out later, to be the only known survivors of the lost legion, and some of them are in England now; but at the time, although no principle could be discovered on which they had been selected, they supposed that

they had been condemned to a further period of captivity; and some even feared that they had been chosen out for execution.

5. Our information about these events is derived for the most part from those routed to Griazovietz, all of whom were released in 1941, and some of whom – notably M. Komarnicki, the Polish Minister for Justice – are now in England.

6. Entrainment of the 10,000 officers from the three camps went on all through April and the first half of May, and the lorries, lined with cheerful faces, which took them from camp to station, were in fact the last that was ever seen of them alive by any witness to whom we have access. Until the revelations made by the German broadcast of April 12th, 1943, and apart from a few words let drop at the time by the prison guards, only the testimony of scribblings on the railway wagons in which they were transported affords any indication of their destination. The same wagons seem to have done a shuttle service between Kozielsk and the detraining station; and on these some of the first parties to be transported had scratched the words 'Don't believe that we are going home', and the news that their destination had turned out to be a small station near Smolensk. These messages were noticed when the vans returned to Smolensk station and have been reported to us prisoners at Kozielsk who were later sent to Griazovietz.

7. But though of positive indications as to what subsequently happened to the 10,000 officers there was none until the grave at Katyn was opened, there is now available a good deal of negative evidence, the cumulative effect of which is to throw serious doubt on Russian disclaimers of responsibility for the massacre.

8. In the first place, there is the evidence to be derived from the prisoners' correspondence in respect to which information has been furnished by officers families in Poland, by officers now with the Polish Army in the Middle East, and by the Polish Red Cross Society. Up till the end of March 1940 large numbers of letters had been dispatched, which were later received by their relatives, from the officers confined at

Kozielsk, Starobielsk and Ostashkov; whereas no letters from any of them (excepting from the 400 moved to Griazovietz) have been received by anybody which had been dispatched subsequent to that date. The Germans overran Smolensk in July 1941, and there is no easy answer to the question why, if any of the 10,000 had been alive between the end of May 1940 and July 1941, none of them ever succeeded in getting any word through to their families.

9. In the second place there is the evidence of the correspondence between the Soviet Government and the Polish Government. The first request for information about the 10,000 was made by M. Kot of M. Vyshinsky on October 6th, 1941. On December 3rd, 1941, General Sikorski backed up his inquiry with a list of 3,845 names of officers included among them. General Anders furnished the Soviet Government with a further list of 800 names on March 18th, 1942. Inquiries about the fate of the 10,000 were made again and again to the Russian Government verbally and in writing by General Sikorski, M. Kot, M. Romer, Count Racynski and General Anders between October 1941 and April 1943. The Polish Red Cross between August and October 1940 sent no less than 500 questionnaires about individual officers to the Russian Government. To none of all these inquiries extending over a period of 2½ years was a single positive answer of any kind ever returned. The inquirers were told either that the officers had been released, or that 'perhaps they are already in Germany', or that 'no information' of their whereabouts was available, or (M. Molotov to M. Kot, October 1941) that complete lists of the prisoners were available and that they would all be delivered to the Polish authorities 'dead or alive'. But it is incredible that if any of the 10,000 were released, not one of them has ever appeared again anywhere, and it is almost equally incredible, if they were not released, that not one of them should have escaped subsequent to May 1940 and reported himself to the Polish authorities in Russia or Persia. That the Russian authorities should have said of any Polish officer in Soviet jurisdiction that they had 'no information' also provokes incredulity; for it is notorious that the NKVD collect and record the

movements of individuals with the most meticulous care.

10. In the third place there is the evidence of those who have visited the grave: first, a Polish commission including among others doctors, journalists and members of the Polish Assistance Committee, a former president of the Polish Academy of Literature and a representative of the Mayor of Warsaw; secondly, another Polish commission which included priests, doctors and representatives of the Polish Red Cross Society; thirdly, an international commission of criminologists and pathologists of which the personnel is given in Annex II. The Report of this Commission forms Annex III to this dispatch, and the reports of the two Polish Commissions add little to it. It is deposed by all that several hundred identifications have been established. All this evidence would normally be highly suspect since the inspections took place under German auspices and the results reached us through German broadcasts. There are fair grounds for presuming that the German broadcasts accurately represented the findings of the Commissions, that the Commissions' findings were at any rate in some respects well founded, that the grounds were sound on which at any rate some of the identifications were made.

11. In the fourth place there is the fact that a mass execution of officer prisoners would be inconsistent with what we know of the German Army. The German Army has committed innumerable brutalities, but the murder by them of prisoners-of-war, even of Poles, is rare. Had the German authorities ever had these 10,000 Polish officers in their hands we can be sure that they would have placed some or all of them in the camps in Germany already allotted to Polish prisoners, while the 6,000 other ranks, policemen and civil officials would have been put to forced labour. In such case the Polish authorities would in the course of two years certainly have got into touch with some of the prisoners; but in fact none of the men from Kozielsk, Starobielsk or Ostashkov have ever been heard of from Germany.

12. Finally there is the evidence to be derived from the confusion which characterizes explanations elicited from or

volunteered by the Soviet Government. Between August 1941 and April 12th, 1943, when the Germans announced the discovery of the grave at Katyn the Russian Government had, among other excuses, maintained that all Polish officers taken prisoner in 1939 had been released. On the other hand, in conversation with the Polish Ambassador a Russian official who had drunk more than was good for him, once referred to the disposal of these officers as 'a tragic error'. On April 16th, immediately after the German announcement, the Soviet Information Bureau in Moscow suggested the Germans were misrepresenting as victims of Russian barbarity skeletons dug up by archaeologists at Gniezdovo which lies next door to Katyn. On April 26th, M. Molotov in a note to the Polish Ambassador in Moscow said that the bodies at Katyn were those of Poles who had at one time been prisoners of the Russians but had subsequently been captured by the Germans in their advance at Smolensk in July 1941 and had been murdered then by them. On a later occasion, and when the German broadcasts gave reason to think that some bodies were sufficiently well preserved to be identifiable, the Russian Government put forward a statement that the Polish officers had been captured by the Germans in July 1941, had been employed upon construction work, and had only been murdered shortly before the German 'discovery' was announced. This confusion cannot easily be understood except on the assumption that the Russian Government had something to hide.

13. The cumulative effect of this evidence is, as I said earlier, to throw serious doubt on Russian disclaimers of responsibility for a massacre. Such doubts are not diminished by rumours which have been current during the last two and a half years that some of the inmates of Kozielsk, Starobielsk and Ostashkov had been transported towards Kolyma, Franz Joseph Land or Novaya Zemlia, some or all of these being killed en route. It may be that this was so, and it may be that some less number than ten thousand odd were destroyed and buried at Katyn; but whether the massacre occurred (if it did occur) in one place or two places or three places naturally makes no difference to Polish sen-

timents. These will accordingly be described without reference to the uncertainty which exists as to the exact number of victims buried near Smolensk.

14. With all that precedes in mind it is comprehensible that the relatives and fellow-officers of the men who disappeared should have concluded that these had in fact been murdered by their Russian captors and should picture their last hours – somewhat as follows – with bitter distress. This picture is a composite one to which knowledge of the district, the German broadcasts, experience of Russian methods and the reports of visitors to the grave have all contributed, but it is not so much an evidentially established description of events as a reconstruction in the light of the evidence – sometimes partial and obviously defective – of what may have happened. But it – or something like it – is what most Poles believe to have happened, and what I myself, in the light of all the evidence such as it is, incline to think happened. Many months or years may elapse before the truth is known, but because in the meantime curiosity is unsatisfied and judgement in suspense, we cannot even if we would – and much less can Poles – make our thoughts and feelings unresponsive to the dreadful probabilities of the case.

15. Smolensk lies some 20 kilometres from the spot where the common graves were discovered. It has two stations and in or near the town the main lines from Moscow to Warsaw from Riga to Orel cross and recross each other. Some fifteen kilometres to the west of Smolensk stands the unimportant station of Gniezdovo, and it is but a short mile from Gniezdovo to a place known locally as Kozlinaya Gora or 'The Hill of Goats'. The district of Katyn, in which this little hill stands, is covered with primeval forest which has been allowed to go to rack and ruin. The forest is mostly coniferous, but the pine trees are interspersed here and there with hardwoods and scrub. The month of April normally brings spring to this part of the country, and by early May the trees are green; but the winter of 1939–1940 had been the hardest on record, and when the first parties from Kozielsk arrived on April 8th, there would still have been occasional patches of snow in deep shade, and of course much mud on

the rough road from the station to The Hill of Goats. At Gniezdovo the prison vans from Kozielsk, Starobielsk and Ostashkov discharged their passengers into a barbed wire cage surrounded by a strong force of Russian soldiers, and the preparations made here for their reception must have filled most of the Polish officers with disquiet, and some indeed with dismay who remembered that the forest of Katyn had been used by the Bolsheviks in 1919 as a convenient place for the killing of many Czarist officers. For such was the case, and a Pole now in London, Janusz Laskowski, tells me that when he was eleven years old he had to listen every evening to an account of his day's work from one of the executioners, Afanaziev, who was billeted in his mother's house. From the cage the prisoners were taken in lorries along a country road to The Hill of Goats, and it must have been when they were unloaded from the lorries that their hands were bound and that dismay gave way to despair. If a man struggled, it seems that the executioner threw his coat over his head, tying it round his neck and leading him hooded to the pit's edge, for in many cases a body was found to be thus hooded and the coat to have been pierced by a bullet where it covered the base of the skull. But those who went quietly to their death must have seen a monstrous sight. In the broad deep pit their comrades lay, packed closely round the edge, head to feet, like sardines in a tin but in the middle of the grave disposed less orderly. Up and down on the bodies the executioners tramped, hauling the dead bodies about and treading in the blood like butchers in a stockyard. When it was all over and the last shot had been fired and the last Polish head punctured, the butchers – perhaps trained in youth to husbandry – seem to have turned their hands to one of the most innocent of occupations: smoothing the clods and planting little conifers all over what had been a shambles. It was of course rather late in the year for transplanting young trees, but not too late; for the sap was beginning to run in the young Scots pines when, three years later, the Polish representatives visited the site.

16. The climate and the conifers are not without

significance. The climate of Smolensk accounts for the fact that, though the Germans first got wind of the existence of the mass graves in the autumn of 1942, it was only in April 1943 that they published to the world an account of what had been unearthed. The explanation is surely this: not that the German propagandists had chosen a politically opportune moment for their revelations, but that during the winter, the ground at Smolensk is frozen so hard that it would have been impossible to uncover corpses without dynamite or such other violent means as would have destroyed the possibility of identifying dead bodies. The winter of 1942–43 was exceptionally mild and the German authorities probably got to work as soon as the soil was sufficiently soft. The little conifers also deserve more attention than they have received. In the first place they are presumptive evidence of Russian guilt; for, considering the conditions under which the German Army advanced through Smolensk in July 1941 in full expectation of early and complete victory, it is most unlikely, if the Polish officers had been murdered by Germans and not Russians, that the Germans would have bothered to cover up their victims' graves with young trees. In the second place, one of these young trees under examination by a competent botanist would reveal beyond any possibility of doubt whether it had been transplanted in May 1940 or some time subsequently to July 1941. Perhaps this test of Russian veracity will presently be made.

17. The political background against which the events described in paragraph 15 are viewed by Poles is by contrast a matter of undisputed history, including as it does all the long story of partitions, rebellions and repressions, the Russo–Polish war of 1919–1920, the mutual suspicions which this left behind it, the unannounced invasion of Poland by Russia in September 1939, the subsequent occupation of half Poland by Russia and the carrying into captivity of some million and a half of its inhabitants. More recently comes the virtual annexation of the occupied eastern parts of Poland, the refusal of the Russian Government to recognize as Polish citizens the inhabitants of the occupied districts, the

suppression of relief organizations for Poles in Russia and the persecution of Poles refusing to change their own for Russian nationality. When Poles learned that in addition to all these misfortunes, round about 10,000 men of the best breeding stock in Poland had (according to Russian accounts) been either dispersed or 'lost' somewhere in the Soviet Union or else abandoned to the advancing German Armies, or had (according to German accounts) been found to have been murdered by the Russians, many of them naturally concluded (though I do not here give it as my own conclusion) that the Soviet Government's intention had been to destroy the very foundations upon which their own Poland could be rebuilt. This sinister political intention imputed by Poles to Russia poisoned the wound and enhanced the suffering of a nation already outraged and dismayed by the conduct of the Soviet Government. Some Poles, remembering Lenin's attitude to the holocausts of 1917 and subsequent years, and probing the dark recesses of Stalin's mind when he took (if take he did) the dreadful decision, compare disciple with master. Lenin would have broken apart the heads of ten thousand Polish officers with the insouciance of a monkey cracking walnuts. Did corpses pitching into a common grave with the precision of machines coming off a production-belt similarly satisfy a nature habituated to manipulate blood and lives with uncompassionate detachment? Some at any rate so interpret Stalin's mind. 'These men are no use to us' they imagine him as saying: 'in fact they are a nuisance and a danger. Here is an élite of talent, here is valour and a hostile purpose. These stallions must not live to sire a whole herd of hostile Christian thoroughbreds. Many of the brood-mares have already been sold to Siberian peasants and the camel-pullers of Kazakstan. Their foals and yearlings can be broken to communist harness. Rid me of this stud farm altogether and send all this turbulent bloodstock to the knackers.'

18. The men who were taken to Katyn are dead and their death is a very serious loss to Poland. Nevertheless, unless the Russians are cleared of the presumption of guilt, the moral repercussions in Poland, in the other occupied coun-

tries and in England of the massacre of Polish officers may well have more enduring results than the massacre itself; and this aspect of things, therefore, deserved attention. As I have as yet seen no reliable reports on public feeling in Poland and German-occupied Europe, my comments will relate only to our own reaction to the uncovering of the graves.

19. This dispatch is not primarily concerned with the reaction of the British public, press or Parliament, who are not in such a good position as His Majesty's Government to form an opinion as to what actually happened. We ourselves, on the other hand, who have access to all the available information, though we can draw no final conclusions on vital matters of fact, have a considerable body of circumstantial evidence at our disposal, and I think most of us are more than half convinced that a large number of Polish officers were indeed murdered by the Russian authorities and that it is indeed their bodies (as well, maybe, as other bodies) which have now been unearthed. This being so, I am impelled to examine the effect on myself of the facts and allegations and to adjust my mind to the shocking probabilities of the case. Since the Polish Government is in London and since the affair has been handled directly by yourself and the Prime Minister with General Sikorski and Count Raczynski, it may seem redundant for me to comment on it as I should naturally do were the Polish Government and I both abroad; but though all important conversations have been between Ministers and the leaders of the Polish Government, my contacts have doubtless been more numerous than yours during the last few weeks with Poles of all kinds and they have possibly spoken to me with less reserve than to yourself. I hope therefore I may without impertinence submit to you the reflections which follow.

20. In handling the publicity side of the Katyn affair we have been constrained by the urgent need for cordial relations with the Soviet Government to appear to appraise the evidence with more hesitation and lenience than we should do in forming a common sense judgement on events occurring in normal times or in the ordinary course of our private

lives; we have been obliged to appear to distort the normal and healthy operation of our intellectual and moral judgements; we have been obliged to give undue prominence to the tactlessness or impulsiveness of Poles, to restrain the Poles from putting their case clearly before the public, to discourage any attempt by the public and the press to probe the ugly story to the bottom. In general we have been obliged to deflect attention from possibilities which in the ordinary affairs of life would cry to high heaven for elucidation, and to withhold the full measure of solicitude which, in other circumstances, would be shown to acquaintances situated as a large number of Poles now are. We have in fact perforce used the good name of England like the murderers used the little conifers to cover up a massacre; and, in view of the immense importance of an appearance of allied unity and of the heroic resistance of Russia to Germany, few will think that any other course would have been wise or right.

21. This dislocation between our public attitude and our private feelings we may know to be deliberate and inevitable; but at the same time we may perhaps wonder whether by representing to others something less than the whole truth so far as we know it, and something less than the probabilities so far as they seem to us probable, we are not incurring risk of what – not to put a fine point on it – might darken our vision and take the edge off our moral sensibility. If so, how is this risk to be avoided?

22. At first sight it seems that nothing less appropriate to a political dispatch than a discourse upon morals can be imagined; but yet, as we look at the changing nature of the international world of today, it seems that morals and international politics are becoming more and more closely involved with each other. This proposition has important consequences; but since it is not universally accepted I hope the following remarks in support of it are not out of place.

23. Nobody doubts that morals now enter into the domestic politics of the United Kingdom, but it was not always so. There was a time when the facts of the government in

London were less often the fruit of consultation and compromise in the general interests of all than of the ascendancy of one class or group of citizens who had been temporarily successful in the domestic arena. It was realization of the interdependence of all classes and groups of the population of England, Scotland and Wales which discouraged the play of intestine power-politics and set the welfare of all above the advantage of the strong. Similar causes are producing similar results in the relations of states to each other. 'During the last four centuries of our modern era,' writes Professor Pollard, 'the last word in political organization has been the nation; but now that the world is being unified by science and culture' the conception of the nation state as the largest group in which human beings are organically associated with each other is being superseded by the conception of a larger, it may be of a European, or indeed of a world-wide unity: and 'the nation is taking its place as the bridge, the half-way house, between the individual and the human family'. Europe and indeed the world are in process of integrating themselves and 'the men and women of Britain', as you said at Maryland, 'are alive to the fact that they live in one world with their neighbours'. This being so, it would be strange if the same movement towards the coalescence of smaller into larger groups which brought about the infiltration of morals into domestic politics were not also now bringing about the infiltration of morals into international politics. This, in fact, it seems to many of us is exactly what is happening and is why, as the late Mr. Headlam Morley said, 'what in the international sphere is morally indefensible generally turns out in the long run to have been politically inept'. It is surely the case that many of the political troubles of neighbouring countries and some of our own have in the past arisen because they and we were incapable of seeing this or unwilling to admit it.

24. If, then, morals have become involved with international politics, if it be the case that a monstrous crime has been committed by a foreign government – albeit a friendly one – and that we, for however valid reasons, have been obliged to behave as if the deed was not theirs, may it not be

that we now stand in danger of bemusing not only others but ourselves: of falling, as Mr. Winant said recently at Birmingham, under St. Paul's curse on those who can see cruelty 'and burn not'? If so, and since no remedy can be found in an early alteration of our public attitude towards the Katyn affair, we ought, maybe, to ask ourselves how, consistently with the necessities of our relations with the Soviet Government, the voice of our political conscience is to be kept up to concert pitch. It may be that the answer lies, for the moment, only in something to be done inside our own hearts and minds where we are masters. Here at any rate we can make a compensatory contribution – a reaffirmation of our allegiance to truth and justice and compassion. If we do this we shall at least be predisposing ourselves to the exercise of a right judgement on all those half political half moral questions (such as the fate of Polish deportees now in Russia) which will confront us both elsewhere and more particularly in respect of Polish–Russian relations as the war pursues its course and draws to its end; and so, if the facts about the Katyn massacre turn out to be as most of us incline to think, shall we vindicate the spirit of these brave unlucky men and justify the living to the dead.

'I have the honour to be, with the highest respect, Sir, Your most obedient, humble Servant, Owen O'Malley.'

Enclosed with this report was a list of missing Polish officers, a list of the personnel comprising the international medical commission on the mass graves at Katyn and the main section of the report of that commission, which is given here:

'From April 28th to April 30th, 1943, a commission composed of leading representatives of forensic medicine at European Universities and other prominent University professors of medicine have conducted a thorough scientific examination of the mass graves of Polish officers in Katyn wood. The discovery of those mass graves, which was recently brought to the attention of the German authorities, prompted Reich's Chief Health Officer, Doctor Conti, to invite experts from various European countries to inspect the Katyn site in order thus to contribute to the clarification of this unique case. Members of the commission personally heard the testimonies of several Russian native witnesses who, among others, confirmed that during the months of March and April 1940 almost daily big railway transports with Polish officers arrived at the station of Gniezdovo, near Katyn, where the Polish prisoners alighted and were then transported in a prisoners' motor van to Katyn wood and were not seen again; the commission further took cognizance of the discoveries and facts thus far established and inspected objects of circumstantial evidence. Accordingly, up to April 30th, 1943, 982 bodies were exhumed, of which approximately 70 per cent have been identified, while papers found on others must first be subjected to careful preliminary treatment before they can be used for identification. Bodies exhumed prior to the commission's arrival were all inspected, and a considerable number of bodies were dissected by Professor Buhtz and his assistants. Up to today seven mass graves have been opened, the biggest of which is estimated to contain the bodies of 2,000 Polish officers. Members of the commission personally dissected nine corpses and submitted numerous specially selected cases to post-mortem. It was confirmed that all those so far exhumed died from bullets in their heads. In all cases, bullets entered the nape. In the majority of cases only one bullet was fired. Two bullets were fired only rarely and only one case was found where three bullets had been fired into the nape. All the bullets were fired from pistols of less than eight mm. calibre. The spot where the bullets penetrated leads to the assumption that the shot was fired with the muzzle pressed against the nape or from the closest range. The surprising regularity of the wounds ... permits the assumption that the shots were fired by experienced hands. Numerous bodies revealed a similar method of tying the hands and in some cases stabs from four-edged bayonets were found on bodies and clothes. The method of tying is similar to that found on the bodies of Russian civilians that were earlier exhumed in Katyn Forest. The assumption is justified that a ricocheted bullet first killed one officer, then went into the body of one already dead in the pit – the shootings apparently being made in ditches to avoid having the bodies transported to graves. The mass graves are situated in clearings in the forest, the ground being completely levelled off and planted with young pines. The mass graves were dug in undulating terrain which consists of pure sand in terraces, and the lowest going down as far as the ground water. Bodies lay, practically without exception, face down, closely side by side and in layers one above the other, clearly ledged methodically at the sides of pits and more irregularly in the centre. The uniforms of the exhumed bodies, according to the unanimous opinion of the commission were, especially with regard to buttons, rank insignia, decorations, form of boots, etc., undoubtedly Polish. They had winter wear. Frequently furs, leather coats, knitted vests and typical Polish officers' caps have been found. Only a few bodies were those of other ranks. One body was that of a priest. The measurements of the clothes correspond with the measurements of the wearer. No watches or rings were found on the bodies, although from the exact date and time found in entries in several diaries, the owners must have had these objects up to their last days, even hours. Comments found on bodies – diaries, correspondence, newspapers – are from the period of the autumn of 1939 to March and April 1940. The latest hitherto established date is that of a Russian newspaper of April 22nd, 1940. There were varying degrees of decomposition of the bodies, differing according to the position of the bodies within the grave and their juxtaposition to each other. A large number of skulls were examined for changes which, according to the experiences of Professor Orsos, are of great importance for the determination of the time of death. These changes consist of various layers of calcareous tuft-like incrustation on the surface of the already loamy brain matter. Such changes are not to be observed on bodies that have been interred for less than three years. But this change was observed to a marked degree on the skull of the body No. 526, which was found with a surface layer in one big mass grave.'

The following comments were added to the report by senior members of the Foreign Office:

'This is a brilliant, unorthodox and disquieting dispatch.

'In the first thirteen paragraphs Mr. O'Malley confined himself to an examination of the evidence as to German or Russian responsibility for the Katyn massacres. This is useful and the material is skilfully assembled. On the evidence available it is, I think, not difficult to share his conclusion that at any rate a strong presumption exists that the Russians were responsible.

'In the next five paragraphs Mr. O'Malley embarks upon what he admits is a "sometimes partial and obviously defective" reconstruction of what may have happened at Katyn, leading up to a final ghoulish vision of Stalin condemning the Poles to the knacker's yard. This passage seems to serve no other purpose than to arouse anti-Soviet passions and prejudices in the reader's mind.

'Mr. O'Malley then applies himself to the question of how passions and prejudices may best be turned to account. By way of a devious argument about the infiltration of morals into international politics he recommends, while recognizing the present necessity of avoiding public accusations of our Russian allies, that we should at least redress the balance in our own minds and in all our future dealings with the Soviet Government refuse to forget the Soviet crime of Katyn. Our future dealings with the Russians should in fact be governed by the moral necessity of "vindicating the spirit of these brave, unlucky men and justifying the living to the dead". In effect Mr. O'Malley urges that we should follow the example which the Poles themselves are unhappily so prone to offer us and in our diplomacy allow our heads to be governed by our hearts. The minutes on Mr. O'Malley's earliest dispatch in U 2011/58/72 suggest that this is the one thing above all to be avoided, at any rate in our dealings wth Soviet Russia.'

(SIR WILLIAM DENIS ALLAN, KCMG, then a member of HM Diplomatic Service.)

'I agree with Mr. Allan's dissection of this dispatch in three very different and unequal parts. I do not think that many people who have been able to follow this question at all closely would disagree with Mr. O'Malley's conclusion that the presumption of guilt rests very strongly on the Soviet Government. It is obviously a very awkward matter when we are fighting for a moral cause and when we intend to deal adequately with war criminals, that our Allies should be open to accusations of this kind and to others relating to the deportation of hundreds of thousands of Poles and to their subsequent treatment in Soviet Russia. However, as Mr. O'Malley says himself, there is no point in our assisting German propaganda on these issues and there is no reason why we cannot maintain our own moral standards and values whilst at the same time endeavouring in every way possible to improve our relations with the Russians and incidentally perhaps to bring about an improvement in Soviet conduct.

'It is unfortunately the case that the Polish case has rather tended to go by default owing to the circumstances in which the Katyn question first became public knowledge.

'It would, therefore, I think, be useful for the facts assembled by Mr. O'Malley in paragraphs 1 to 13 to be circulated at all events to the Cabinet. But I cannot help feeling that this subsequent imaginative reconstruction of the scene in paragraphs 14 to 17, and more particularly paragraph 17, and his moral observation in paragraphs 19 to 24 cast very little light upon this problem and merely leave the reader with the impression that Mr. O'Malley is working up the maximum prejudice against the Soviet Union. The last paragraphs of this dispatch therefore tend to discount the impression left by the introductory factual paragraphs. I know that Mr. O'Malley is very anxious that this dispatch should be circulated. I think myself that there would be advantage in printing and circulating to the War Cabinet paragraphs 1 to 13 only without the last sentence of paragraph 13 and without the passages I have marked in paragraphs 7 and 10.'

(SIR FRANK KENYON ROBERTS, Foreign Office, 1937–45.)

'I should be inclined to print this as it stands (except the first enclosure) and circulate to King and War Cabinet only. It is a powerful piece of work and deserves to be read.'

W. STRANG
(Lord William Strang, then Assistant Under-Secretary of State in the Foreign Office.)

'I agree.'

O. SARGENT
(Sir Orme Sargent, then Deputy Under-Secretary of State in the Foreign Office.)

'This is very disturbing. I confess that, in cowardly fashion, I had rather turned my head away from the scene at Katyn – for fear of what I should find there.

'There may be evidence, that we do not know of, that may point in another direction. But on the evidence that we have, it is difficult to escape from the presumption of Russian guilt.

'This of course raises terrible problems, but I think no one has pointed out that, on the purely moral plane, these are not new. How many thousand of its citizens has the Soviet régime butchered? And I don't know that the blood of a Pole cries louder to Heaven than that of a Russian. But we have perforce welcomed the Russians as Allies and have set ourselves to work with them in war and peace.

'The ominous thing about this incident is the ultimate political repercussion. How, if Russian guilt is established, can we expect Poles to live amicably side by side with Russians for generations to come? I fear there is no answer to that question.

'And the other disturbing thought is that we may eventually, by agreement and in collaboration with Russians, proceed to the trial and perhaps execution of Axis "war criminals" while condoning this atrocity. I confess I shall find that extremely difficult to swallow.

'However, quite clearly for the moment there is nothing to do be done. As to what circulation we give to this explosive material, I find it difficult to make up my mind. Of course it would be only honest to circulate it. But as we know (all admit) that the knowledge of this evidence cannot affect our course of action, or policy, is there any advantage in exposing more individuals than necessary to the spiritual conflict that a reading of this document excites?'

A.C.
(Rt. Hon. Sir Alexander Cadogan, then Permanent Under-Secretary of State for Foreign Affairs.)

The following report, dated February 11th, 1944, was sent to Sir Anthony Eden, the then Foreign Secretary:

Sir – On January 24th the Soviet Government issued the report of a special commission appointed for 'ascertaining and investigating the circumstances of the shooting of Polish officer prisoners by German Fascist invaders in the Katyn Forest'. This report appears in full in the *Soviet War News* of January 27th, 28th, and 31st and February 1st, runs to some 20,000 words, and finishes with the conclusions which are enclosed herein. Having dealt with the German account of this affair at some length in my dispatch No. 51 of May 24th, 1943, I ought perhaps now to deal with the question of what new light, if any, is thrown upon it by our Allies who, having regained possession of Smolensk, have been able to revisit the scene of the massacre and make an inquiry on the spot.

2. There was a difference between the methods employed by the German Government on the one hand and the Soviet Government on the other for convincing the world of the truth of the conclusions which each has levelled against the other. The Germans relied primarily upon the findings of an international commission of fourteen pathologists and criminologists of whom two came from Germany, eleven from satellite or occupied states, and one from Switzerland. Basing itself on the findings of this body, the German Government told its story to the world through every available publicity agency, and they reinforced their case by bringing to Katyn a purely Polish delegation composed of

well-known Poles from many different professions and classes of society, a delegation from the Polish Red Cross Society, and delegations from Lodz and Poznan. The Russian Government on the other hand relied mainly upon the report of a purely Russian commission composed of eight Government officials who had the assistance of a medico-legal sub-commission composed of five Russian scientists. The Russian Government and the German Government, however, acted alike in this, that they both invited foreign journalists to visit the scene of the crime, and both did their best to make the visit a pleasant one. The most up-to-date sleeping-cars were provided by the Russians and aeroplanes by the Germans for the guests; in both cases, after a busy day among the corpses, these were served with smoked salmon, caviare, champagne and other delicacies. In both cases a religious ceremony terminated the proceedings.

3. No definite conclusion can, I think, be drawn from the differences between German and Russian procedure, except perhaps that we shall be slightly more inclined to credit the opinion of the international experts brought to the spot by the Germans than the opinion of a scientific sub-commission composed exclusively of Russians; for since it would clearly have strengthened their case if the Soviet Government had invited British and American scientists to participate in the investigation, one can only suppose that a guilty conscience prevented them from doing so. This inclination is strengthened by the facts, first, that Polish visitors to the graves (including members of the Underground Movement) who hate Germans and Russians equally were in no doubt that the latter had carried out the massacre; and secondly, that the journalists who accompanied the Russian investigators from Moscow, with the exception of Miss Kate Harriman, were not favourably impressed by the Russian evidence or the means by which it was elicited.

4. Both Germans and Russians relied, among other things, upon two classes of testimony; first, verbal testimony given at first or second hand by individuals who might be supposed to have personal knowledge of what occurred at Katyn in April and May 1940 (according to the Russian story); and

secondly, the findings of experts who examined the corpses. It would, I think, be futile to try to appraise the trustworthiness of the testimony of witnesses examined by either the German Government or the Russian Government. Both were in a position to intimidate the soldiers, servants, peasants or other local residents who were called upon to give evidence, and both are notoriously prone to use intimidation. Both allege that material witnesses had been murdered by the other side. The Germans, for instance, say that the Soviet Government itself gave orders for the destruction of the executioners employed by them; while the Russians affirm that the Gestapo liquidated no less than 500 Russian prisoners who had been ordered to open the graves at Katyn and assist with the examination of the corpses. It was for this reason that my dispatch No. 51 made no reference to any part of the verbal evidence given to the German investigators; and for the same reason I do not propose to discuss similar evidence given to the Russian investigators although it occupies not less than nine-tenths of their report.

5. Since I enclosed in my dispatch No. 51 the findings of the German (international) Scientific sub-commission, it is only fair that I should annex to the present dispatch the findings of the Russian Scientific sub-commission (see enclosure No. 2). The following are the most important discrepancies between the two. The German sub-commission claims to have exhumed 982 bodies: the Russians 925. The Germans say that 'a considerable number of the bodies were dissected'; the Russians say 'no external examination of the bodies ... and no medico-legal examination of the bodies ... had been effected previously'. The Germans say that 'there are varying degrees of decomposition of the bodies; that a large number of skulls were examined' for certain changes which only occur three years after death, and that 'this change was observed to a marked degree on skull No. 526': the Russians say that 'there are absolutely no bodies in a condition of decay or disintegration', that the bodies had not remained in the earth 'for long' and that 'the shooting dates back to ... between September and December 1941.' The Germans say the latest document found on any corpse was

dated April 22nd, 1940; the Russians say that numerous documents were found with dates between September 12th, 1940, and June 20th, 1941. It would be rash to draw any conclusions from these discrepancies; but it would be very interesting if His Majesty's Minister in Berne could get an opinion of the whole matter from Dr. Naville, Professor of Forensic Medicine at Geneva, who was a member of the German sub-commission, and is apparently the only neutral and accessible expert from either side.

6. Dismissing as more or less unreliable the verbal accounts of supposed eye-witnesses and the findings of the scientific commissions on both sides, let us summarize the Russian story and see whether it affords reason for doubting the conclusion tentatively reached in my former dispatch on the subject, namely that it was by order of the Soviet Government that the Polish officers were massacred.

7. The Russian report may be summarized as follows: Before the capture of Smolensk by the Germans, Polish prisoners were quartered in three camps 25 to 45 kilometres west of Smolensk. After the outbreak of hostilities the camps could not be evacuated in time, and all the Polish war prisoners as well as some members of the guard were taken prisoner by the Germans. Polish prisoners were seen working on the roads round Smolensk in August and September 1941 but not later. German soldiers frequently combed the neighbouring village for escaped Polish prisoners. Access to the localities where the executions took place were strictly barred, but lorry-loads of Polish prisoners were often seen being driven thither and many shots were heard. The report then passes on to the spring of 1943 when the Germans were alleged to have been preparing the ground for the announcements made on their broadcast system on April 12th of that year, and states that witnesses were tortured by the Germans into giving false evidence of Russian culpability; that 500 Russian prisoners, subsequently murdered, had been employed in March 1943 by the Germans to dig up the corpses and to introduce forged documents into their pockets, and that lorry-loads of corpses were brought to Katyn in March 1943. In short, the Russian case amounts to this: that the occupants of the

camps at Kozielsk, Starobielsk and Ostashkov were moved in April and May 1940 to three Russian labour camps near Smolensk, captured by the advancing German armies in July 1941, and shot at various dates during the subsequent four months.

8. If the evidence of the Soviet Government's witnesses and experts could be trusted, it would be just possible to believe in the truth of the Russian story; but it would nevertheless be very difficult to do so because it makes at least one essential assumption which is incredible, and because it leaves altogether unexplained at least one indisputable set of facts which urgently require explanation before we can accept the Soviet Government's account of events.

9. The Russian story assumes that about 10,000 Polish officers and men, employed on forced labour, lived in the district of Smolensk from April 1940 till July 1941 and passed into German captivity when the Germans captured it in July 1941 without a single one of them having escaped or fallen again into Russian hands or reported to a Polish consul in Russia or to the Polish Underground Movement in Poland. This is quite incredible; and not only is it incredible to anyone who knows anything about prisoners-of-war labour camps in Russia, or who pictures to himself the disorganization and confusion which must have attended the Russian exit and German entry into Smolensk, but the assumption which I have described as essential to the Russian case is actually destroyed by the words of the Russian investigating commission itself. The commission asserts that many Polish prisoners did in fact escape after the district of Smolensk had been overrun by the Germans, and describes the frequent 'round-ups' of escaped prisoners which the Germans organized. The Russian story gives no explanation of why in these circumstances not a single one of the Poles who were allegedly transferred from Kozielsk, Starobielsk and Ostashkov to the labour camps Nos. 1 O.N., 2 O.N. and 3 O.N. has never been seen or heard of alive again.

10. So much for the assumption essential to the credibility of the Russian story. The unexplained set of facts is the same set of facts which has dominated this controversy

throughout, namely that from April 1940 onwards no single letter or message was ever received by anybody from the Poles who were until then at Kozielsk, Starobielsk and Ostashkov (excepting the 400 to 500 sent to Griazovietz); that no single inquiry about these men out of some 500 actually addressed by the Polish Red Cross Society to the Soviet authorities was ever answered, and that no inquiries by representatives of the Polish Government elicited any definite or consistent information about them from the Soviet Government. If they had, as the Soviet Government now allege, been transferred from Kozielsk, Starobielsk and Ostashkov to camps Nos. 1, 2 and 3 O.N., why did not the Soviet Government say so long ago?

11. To all this I am afraid I can only reply, as I did in my previous dispatch on the same subject, that, while 'we do not know for certain who murdered the Polish officers buried at Katyn ... the cumulative effect of the evidence is to throw serious doubts on Russian disclaimers of responsibility'. The defective nature of the report now issued by the Russian commission of inquiry makes these doubts even stronger than they were before. Stronger anyhow in the view of well informed persons in the United Kingdom, for having made inquiries through appropriate channels, I am satisfied that the great majority of responsible British journalists have during the last nine months come round to the same opinions as I have held myself throughout. Consistently with this, the Russian report was coldly received by the British press.

12. Let us think of these things always and speak of them never. To speak of them never is the advice which I have been giving to the Polish Government, but it has been unnecessary. They have received the Russian report in silence. Affliction and residence in this country seem to be teaching them how much better it is in political life to leave unsaid those things about which one feels most passionately.

I have the honour to be, with highest respect, Sir, Your most obedient humble Servant.

Owen O'Malley.'

Mr. O'Malley's reports then, contain the vital information that the Government has known but tried to ignore for thirty-five years. The war has been over for thirty-two of those years, and the political balance now is not nearly so delicate as when the information was first received. More than ever before, we should ask ourselves with Mr. O'Malley 'whether representing to others something less than the whole truth so far as we know it, and something less than the probabilities so far as they seem to us probable, we are not incurring a risk of what – not to put too fine a point on it – might darken our vision and take the edge off our moral sensibility'.

APPENDIX 2

PROFESSOR SIR DOUGLAS SAVORY'S SPEECH IN THE HOUSE OF COMMONS NOVEMBER 6TH, 1952

I AM quite sure that the speech made by the hon. Member for Maldon (Mr. Driberg) will be adequately replied to by the representatives present on the Treasury Bench. The subject with which I wish to deal is something entirely different.

It will be in the recollection of this House that a Motion appeared on the Order Paper before the Recess which was signed by no fewer than 123 hon. Members. They represented all parties, and the Motion certainly would have received a great many more signatures from sympathizers on the Government benches had they been allowed to sign the document. I was surprised to learn that it was impossible even for Parliamentary Private Secretaries to sign a Motion of this kind.

If the House will bear with me, I should like to make a personal explanation of how it was that I became so deeply interested in this question. When the terrible revelations came out as to the massacre at Katyn of several thousand Polish officers, my interest was aroused. After reading through special numbers of the *Soviet War News* in which an attempt was made to explain away these massacres, I had very serious doubts as to the truth of those statements. They were inconsistent with one another and it was noticeable that the commission which had inquired into the matter was composed exclusively of Russians. Not a single international medical authority was called in to examine the question.

I therefore felt a very great desire to ascertain the truth, and in spite of the attacks that have been made upon me, I wish to say here that I acted entirely on my own initiative. No Minister of any Government whatsoever asked me to undertake this inquiry. I can say honestly that my one desire was to ascertain the truth and find out the facts.

I first of all went to the Polish Minister of Information in Stratton Street, Professor Kot, and I am very grateful to him for placing at my disposal all the original documents, all the photographs which he had, and any particular paper that I required was at once placed at my disposal.

I devoted my whole time for several weeks to studying this question, and I have in my possession a very large number of photographs. I eventually drew up my report which was intended to be – and I am sure it was – absolutely impartial and factual. In fact, it may be considered rather dull because it gave a very careful enumeration of the facts.

I immediately put this report into the hands of the Prime Minister and the Foreign Secretary. The Foreign Secretary received me with great cordiality and promised me that this document should be placed in the archives of the Foreign Office. When the Labour Government came into power and I understood that this question of the Katyn massacre was going to be brought up before the Nuremberg military court of justice, I asked for a personal interview with the late Mr. Ernest Bevin. He received me with the utmost kindness, and after I had given him a summary of my report and handed it to him, he said: 'Savory, do you see that basket there?' I said 'Yes.' 'Well,' he said, 'into that basket are placed all the papers and documents which I shall have to read before going to bed tonight, and you see I am going to place your report in that basket.' He was as good as his word, because the very next day he sent me a message saying that my report was being sent to Nuremberg where, I have been informed, it was very carefully considered.

It will be within the recollection of the House that Poland was invaded on September 1st, 1939. But while that was expected, what was a complete surprise was an attack on September 17th by the Soviet forces. The Soviet Government had a treaty of non-aggression with Poland, and they suddenly crossed the frontier declaring that they were coming to the assistance of the Poles. They broadcast this everywhere. They posted up proclamations, 'We are coming to help you against the German aggressors.' The Poles believed them. Many of the Polish Regiments welcomed them, and the result was that without any resistance these Polish regiments and officers were surrounded and carried off to Russia.

Then a few days later – to be precise, on September 28th, 1939 – was published that amazing treaty which we know now as the Molotov–Ribbentrop Treaty. Let me refer to one sentence – perhaps the most important sentence – in the terms of this treaty. Under this Molotov–Ribbentrop pact of September 28th, 1939, the whole of Poland was to be divided between Russia and Germany, Germany taking roughly 72,000 square miles with a population of 22 million and Russia taking roughly 77,000 square miles with a population of 13 million.

In other words, a fourth partition of Poland took place. Poland, which in the eighteenth century had undergone a three-fold partition, denounced by the greatest Ulster historian Lecky as being the worst international crime which had ever been committed up to that date, was once more partitioned between these two aggressors who had both signed treaties of non-aggression with Poland.

Altogether 181,000 soldiers were carried off as prisoners to Russia. The secret police took the utmost care to segregate from the great mass of Polish troops the officers and the leading intellectuals, who were concentrated in three camps, the camps of Kozielsk, Starobielsk and Ostashkov. The camp at Kozielsk was by far the most important. There were placed officers of the highest rank, the leading physicians and leading Polish citizens. These gentlemen were subjected to a whole series of interrogations. In fact, the inquiries lasted six months, from September–October when they were captured in Poland up to March of the following year.

These investigations were extremely minute. For long hours during the night these men were questioned, and from the 21 officers who survived and who have given evidence it is perfectly clear that what they wanted to do was to find out

222

the potential leaders of Poland in case of a resurrection of that unfortunate country. But further, they hoped that by their persuasion – sometimes a very forcible persuasion – they would be able to convert as many as possible of them to becoming Communists. Let it be said to the honour of the Polish Army and the Polish officers that, in spite of the immense pressure which was brought to bear upon them, only six were persuaded to join the Soviet forces. The others remained true to their allegiance. Four hundred were taken from these three camps to another camp at Griazovietz, because it was believed that they were not quite hopeless and that it might still be possible to convert them to Communism.

Apart from those 400 survivors not a word has been heard of the 15,000 Polish officers who were imprisoned in those three camps. In the month of March the interrogations and the investigations came to an end. Every day from the camp at Kozielsk – and also from the other camps, but I am dealing especially with this particular camp – 200 officers were taken away in a very mysterious fashion. The rumour was spread in the camps that they were being sent home. This was believed by the Poles and there was a certain amount of competition to be in the first of those various batches which were being sent. They were brought to Katyn, where they were massacred wholesale. I shall describe that massacre a little later. It is very important.

For the moment I desire to refer to the extraordinary *coup de théâtre* which now took place. These allies, who had partitioned Poland between them, now became enemies and, on June 22nd, 1941, Hitler invaded Russia. The Russians were driven back with extraordinary rapidity. Within two months they were found retreating right into the Ukraine, with the result that they looked round for help, and they thought at once of these Polish soldiers whom, by a most signal breach of faith only worthy of such a people, they had carried off.

They therefore got into touch with the Polish Government in London and made an agreement with that Government that all Polish soldiers should be set free and that a

Polish Army should be reconstituted under General Anders. The question was, who was to direct this army? Professor Kot, whom I got to know as Polish Minister of Information here in London, was Polish Ambassador and he was constant in his efforts to discover the whereabouts of these officers. In October and November he had lengthy interviews with Molotov and Vyshinsky and finally, in December, he had a personal interview with Marshal Stalin. He said to Marshal Stalin: 'We want the Polish officers restored to us in order that we may organize the army which we are placing at your disposal.' Marshal Stalin replied: 'But we have released all the officers.' Professor Kot said: 'I ask you – I implore you – Mr. President, to set free the officers we need for organizing our army because, with the exception of the 400 from Griazovietz, not a single one had been discovered.'

The Polish Prime Minister – the very distinguished General Sikorski – and General Anders had a further interview with Marshal Stalin and gave him a list of several thousand officers, which they had written out from memory, and asked that those officers might be restored. Stalin telephoned to the Secret Police. What reply he received from them he did not venture to vouchsafe either to General Sikorski or to General Anders. All he said was, 'Inquiries shall be made.' In spite of every effort made by General Anders to try to trace these officers in Poland, not a single one could be found.

Then came another extraordinary *coup de théâtre*. On April 13th, 1943, the Germans broadcast the discovery which they had made of these mass graves at Katyn, where no fewer than 4,000 Polish officers in full uniform were unearthed. This broadcast naturally caused a sensation throughout the whole world. The Soviet reply to this revelation is worth hearing, because it is so typical of Soviet methods. On April 15th, 1943, the Soviet Information Bureau stated:

'In their clumsily concocted fabrication about the numerous graves which the Germans allegedly discovered near Smolensk, the Hitlerite liars mentioned the village of

Gniezdovo. But, like the swindlers they are, they are silent about the fact that it was near this village that the archaeological excavations of the historic Gniezdovo burial place were made.'

That is the explanation and that is the defence of the Soviet Government – that there was confusion between the mass graves of these Polish officers and the historic excavations which had been made in the neighbourhood.

On receiving these reports, Lt.-General Kukiel, Polish Minister of National Defence, demanded that there should be an investigation by the International Polish Red Cross. It was surely a very reasonable demand to make, but what was the sequel? A few days later Molotov addressed a letter to the Polish Ambassador in Moscow, as follows:

'You have now joined the Hitlerites. You have believed these slanders which have been promulgated against the Russians. We therefore break off all diplomatic relations.'

However, the Germans insisted on having a very careful inquiry made and 12 distinguished professors from neutral countries – [An HON. MEMBER: 'The Germans asked for the inquiry.'] – the Germans asked for the inquiry, of course; it was the Germans who discovered these graves. The Germans summoned a tribunal consisting of 12 of the most distinguished international professors of anatomy, criminologists and so on, who arrived on the spot and carried out an investigation. I have read the whole of their report and I was especially impressed by the statement, in beautiful French by Professor Naville, Professor of Medicine at Geneva University. In any case, these 12 international experts signed a unanimous report that the massacre must have taken place – I could give hon. Members all the details and the proofs but I do not want to take up time – not later than March or April 1940, when the Russians were still in occupation of Smolensk.

MR. S. SILVERMAN:

Were these the same distinguished gentlemen who at a later date inspected the camp at Auschwitz, where six million people were murdered, and were unable to find anything wrong?

SIR D. SAVORY:

I cannot answer the hon. Member. That question seems to me to be altogether irrelevant. All I can say is that these great men drew up the unanimous report that the massacre must have taken place not later than March or April 1940.

The Russians had made the profound mistake of burying the 4,000 officers in their uniforms. Their shoulder straps – I have the photographs and would like to show them to any hon. Member who may wish to see them – showed exactly what their ranks were – general, colonel, major, lieutenant, and so on. On their bodies were found letters from their friends, none of them of a later date than April 28th, 1940, and letters which they had written home but which had never been posted. There were also certificates showing that some of them had been awarded the Silver Medal and that some of them even possessed the Virtuti Militari, which is the Polish equivalent of the Victoria Cross.

The fact that they were wearing overcoats and mufflers showed that the massacre must have taken place at about the time I have stated, for climatic conditions in Russia are still very cold in March and April. In any case, there are the proofs and there are the photographs. The 4,000 have been disinterred and from the indications found on their bodies it was possible to draw up a complete list, of which I have a copy.

The question was brought up at Nuremberg. The gentleman who wrote attacking me in the *Daily Telegraph* asked why I did not rest content with the trial which was taking place there. I have read the whole of the evidence on July 1st and 2nd, 1964. Only three witnesses were allowed to be summoned on both sides. There was a very complete cross-examination, and one cannot help paying a tribute to the impartiality of the British presiding judge, but the result was absolutely unconvincing.

The Russians were unable to prove anything. In fact, when it came to summing up the evidence, they omitted all reference to the Katyn massacre. They had accused Field Marshal Goering of being the principal culprit, but when it came to the summing up they made no allusion whatsoever to the Katyn massacre. Therefore, it was left an open question.

I maintain that it is to the honour of the House of Representatives of the United States that they did not rest content with this blank verdict. They appointed a Select Committee consisting of four Democrats – the appointment was made by the Speaker – and three Republicans, and they have carried out one of the most exhaustive investigations in history.

I want briefly to tell the House what they have done. They have held numerous sittings in Washington, Chicago, London, Frankfurt-am-Main, Berlin and Naples. They heard altogether 81 witnesses and received more than 100 depositions from witnesses who, for some reason or another, were not able to appear at the sittings. They have published the evidence in five huge white books. Has even a Select Committee of the House of Commons ever carried out such an exhaustive investigation covering five large volumes? I have those white books in my room and would be delighted to show them to any hon. Member. I cannot help admiring the careful way in which these gentlemen carried out the investigation; it was extremely careful and impartial, and extremely judicial.

What is their verdict? It is:

'This Committee unanimously finds beyond any question of reasonable doubt that the Soviet NKVD' –

that is, the People's Commissariat of Internal Affairs –

'committed the mass murders of the Polish officers and intellectual leaders in the Katyn Forest, Smolensk, Russia.'

Let hon. Members listen to this:

> 'Throughout our entire proceedings there has not been a scintilla of proof or even any remote circumstantial evidence presented that could indict any other nation in this international crime.'

I hope the British Government will support the American deputation before the United Nations. I appeal to the Foreign Secretary when he goes over there to bring up this question and to support the American deputation in demanding that this evidence shall be submitted to an international tribunal. I should like the Foreign Secretary to know that I was in Washington in January and May this year and I assure him that the interest in the question was by no means confined to people of Polish origin.

I urge Her Majesty's Government now to make an immediate protest against the conspiracy of silence which has for 12 years shrouded the terrible mystery of the murder and the disappearance of 15,000 Polish officers taken into captivity by the Red Army in the autumn of 1939.

Let us protest against the silence of Christian nations and let us make an appeal against this moral wrong. Let us cry for justice in connection with the foul massacre of innocent victims in one of the most barbaric of all war atrocities. Let us realize that the Katyn crime is a moral sin against humanity and against every Christian concept of the dignity of man.

I beg the Foreign Secretary when he goes over to New York tomorrow to support the proposal that an international tribunal should be formed under the auspices of the United Nations to conduct an investigation. Let them consider the five white books containing this immense catalogue of evidence. Let them conduct an inquiry as a warning that the free world is no longer disposed to tolerate or condone such a flaunting of international law and such a deprivation of the divine dignity of human beings as has been shown by these deplorable events.

INTERIM REPORT OF THE US CONGRESSIONAL SELECT COMMITTEE, JULY 2ND, 1952

SELECT COMMITTEE TO CONDUCT AN INVESTIGATION AND STUDY OF THE FACTS, EVIDENCE, AND CIRCUMSTANCES OF THE KATYN FOREST MASSACRE

RAY J. MADDEN, Indiana, *Chairman*

DANIEL J. FLOOD, Pennsylvania GEORGE A. DONDERO, Michigan

FOSTER FURCOLO, Massachusetts ALVIN E. O'KONSKI, Wisconsin

THADDEUS M. MACHROWICZ, Michigan TIMOTHY P. SHEEHAN, Illinois

JOHN J. MITCHELL, *Chief Counsel*

ROMAN C. PUCINSKI, *Chief Investigator*

BARBARA R. BOOKE, *Secretary*

CONTENTS

THE KATYN FOREST MASSACRE

July 2nd, 1952. – Committed to the Committee of the Whole House on the State of the Union and ordered to be printed.

Mr. MADDEN, from the Select Committee to Conduct an Investigation and Study of the Facts, Evidence, and Circumstances of the Katyn Forest Massacre, submitted the following:

INTERIM REPORT

[Pursuant to H. Res. 390 and H. Res. 539]

I. INTRODUCTION
A. CREATION AND PURPOSE OF SELECT COMMITTEE TO INVESTIGATE KATYN FOREST MASSACRE

On September 18th, 1951, the House of Representatives unanimously adopted House Resolution 390. This resolution provided for the establishment of a select committee of Congress and authorized it to conduct a full and complete investigation concerning an international crime committed against soldiers and citizens of Poland at the beginning of World War II. This committee was given the responsibility to record evidence, take testimony, and study all facts and extenuating circumstances pertaining directly or indirectly to the barbarous massacre of thousands of Polish Army officers and civilian leaders buried in mass graves in the Katyn Forest on the banks of the Dnieper in the vicinity of Smolensk, USSR.

B. ORGANIZATION OF THE COMMITTEE

The Speaker of the House of Representatives appointed the following members to this committee: Ray J. Madden (Democrat) Indiana, chairman; Daniel J. Flood (Democrat) Pennsylvania; Foster Furcolo (Democrat), Massachusetts; Thaddeus M. Machrowicz (Democrat), Michigan; George A. Dondero (Republican), Michigan; Alvin E. O'Konski (Republican), Wisconsin; and Timothy P. Sheehan (Republican), Illinois. The committee selected John J. Mitchell for counsel, Roman C. Pucinski as investigator, and Barbara Booke as secretary.

C. PROCEDURE

This committee was confronted with the difficult task of determining whether the Germans or the Soviets were responsible for this colossal crime. Both countries had accused each other.

The task assigned this committee is without precedent in the history of the United States House of Representatives. But likewise without precedent is the fact that never before in the history of the world have two nations accused each other of such an atrocious crime with the identity of the nation actually guilty never having been sufficiently established.

Until the creation of this committee, this crime was destined to remain an international mystery and the conscience of the world could never have rested.

Fully aware then that this was the first neutral committee ever officially authorized by any government to investigate the Katyn massacre, this committee divided its investigation into two phases:

(1) Assemble evidence which would determine the guilt of the country responsible for the mass murder of these Polish Army officers and intellectuals in the Katyn Forest.

(2) Establish why the Katyn massacre with all of its ramifications never was adequately revealed to the American people and to the rest of the world. The committee likewise included in this phase an effort to determine why this crime was not adjudicated at the Nuremberg trials – where it should have been settled in the first instance if the Germans were guilty.

It was unanimously agreed by the committee that phase I of the investigation would be undertaken first and this interim report will include an analysis only of this phase. Testimony heard thus far has of necessity touched on phase II but additional study will be required before any conclusions can be reached.

This committee, for instance, heard testimony which clearly indicates certain reports and records relating to this massacre which were compiled by American observers had either disappeared or had been misplaced. What effect, if any, these reports might have had on this country's postwar foreign policy if the missing reports had been known and properly evaluated by all top level United States agencies will be the subject of subsequent hearings. The committee's conclusions on phase II will be incorporated in its final report.

D. HEARINGS

The committee's first public hearing was held in Washington on October 11th, 1951. It heard the testimony of Lt.-Col. Donald B. Stewart, a United States Army officer, who, as a German prisoner-of-war, was taken by the Germans to view the mass graves at Katyn in May 1943. (See pt. I of the committee's published hearings.)

The next set of hearings was held in Washington on February 4th, 5th, 6th, and 7th, 1952. Seven witnesses appeared and rendered an account of their knowledge relating to the Katyn massacre. (See pt. II of the published hearings.)

In Chicago on March 13th, 14th, 1952, eight other witnesses were heard by this committee. (See pt. III of the published hearings.)

In London on April 16th, 17th, 18th, and 19th, 1952, 29 witnesses were heard. (See pt. IV of the published hearings.)

In Frankfurt, Germany, on April 21st, 22nd, 23rd, 24th, 25th, and 26th, 1952, 27 witnesses were heard. (See pt. V of the published hearings.)

In Berlin, Germany, on April 25th, a sub-committee heard testimony from members of the German Commission on Human Rights and received approximately 100 depositions which had been taken by that organization.

In Naples, Italy, on April 27th, testimony of Dr. Palmieri was heard.

In Washington on June 3rd and 4th, 1952, testimony was heard from five witnesses.

In the course of the hearings held by this committee to date, testimony has been taken from a total of 81 witnesses; 183 exhibits have been studied and made part of the record, and more than 100 depositions were taken from witnesses who could not appear at the hearings. In addition, the committee staff has questioned more than 200 other individuals who offered to appear as witnesses but whose information was mostly of a corroborating nature.

E. LETTERS OF INVITATION

The committee unanimously agreed that in order to make this a full, fair, and impartial investigation, it would be willing to hear any individual, organization, or government having possession of factual evidence or information pertaining to the Katyn massacre.

Letters of invitation were forwarded to the Government of the USSR, the Polish Government in Warsaw, the Polish Government-in-Exile in London, and the German Federal

Republic. The German Federal Republic and the Polish Government-in-Exile accepted the invitation.

The Soviet Government rejected the invitation of the committee with the statement that a Special Soviet Commission (composed of all Russian citizens) had thoroughly investigated the Katyn massacre in January 1944 and consequently there was no need for reopening the issue. However, the Soviet Government did attach to their reply the special commission's report and it later was made part of the permanent record of this committee. (See pp. 223 through 247, pt. III of the published hearings.)

The Polish Government in Warsaw transmitted to the American Embassy a note likewise rejecting the committee's invitation, part of which is quoted as follows:

> The attitude of the Polish Government re the activities of this committee was expressed in the declaration of the Polish Government published on March 1st, 1952, and the Polish Government does not intend to return to this matter again.

The entire note may be found on page 504 of part IV of the public hearings of this committee.

The attitude of the Polish Government as quoted above was revealed by the vicious propaganda blast issued in the form of a press release and circulated to all newspaper correspondents by the Polish Embassy in Washington. The chairman of the committee published this press release in its entirety in the Congressional Record on March 11th, 1952, and called upon the Secretary of State to take prompt action relative to the propaganda activities of the Polish Embassy here in Washington. The Secretary of State on March 20th, 1952, delivered a stern reprimand to the Polish Embassy regarding such press releases and greatly restricted its activities in this field.

F. HOUSE RESOLUTION 539

The first two series of hearings definitely established in the minds of this committee that it would be impossible to conduct a thorough investigation without obtaining the testimony of available witnesses in Europe. Consequently, the committee went before the House of Representatives on March 11th, 1952, with House Resolution 539 which amended the original, House Resolution 390, and requested permission to take testimony from individuals and governments abroad. The House approved House Resolution 539 on March 11th, 1952.

G. FINDINGS

This committee unanimously agrees that evidence dealing with the first phase of its investigation proves conclusively and irrevocably the Soviet NKVD (Peoples' Commissariat of Internal Affairs) committed the massacre of Polish Army officers in the Katyn Forest near Smolensk, Russia, not later than the spring of 1940.

This committeee further concludes that the Soviets had plotted this criminal extermination of Poland's intellectual leadership as early as the fall of 1939 – shortly after Russia's treacherous invasion of the Polish nation's borders. There can be no doubt this massacre was a calculated plot to eliminate all Polish leaders who subsequently would have opposed the Soviets' plans for communising Poland.

APPENDIX 4

EXTRACT FROM US CONGRESSIONAL RECORD

CONGRESSMAN DERWINSKI'S SPEECH IN THE HOUSE OF REPRESENTATIVES, MAY 14TH, 1962

MR. DERWINSKI: Mr. Speaker, for over a year I have been pleading with the majority party leaders and the State Department to approve the creation of a special House Committee on Captive Nations.

One of the precedents for the creation of this special committee is the select House committee which investigated the Katyn massacre. This select committee proved beyond all doubt that the Soviet Union had murdered in cold blood approximately 15,000 Polish prisoners-of-war in the Katyn Forest area of the Ukraine in 1940.

I submit for the Record an article entitled 'Awaiting the Public Prosecutor', which was published in the April issue of the Republic of Poland publication, written by Mr. Jan Walewski, a member of the Council of the Republic of Poland – a parliamentary body in exile. I believe this article to be especially pertinent at this time not only because it dramatizes and recalls the crime of the Katyn massacre but also emphasizes the practicality of a special House committee. I feel, Mr. Speaker, that the creation of a Captive Nations Committee will provide an even more effective instrument to expose Soviet colonialism in Eastern Europe; that this committee would be a great contribution to the House in the field of world knowledge, and would receive support from freedom-loving citizens here in the United States and in all corners of the free world. The article follows:

Ten years ago, in April 1952 a select committee of the US Congress arrived in London in order to take the testimony of witnesses in respect of the Katyn massacre. The month of April has a bloodstained page in the history of Poland's martyrdom, for that month is bound up with a most notorious and ghastly war crime – the Katyn massacre.

In April for many years past, Poles in the free world have held solemn mass meetings dedicated to the memory of the victims of the Katyn crime while at the same time reminding the world that this crime against Poland and all humanity still awaits judicial trial and that the culprits remain unpunished.

The 22nd anniversary of the Katyn massacre falls due this year. It would be well therefore to review the facts of this crime and the action undertaken by the Polish Government-in-exile to have the culprits identified and a final judgement pronounced.

The Poles in the homeland and abroad were disquietened in 1940 by the cessation of correspondence as from April with the Polish prisoners-of-war held by the Russians in three camps: Kozielsk, Starobielsk and Ostashkov. These prisoners numbered about 15,000 and for the most part comprised officers captured by the Red Army after it invaded Poland on September 17th, 1939. It later transpired that this aggression was the execution of that secret and treacherous agreement, the Ribbentrop–Molotov pact.

After the German attack on Russia and following the resumption of diplomatic relations between the Polish Government and the Soviet Government, both the Polish Government in London and the Polish military authorities in the Soviet Union began a search for the missing prisoners-of-war in August 1941, but in vain. The leading representatives of the Soviet Government gave nothing but mendacious or evasive replies when questioned on the subject. During the autumn of 1941, barely 400 of the missing prisoners-of-war were traced.

In April 1943, mass graves containing the bodies of over

4,000 Polish officers, murdered in atrocious fashion, were found in Katyn Forest, near Smolensk. In view of this shocking discovery, the Polish Government asked the International Committee of the Red Cross in Geneva to undertake an impartial investigation of the matter. The relevant Polish note was handed to Mr. Paul Ruegger, representative of the International Committee of the Red Cross, by Prince Stanislaw Radziwill, delegate of the Polish Red Cross in Switzerland, on April 17th, 1943. The Soviet Government, however, strongly protested against such an investigation and the International Committee could not therefore accept the mission. And then, a few days later, during the Easter holidays of that year, the Soviet Government broke off diplomatic relations with the Polish Government in London, simultaneously launching a slanderous campaign against that Government, of which General W. Sikorski was Prime Minister at the time.

The Polish white book

Gloomy times ensued for Poland and the Poles. At the Moscow, Teheran, and Yalta Conferences with the Soviets, the Western Allies abandoned the lofty principles of the Atlantic Charter and the commitments they had accepted; with Poland unrepresented at these negotiations, the Western Powers decided the fate of that country – their oldest and most loyal ally. As an outcome of the Yalta resolutions, the Communist régime imposed upon Poland by Moscow was recognized by the Western Allies in July 1945 simultaneously with the de-recognition of the constitutional Government of the Republic of Poland which had functioned in France since October 1st, 1939, and then, after the collapse of France, in London as from June 1940.

Despite these dire experiences, the Polish Government ceaselessly worked on the elucidation of the Katyn massacre. One of the first tasks undertaken by the government of Tomasz Arciszewski was the appointment, in December 1944 of a special committee for investigating the disappearance of 15,000 Polish prisoners-of-war in the Soviet

Union. The members of the committee were Gen. Marian Kukiel, Minister of National Defence; Adam Tarnowski, foreign minister; and Prof. Adam Pragier, Minister of Information and Documentation, while a team of experts headed by Profs. W. Sukiennicki and M. Heitzman, studied the matter on the basis of the collected evidence and documents. The findings of this committee were published in February 1946, in a work entitled 'Facts and Documents Concerning the Polish Prisoners-of-War Captured by the USSR. During the 1939 Campaign'. This Polish white book was presented to the attention of the Western members of the International Military Tribunal at Nuremberg in time for the proceedings and, years later, was incorporated as part VI of the American congressional Katyn hearings of 1952.

At the Nuremberg trial

During the trial of the principal German war criminals by the International Military Tribunal at Nuremberg, when the charge that Polish prisoners-of-war were murdered in Katyn Forest was also examined since it figured in the indictment, supplementary documentation was presented on July 2nd, 1946, to the President of the Tribunal. This consisted of 34 documents compiled by the Polish Foreign Ministry in London in 1946 under the title of 'Report on the Massacre of Polish Officers in the Katyn Wood'. Polish documentary material on Katyn was undoubtedly taken into consideration by the Nuremberg Tribunal when this body announced it could find no basis for ascribing guilt for the Katyn massacre to the German war-criminals under trial.

The struggle for the truth continues

A book in Polish entitled *Zbrodnia Katynska w Swietle Dokumentow* (The Katyn Crime in the Light of Documents) was published in London in 1948, while the Polish press in the free world wrote more and more often about this crime.

Action for establishing the facts of the Katyn massacre made further progress in 1949. The Polish Association of

Former Soviet Political Prisoners was founded in London on April 2nd, 1949; one of the chief aims of this organization is the general dissemination of information on the Katyn massacre and the demand that this crime be judicially investigated.

The American Committee for the Investigation of the Katyn Massacre, Inc. was established soon after in New York on the initiative of several eminent American personalities with the intention of organizing a public trial dealing with the Katyn massacre. Former US Ambassador to Poland, Arthur Bliss Lane stood at the head of this committee, with Clare Boothe Luce, Dorothy Thompson, Gen. William J. Donovan, Allan W. Dulles, Max Eastman, James A. Farley, Blair F. Gunther, Charles Rozmarek, George E. Sokolsky, and others as members of that body.

The National Council of the Polish Republic unanimously passed its Katyn resolution during a session in London on September 5th, 1949, on the motion of the Polish Government-in-exile. This resolution expressed gratification that the initiative for an independent investigation of the Katyn massacre had been undertaken in the United States; it also expressed confidence that 'people with sufficient moral strength would be found in the free world, able to bear the burden of struggle for the truth and to wage this struggle victoriously'.

The first American solemn mass meeting in memory of the victims of the Katyn massacre was held on September 18th, 1949. It was initiated by post No. 15 of the Polish Army Veterans Association of America, headed by Vincent A. Basinski, a member of the London Association of Former Soviet Political Prisoners. The meeting was held in Gary, Ind., under the patronage of HE August Zaleski, legitimate President of the Polish Republic. Among the speakers were Representative Ray J. Madden of Gary, Ind., Democrat, and the Reverend Walerian S. Karcz, chaplain to the Polish Army Veterans Association of America.

The turning point in efforts for establishing the facts of the Katyn massacre occurred in 1951. The American committee headed by Arthur Bliss Lane had been active for two years, doing sterling work in amassing evidence and effectively combating the indifference shown in this matter. News to the effect that UN soldiers captured by the Communists in Korea were being 'Katynized' began to reach America from the Far East. The idea of appointing a congressional select committee for the investigation of the Katyn massacre arose in Chicago – where the organized life of Americans of Polish descent is centred. Credit for this initiative is due to Representative Timothy P. Sheehan, Republican, of Chicago, who introduced the original resolution (H. Res. 282) in the House of Representatives on June 26th, 1951, asking for a complete congressional investigation of the Katyn massacre. Mr. Julius Epstein, executive secretary of Arthur Bliss Lane's committee, drew the attention of American public opinion to this important development in the Katyn case when he wrote on the subject in the *New York Times* of July 9th, 1951. Joseph Mackiewicz's *The Katyn Wood Murders* was published in book form in London during the same month. In the meantime, the appointment of a congressional Select Committee on the Katyn Massacre was becoming ripe for action. Resolutions on this subject were also introduced by Representatives Madden, Flood, Machrowicz, and Latham. But Representative Ray J. Madden, of Gary, Ind., bore away the palm. An attorney at law by profession, member of the American Legion and for many years a member of the Committee on Rules of the House of Representatives (on whose decision the creation of select committee is chiefly dependent), Representative Madden had interested himself in the Katyn case since 1949 and acquired a thorough knowledge of it. His second resolution (H. Res. 390, dated August 15th, 1951) was referred to the Committee on Rules which on August 16th, 1951, unanimously adopted his resolution for creating a select committee composed of seven Members of the House of Representatives to investigate the Katyn Forest massacre.

On September 18th, 1951, the second anniversary of the commemorative mass meeting in Gary, Ind., the US House of Representatives held a debate during which 16 speakers addressed the House and in the outcome unanimously adopted Representative Madden's resolution (H. Res. 390), introduced by the chairman of the Committee on Rules, and dean of the House of Representatives, Representative Adolph J. Sabath, of Chicago.

The select committee consisted of the following Representatives: Ray J. Madden, Democrat, of Indiana, chairman; Thaddeus M. Machrowicz, Democrat, of Michigan, Foster Furcolo, Democrat, of Massachusetts, Daniel J. Flood, Democrat, of Pennsylvania, George A. Dondero, Republican, of Michigan, Alvin E. O'Konski, Republican, of Wisconsin, and Timothy P. Sheehan, Republican, of Illinois, Representative Machrowicz, who is of Polish descent, was made vice-chairman.

The select committee began its investigation by hearing the evidence of a number of witnesses, first in Washington and then in Chicago. At the beginning of 1952, the chairman of the committee sent letters inviting the co-operation of the Polish Government in London, the Soviet Government, the Communist 'government' in Warsaw, and of the German Federal Republic authorities.

The murderers' cynicism and their stooges' perfidy

The Soviet authorities refused their co-operation and in their memorandum of February 29th, 1952, stated:

'The question of the Katyn crime had been investigated in 1944 by an official commission, and it was established that the Katyn case was the work of the Hitlerite criminals, as was made public in the press on January 26th, 1944. For eight years the Government of the United States did not raise any objections to such conclusion of the Commission until very recently.'

The example of the Soviet Union was followed by

Warsaw which, through the intermediary of its Ambassador, likewise refused its co-operation and referred to a reply made by Cyrankiewicz on March 1st, 1952, in a PAP press release. He described the activity of the congressional select committee as a 'stage-managed farce and one of the links in the propaganda action of the US Government, the provocative aims of which are obvious and are part of aggressive war preparations'.

Katyn – on the conscience of the world!

As already stated, it was in April 1962 that the members of the Select Committee To Investigate the Katyn Forest Massacre arrived in London. Thirty Polish witnesses were heard during the course of four days. A great mass meeting of Poles was held in London commemorating the 12th anniversary of the Katyn massacre on April 19th, 1952; it was attended by the legitimate President of the Polish Republic, and Representatives Madden, Flood, and Machrowicz also addressed the assembly. On behalf of the US Congress, Chairman Madden assured his Polish listeners that the murder of Polish prisoners-of-war in Soviet Russia shall not go unpunished and that Congress not only will pronounce a verdict but see to it that justice be done and the perpetrators pay for their crime. 'Katyn,' said Representative Madden, 'is not only a Polish issue, but one that affects the conscience of the entire civilized world, being at the same time a threat to this world.'

The select committee returned to Washington on the conclusion of its investigations in Europe and drew up its interim report.

President Zaleski's Cablegram

Having received news that this phase of the investigation had been concluded, the legitimate President of the Polish Republic sent a cablegram of thanks to Chairman Ray J. Madden. The text of this message was published on July 3rd, 1952, in the Congressional Record (A479), and on July 7th the press bulletins of the US Information Service included the following item from Washington as given in the daily wireless bulletin of the US Embassy in London (No. 1916, July 7th, 1952):

'Katyn: Exiled president expresses Poland's gratitude at US Findings

'Washington, July 7th. – The head of the Polish Government-in-exile believes the special committee of the US House of Representatives has rendered a great service to humanity by establishing that the Soviet Union was responsible for the massacre of 15,000 Polish Army officers in the spring of 1940.

'President August Zaleski, in a cable from London to the head of the committee, Representative Ray J. Madden, of Indiana, said:

' "By exposing this plot to eliminate those who subsequently would have opposed the communising of Poland, you have rendered a great service not only to Poland but to humanity as a whole."

'Representative Madden's group based its findings on nine months of investigations and testimony in the United States and Europe. It recommended that the United Nations General Assembly take action on the crime before the International Court of Justice.

'The committee asserted in its report to the full House:

' "Throughout our entire proceedings there has not been a scintilla of proof or even any remote circumstantial evidence presented that would indicate any other nation in this international crime."

'President Zaleski congratulated Mr. Madden and the other members of the committee on the results of their probe into "the ghastly crime perpetrated on Polish prisoners-of-war."

'His message added:

' "Your action proves that the US Congress stands always as a defender of justice and righteousness. I am sure that I express the sentiments of the whole Polish nation when I express to you and your colleagues our most sincere thanks."

'The House committee found after its long investigation that: "Beyond question of reasonable doubt, the Soviet NKVD, secret police, committed the mass murders of the Polish officers and intellectual leaders in the Katyn Forest." '

Final report of the select committee on the Katyn Massacre

The American elections in the autumn of 1952 brought victory to the Republicans, and the select committee then heard some more important witnesses including Robert H. Jackson, Associate Justice, US Supreme Court, former Under Secretary of State, Sumner Welles, former American Ambassadors George H. Earle, W. A. Harriman, Arthur Bliss Lane, and Adm. William H. Standley, and S. Mikolajczyk, president of the International Peasant Union. The committee concluded its labours as the terms of the 82nd Congress of the United States was drawing to a close. The select committee held a press conference on December 22nd, 1952, when it released the text of its final unanimous recommendation that the House of Representatives approve the committee's findings and adopt the following resolution:

1. Requesting the President of the United States to forward the testimony, evidence, and findings of this committee to the US delegates at the United Nations;

2. Requesting further that the President of the United States issues instructions to the US delegates to present the Katyn case to the General Assembly of the United Nations;

3. Requesting that appropriate steps be taken by the General Assembly to seek action before the International World Court of Justice against the Union of Soviet Socialist Republics for committing a crime at Katyn which was in violation of the general principles of law recognized by civilized nations;

4. Requesting the President of the United States to instruct the US delegation to seek the establishment of an

international commission which would investigate other mass murders and crimes against humanity.

We now come to the year 1953. In the United States, the Republicans headed by President Eisenhower took over the reins of Government. The 83rd Congress likewise had a Republican majority. The new US administration took steps to end the war in Korea in accordance with General Eisenhower's election pledges. Representative Madden's recommendation that the Katyn case be followed up before the forum of Congress was presented at the beginning of the year, but it was shelved – on the request of the Department of State – by a majority vote of the Foreign Affairs Committee in the House of Representatives on June 18th, 1953.

The report of the Congressional Select Committee on the Katyn Massacre, which comprised 2,437 pages of testimony and other evidence, still awaits action.

The Polish Nation now has at its disposal a wealth of evidence against the perpetrators of this ghastly murder of Polish prisoners-of-war amassed chiefly by official representatives of the American Nation.

The Katyn crime has not been forgotten. The Poles in the free world ceaselessly recall it to mind.

The following events in some connection with the Katyn massacre have taken place since 1953:

February 12th, 1953: Ambassador Henry Cabot Lodge, Jr., US representative to the United Nations, sent the select committee's final report on the Katyn Forest massacre to the UN Secretary General for distribution to all members of the United Nations.

March 25th, 1953: Ambassador Lodge, speaking at a meeting of the Political Committee of the General Assembly of the United Nations on the Katyn massacre, pointed out that the investigation of the congressional select committee demonstrated that responsibility for this crime lies with the shameful NKVD (secret police) of the Soviet Government.

May 8th, 1956: Representative Timothy P. Sheehan, of Chicago, informed the House of Representatives that he had sent a cablegram to Jozef Cyrankiewicz, 'Prime Minister of the Communist Polish People's Republic', stating he was prepared to come to Poland and present the Katyn evidence collected by the congressional select committee during 1951–52. Press agencies had just announced that the Warsaw régime intended to appoint a special committee to investigate the Katyn crime. As could be expected, no such committee was set up in Warsaw, and Representative Sheehan received no reply to his cablegram.

July 26th, 1956: Six members of the congressional Select Committee on the Katyn Massacre (Representatives Madden, Flood, Machrowicz, Dondero, O'Konski, and Sheehan) sent a letter to Khrushchev (reported by the press on August 6th, 1956) urging him publicly to admit Stalin's guilt of the Katyn massacre. There was no answer to this letter, too.

October 1956: Demonstrators in the streets of Warsaw raised the cry of 'Rokossovski, go to Moscow' amidst the insistent chant of 'Katyn, Katyn, Katyn'. Konrad Syrop wrote of this in his *Spring in October* (London, 1957).

July 20th, 1957: A German weekly, the 7 Tage of Karishruhe/Baden, published a 'Soviet document'. This was the photostat of a report of the Minsk NKVD (secret police) dated June 10th, 1940, and dealing with the liquidation of three camps for Polish prisoners-of-war. Apart from the dates of this 'liquidation' of the camps, this report gives the names of the military formations which provided the 'guard' for this operation. If this document is authentic, it clears up a mystery unsolved since 1940, viz. where the prisoners-of-war in the Starobielsk and Ostashkov camps were murdered.

September 1957: Two volumes of Stalin's correspondence with the Presidents of the United States and the Prime Ministers of Great Britain during the war were published in Russian. This edition was prepared by a commission presided over by Minister A. A. Gromyko but there is also an English edition in one volume, published in 1958 and entitled *Stalin's Correspondence with Churchill, Attlee, Roosevelt, and Truman, 1941–45*. It follows from this official Soviet publication that the Soviet Government note of April 25th, 1943, breaking off diplomatic relations with the Polish Government and signed by Molotov included the verbatim text of

Stalin's letter of April 21st, 1943, to President Roosevelt and Prime Minister Churchill. Moscow continues to uphold Stalin's version of April 1943 as regards the Katyn massacre. For, in a footnote added in 1957 to Document No. 150 – Stalin's letter of April 21st, 1943, to Churchill in which he accused the Polish Government of inimical action against the Soviet Union in connection with the Katyn massacre – the 'Katyn' footnote (item 67 in the Russian edition and 59 in the English one) reads as follows:

'The allusion is to the anti-Soviet slander campaign which the Hitlerites launched in 1943 over the Polish officers whom they themselves had massacred at Katyn, near Smolensk.'

The Mala Encyklopedia Powszechna (Small Universal Encyclopedia) published in Warsaw in 1958 repeats this Soviet version, for under the entry 'Katyn' we read:

'Locality in the Smolensk region of the Russian Soviet Federal Socialist Republic, site of the mass graves of several thousand Polish officers interned since 1939 in the Soviet Union and murdered by the Hitlerites after they occupied these areas.'

Among the most recent enunciations on the Katyn massacre, mention must be made of one made by Wladyslaw Gomulka not long ago. Speaking in Warsaw on the 20th anniversary of the formation of the present Polish Communist Party (Polish Workers Party), he said that Katyn was 'a Goebbels provocation' exploited by the Polish Government in London in order to justify severing relations with the Soviet Union.

This statement shows that the so-called de-Stalinization proclaimed by Khrushchev does not extend to the Katyn murders. It also provides further proof that Gomulka and the Communist régime in Warsaw are dependent on Moscow.

BIBLIOGRAPHY

For those who wish to verify the statements contained in this book, the following documents and books are recommended:

I.   *Der Massenmord im Walde von Katyn – Ein Tat-sachenbericht.* A short pamphlet of 6 pages only, and with a further 26 pages of pictures. Undated and with no indication of publisher. Probably originating from NSDAP in 1943.

II. *Amtliches Material zum Massenmord von Katyn.* The official German Government Report, published in Berlin in 1943. (Copy in the possession of the Polish Library, London.)

III. *Soviet War News,* No. 541 dated April 17th, 1943.

IV. Indictment presented to the International Military Tribunal sitting at Berlin on October 18th, 1945, pursuant to the agreement by the Governments of the United Kingdom of Great Britain and Northern Ireland, of the United States of America, of the Republic of France and of the USSR for the prosecution and punishment of Major War Criminals of the European Axis. London HM Stationery Office. Treaty Series No. 27 (page 22). 1946.

V.   Document: *The Mass Murder of Polish Prisoners of War in Katyn.* Produced in London by the Polish Government in Exile. March 1946 (then marked 'Most Secret').

VI. Judgement of the International Military Tribunal in the trial of the Major German War Criminals (with dissenting opinion of the Soviet members). Nuremberg 30/9 and 1//46 HM Stationery Office, London.

VII. *La Tribune de Genève.* Issue of January 20th, 1947.

VIII *The Inhuman Land.* A book by Count Josef Czapski. Chatto & Windus. 1951.

IX. *The Katyn Wood Murders.* A book by Josef Mackiewicz. The World Affairs Book Club, London. Undated.

X. *Katyn – Ein ungesuhntes Kriegsverbrechen gegen die Wekrkraft eines Volkes.* Pamphlet published by Wehrwissenschaftlicher Verlag Walther de Bouche. Munich. 1952.

XI. *The Katyn Forest Massacre.* Final Report of the Select Committee to conduct an Investigation and study the facts, evidence and circumstances of the Katyn Forest Massacre (Pursuant to House Resolutions 390 and 539 of the 82nd Congress). Washington, 1952.

XII. Speech of the late Professor Sir Douglas Savory, MP, in the British House of Commons. Hansard (Commons) November 6th, 1952 Columns 333–341 (see Appendix No. 1 of this book).

XIII. *Crimes Discreetly Veiled.* A book by F. J. P. Veale. Cooper Book Company, 293 Grays Inn Road, London, W.C.1. 1958.

XIV. *Death in the Forest,* by J. K. Zawodny – University of Notre Dame Press, 1962.

XV.   Congressional Record, Vol. 108, dated 14.5.1962, page
7643 (see Appendix No. 3 of this book).

XVI.   *The Crime of Katyn – Facts and Documents*. Published by the Polish Cultural Foundation, London,
1965.

Note: A full bibliographical list, containing 25 documents
and 60 books is available from the Polish Library, 9 Prince's
Gardens, London, S.W.7.

THE END

MARCH BATTALION BY SVEN HASSEL

Into the screaming inferno of the Russian Front were thrown the Tank Battalions of Hitler's Penal Regiments – men whose lives were considered expendable by the German high command.

And because they were treated as animals, they learned to live like animals – to steal and cheat and whore in the manner of beasts – to fight, not only the enemy but each other – to die brutally and bloodily . . .

These were the men sacrificed in the Führer's Russian Offensive . . . The men of the MARCH BATTALION

o 552 08528 6   65p

S.S. GENERAL BY SVEN HASSEL

Stalingrad, the universal grave . . . Stalingrad, where one German soldier died every minute, while back in Germany a madman strutted and screamed himself hoarse: 'Fight to the last man, the last bullet!'

The 27th Panzers in Hitler's Penal Regiment had fought through the winter in the hell-hole that was Stalingrad. Now there were few survivors from the last massive Russian attack. Weary and nauseated by the horrors they had seen on the Russian front, they crawled into a bunker near the banks of the Volga. Then the brutal S.S. general arrived . . .

o 552 08874 9   65p

THEY CAME FROM THE SKY by E. H. Cookridge

The Special Operations Executive was created by Churchill in the Summer of 1940 to 'set Europe ablaze'. Working secretly behind enemy lines to 'sabotage and subvert', they operated all over Europe, and some of the most active agents were in the French Section. It was dangerous work, and many agents did not return: a few, like Christine Granville, became famous names, but for the most part their exploits remain unsung. Here now are the stories of three members of the French Section – true stories that make more exciting reading than any novel . . . They had little training, and their unconventional methods were frowned on by the top brass of the Army, but what they lacked in style, they more than made up for in courage and initiative . . .

0 552 10136 2   75p

THE SAVAGE CANARY by David Lampe

The Danish resistance movement was described by Montgomery as 'second to none'.

   The Savage Canary is a fantastic but true account of the Danish efforts to help the Allies and cripple Germany in the Second World War. By May 1945, illegal newspapers had published a total of about 26 million issues; illegal broadcasts were transmitted regularly; boats were running a timetable service between Britain, Sweden and Denmark and 7,000 Jews had been shipped to safety. German ships were unable to move from Danish harbours; a vast number of German troops were kept from the main fighting points by Danish sabotage of the railways and aerodromes. This book, the story of an impudent, almost foolhardy heroism, is a salute to the people of Denmark.

0 552 10101 X   65p

A SELECTED LIST OF WAR BOOKS
PUBLISHED BY CORGI

All these books are available at your bookshop or newsagent, or can be ordered direct from the publisher. Just tick the titles you want and fill in the form below.

CORGI BOOKS, Cash Sales Department, P.O. Box 11, Falmouth, Cornwall.

Please send cheque or postal order, no currency.
U.K. send 19p for first book plus 9p per copy for each additional book ordered to a maximum charge of 73p to cover the cost of postage and packing.
B.F.P.O. and Eire allow 19p for first book plus 9p per copy for the next 6 books thereafter 3p per book.
Overseas Customers: Please allow 20p for the first book and 10p per copy for each additional book.

NAME (Block letters) ....

ADDRESS ....

(MAY 77) ....

While every effort is made to keep prices low, it is sometimes necessary to increase prices at short notice. Corgi Books reserve the right to show new retail prices on covers which may differ from those previously advertised in the text or elsewhere.